ROCHAMBEAU

ROCHAMBEAU

By *Arnold Whitridge*

COLLIER BOOKS

A Division of Macmillan Publishing Co., Inc.

NEW YORK

COLLIER MACMILLAN PUBLISHERS

LONDON

Macmillan Publishing Co., Inc.
866 Third Avenue, New York, N.Y. 10022
Collier-Macmillan Canada Ltd.

Rochambeau is published in a hardcover
edition by Macmillan Publishing Co., Inc.

Library of Congress Catalog Card Number:
65-21462

First Collier Books Edition 1974

Printed in the United States of America

TO MY GRANDCHILDREN

IN THE HOPE

THAT THE PRESENT AND THE FUTURE,

HOWEVER ENGROSSING,

WILL NOT PRECLUDE A GLANCE

AT THE PAST

Illustrations

Acknowledgments

F IRST OF ALL, I wish to express my very special thanks to Mrs. John Nicholas Brown of Providence, Rhode Island, a leading authority on French military history who had herself been planning to write a book on Rochambeau, and who very generously surrendered the field to me when she heard of my projected biography. I am also grateful to her for allowing me to reproduce two engravings from her matchless collection of books, manuscripts, paintings, engravings and drawings dealing with French military history.

I am also particularly indebted to Mr. Paul Mellon and to his librarian, Mr. Willis Van Devanter. Mr. Mellon put his recently acquired collection of Rochambeau manuscripts at my disposal, and Mr. Van Devanter made it possible for me to use the manuscripts under the pleasantest conditions. Monsieur André Cambier in Paris guided my footsteps through the mazes of the Archives Nationales and the Archives de la Guerre. I am also grateful to various members of the Rochambeau family who arranged for me to visit the Château de Rochambeau and to examine many of the family documents. My work in Paris was facilitated by Monsieur Edouard Morot-Sir, the "Conseiller Culturel" of the French Embassy in Washington.

My acknowledgments and thanks are due to the following libraries: the New York Public Library, to whom I am particularly indebted for the use of the Frederick L. Allen Room, the Yale University Library, the Princeton University Library, the Division of Manuscripts of the Library of Congress, the Morgan Library, the New York Society Library, and the libraries of the University Club of New York and the Century Association.

ROCHAMBEAU

One

IN THE SPRING of the year 1725 Louis XV, the King of France, was respectfully informed by his ministers that the time had come for him to marry. He was fifteen years old. For two years he had been betrothed to the Infanta of Spain, but as she was only seven, and as for reasons of state it was important that there be an heir as soon as possible, the ministers changed their minds about the Spanish marriage and the Infanta was hurriedly returned to Madrid.

The Duc de Bourbon, the young King's mentor, presented him a list of princesses for his consideration, strongly recommending that he pick Marie Leczinska, daughter of Stanislas, dethroned King of Poland. Elizabeth of Russia, the future Czarina, would have been a more glittering match, as would have been Anne, the older daughter of the Prince of Wales, but there were objections to both. Elizabeth was the daughter of a drunken father, and she herself was said to be mentally unstable. The English princess had the misfortune to have been born a Lutheran, and since the Hanoverians were the most determined heretics in Europe, there was no hope of her being converted to Catholicism. A Lutheran Queen of France was unthinkable. The choice, therefore, narrowed down to the Polish princess. It was true that her father had been ousted from his throne by the Elector of Saxony and that she brought no dowry with her and no political connections, but there were other compensations.

If Marie Leczinska was a beggar maid, she was a very attractive one, not beautiful perhaps but blessed with a good figure, a lovely complexion, and the ability, not always characteristic of princesses, to face the most critical society in the world without embarrassment. She was older than the King, but that made no difference.

Louis XV was enchanted with Marie, as was everybody else. They were married in Fontainebleau on September 4, the day after she arrived. The long journey from Strasbourg, where her father had set up his court, had been exhausting. It had rained most of the way and the coaches had been stuck in the mud, but the royal party arrived in good spirits; and even though the evening celebrations were spoiled by the bad weather, nothing could dampen the young King's ardor. He had fallen in love with a portrait, and the original was even more irresistible. The guests might complain of the rain but not the young couple. It was a good excuse for cutting short the formalities demanded by Court etiquette before they could be left to themselves. Never again would the King enjoy such carefree happiness.

The little Polish princess lost no time in doing what was expected of her. Twin girls came first, followed by another girl, but in 1729 she gave birth to an heir, the father of Louis XVI. The King was enraptured. He had been discouraged by the third daughter, though he was considerate enough to hide his disappointment. He and the Queen could now laugh at their forebodings. *"On n'a jamais aimé comme je l'aime,"* she wrote her father the day after the first son was born.

Unfortunately for France as well as for Marie Leczinska, the King's eyes soon began to stray elsewhere. Constancy was not in his nature. He delighted in society, in the company of artists and scholars, while the Queen, soon worn out with childbearing, never wanted to go anywhere or to see anybody. But in 1725 they were young and they were in love. Madame de Pompadour and Madame du Barry were still well below the horizon.

Altogether the Queen bore ten children, of whom seven survived. The charming young couple, with their rapidly increasing family, were the symbol of a new and more robust France, a France that had recovered from the exhausting wars of Louis XIV and that looked forward with supreme confidence to whatever the future held. Painters, sculptors, goldsmiths, and furniture-makers began devoting themselves again to the embellishment of Versailles, and on a lower plane the houses of rich and poor alike became more comfortable than they had ever been before. The imposing grandeur of the *grand monarque* gave way to the intimacy, the charm, the *douceur de vivre* of the eighteenth century.

National prosperity was founded on a broader base. In Paris alone, ten thousand houses were built in the first thirty years of the new King's reign, and in these new houses, however elegant they may have been, more space was devoted to small "livable" rooms than to the spacious apartments of an earlier age, designed primarily for entertaining. The seventeenth century had admired paintings of mythological scenes and, though the popularity of Boucher proves that such paintings were still in demand, there was a growing market for such artists as Chardin and Greuze who were more absorbed by everyday life than by the Junos and Jupiters, or even the Cupids, that delighted the older generation. The traditionally French virtue of *bon sens* was beginning to assert itself.

Abroad as well as at home, the subjects of Louis XV had every reason to be proud of their young King, and of their country. Versailles set the tone for every court in Europe, and the French language came to be recognized as the language of educated men the world over. Other nations, said Voltaire in speaking of the early years of Louis XV, looked to the French Court as the arbiter of Europe, all the more so since Cardinal Fleury, soon to become the King's first minister, was known to be a man whose whole policy was founded on the avoidance of war. Across the Channel, the government of George I under the guiding hand of Sir Robert Walpole seemed equally dedicated to maintaining the peace. By 1725, the major powers in Europe had been enjoying a general respite from war for twelve years, ever since the Treaty of

Utrecht, when King Philip of Spain renounced his claim to the French throne. At the same time Louis XIV had agreed to recognize the Protestant succession in England and to give no further aid to the Stuarts.

In this short interim of peace, when it seemed that the major causes of war had all been eliminated, France continued to reach out overseas without yet arousing the antagonism of other nations. Trade with the West Indies had never been more lucrative, and the island of Santo Domingo alone was soon supplying half the sugar consumed in Europe. To meet this ever-growing demand, the ship-owners of Nantes transported thirty thousand Negroes in one year. On the mainland, France was steadily consolidating her hold on the Gulf of Mexico. Mobile was founded in 1702, New Orleans in 1718. Quebec and the Gulf ports were then connected by a series of forts which sufficed for communication and for the establishment of a claim to the Mississippi Valley. French zeal and enterprise had seized upon the heart of the Continent, and it seemed probable that the English settlements might be confined to the coast. Since the colonists showed none of the French genius or appetite for exploration, there was no compelling reason to believe that a war between France and England was inevitable.

During the brief period when France was recovering from one war before plunging into another, when the young King was studying the portraits submitted to him of the Polish princess he was soon to marry, an incident of no apparent significance took place in the little town of Vendôme that was destined to change the course of modern history. Here, on July 1, 1725, Marie-Claire-Thérèse Bégon, wife of the Marquis de Rochambeau, gave birth to a third son, Jean-Baptiste-Donatien de Vimeur Rochambeau.

Unlike most famous men who in their old age feel impelled to write their memoirs, Jean-Baptiste-Donatien is tantalizingly reticent about his childhood. Nor does he think it necessary to tell us anything about his mother and father. After the first two or three pages we accept the fact, regretfully, that here is a man concerned

only with facts. Moods, impressions, the trivial incident that may
turn out to be so significant in the formation of character, are not
worth recording. Rochambeau is the least introspective of men.
Posterity, he seems to say, will not be interested in me as a human
being. It will be interested only in what I have to say about those
great events in which I played some part.

Rochambeau's father and mother would no doubt have been the
first to agree with him. They were both, so far as we can tell,
matter-of-fact people. Of his mother we know little except that she
came of a well-known naval family. Her uncle Michel Bégon was
appointed by Colbert *Intendant* Commissioner of the French Islands in America. In 1683 he landed in Santo Domingo and, after
restoring order in that island, went on to Martinique. Bégon seems
to have been interested in botany as well as naval affairs, for in
Martinique he discovered and gave his name to the familiar flower
now to be seen in every public park in France.

Through his mother, one of those capable Frenchwomen who
are always adding to the family estate, Rochambeau probably in-
herited his talent for administration. From his father, a less complicated character, judging by his portrait, would seem to have
come that unquestioning allegiance to church and state of which
unfortunately Louis XVI never learned to avail himself. One of his
ancestors, Jean de Vimeur, had been killed at the Battle of Man-
sura in the First Crusade. Another De Vimeur, captain of a company of archers, was standing by the side of Henri III when he was
assassinated. A few years later he crops up again at the defense of
Laon, where the Duc de Guise granted him a substantial pension
to "recompense him for the losses he had suffered in his profession, likewise for the three horses he had had killed under him."
His grandson, René de Vimeur, was enrolled in the second company of musketeers commanded by François Colbert, brother of
the Comptroller of Finances. In a letter to his family in January
1668, this René de Vimeur wrote: "We held an inspection last
Tuesday in the courtyard of the Louvre where I was promoted to

sergeant; when I thanked the King, for it was he who promoted me, he did me the honor to say that he knew I was of a good house, and that I had served with distinction. This is due to the generosity of Monsieur de Colbert to whom I am deeply indebted."

With the King's permission he later withdrew from the company of musketeers and got himself appointed to a mission in the French Indies. In this case the mission seems to have involved harrying the colonies of other nations. In an action against the Dutch on the Coromandel coast he was wounded, captured, and after five years invalided home, "happy," he said, "to have seen France once again before dying."

Such was the fighting stock from which Rochambeau came. With the exception of his mother's uncle, Michel Bégon, his ancestors were men of action rather than intellectuals, men who took to war on land or sea as the natural way of life. His father, the Marquis, was crippled at birth, which prevented him from following in their footsteps. Incapable of military service but intensely loyal to the King, he was appointed a Knight of the Order of the Holy Sepulchre, Governor of the Castle of Vendôme, and chief bailiff of the Duchy. These honorary positions, gratifying as marks of royal consideration, hardly compensated for the life of inactivity to which he was condemned, and he must have looked forward with some eagerness to the day when his sons would resume the normal life of their forefathers, a life from which he himself had been so cruelly barred.

Since the two older boys died in childhood, the hopes of the family became centered on Jean-Baptiste. At the age of five he was sent to the College of the Oratorian Fathers, a school later attended by Balzac, who describes it as "a spiritual prison house." Rochambeau characteristically has nothing to say about it except that the good Fathers were suspected of Jansenism, a doctrine the Bishop of Blois considered so dangerous that he persuaded the Marquis to transfer his son to a school in Blois where he would be educated by Jesuits.

According to Balzac, parents were not allowed to visit their children, and the children were not allowed to leave the College until they went home for good. The only recreation permitted was a long walk every Thursday. On one of these occasions he visited the Château of Rochambeau, six miles outside the town, which remained in his mind ever afterward as the château of his dreams. However strict the Oratorian Fathers may have been, and they were certainly less strict than the Jesuits, they chose a most enticing spot for their school. The Loir, a pleasant meandering river, flows around the walled-in buildings. The College, which has now become the Lycée Ronsard, is smaller than it was in Rochambeau's day, and the walls have disappeared, but the gardens Balzac speaks of, planted along the several branches of the river, have been enlarged and are now open to the public.

Whether or not the five-year-old Rochambeau was as unhappy at school as Balzac, Vendôme itself and the surrounding country certainly had a great hold on his affections. He never commits himself in his memoirs, but in his private letters to Washington and to others he confesses his happiness in being home, and the wrench to his spirit when, at the King's bidding, he is called upon to leave it. Having grown up in the shadow of the castle of which his father was Governor, how could any good Vendômois—particularly a Vendômois with a sense of history—not be conscious of being rooted in the past? "History," he learned from the Oratorians, "is the foundation of learning; it is the theater where all men are spectators."

The castle, long considered impregnable, from which the old Counts of Vendôme defied the attacks of their neighbors of Tours and Angers, had been founded by Geoffrey Martel, ancestor of the Plantagenets. At one time this famous warrior held possession of Anjou as well as of Vendôme; at the end of his life, conscious of his many misdeeds, he decided to make sure of a safe entry into paradise and earn the eternal gratitude of his fellow citizens by building them a noble abbey. Today the lover of great architecture visits Vendôme to study the towers of the Abbey of the Trinity, from one of which the master builder of Chartres is said to have drawn his inspiration, but Geoffrey Martel bequeathed to his abbey something he must have felt was infinitely more precious than the structure itself. He gave to it the "Holy Tear" which Christ shed on hearing of the death of Lazarus.

The *Sainte Larme de Vendôme* had an interesting history.[1] It had been received by an angel, enclosed in a transparent stone without any opening, and given to Mary Magdalen. Everybody knows how Martha, Mary Magdalen, the Apostle James, and the resuscitated Lazarus, driven out of Palestine by their enemies, put to sea in a rudderless boat and were miraculously driven by the winds to the coast of Provence. The still-restless James put out to sea again and eventually reached the coast of Spain, where his boat can be seen today turned into stone, near Padron, the port for Santiago de Compostela. The others settled in France, where Mary Magdalen made ample amends for past sins and bequeathed to the Bishop of Aix the "Holy Tear," the only treasure she possessed. From Aix the precious relic found its way to Constantinople, where Geoffrey Martel discovered it and brought it back to Vendôme to become the crowning glory of his abbey. Vendôme thus became one of the great shrines of Europe, the place above all others recommended for those suffering from diseases of the eye. With the outbreak of the Revolution, the "Tear" disappeared. Some godless men questioned its authenticity, and though Rome was prepared to conduct an inquiry into the provenance, it was never heard of again.

Such were the stories Rochambeau grew up with, stories of the prowess of his ancestors, of Geoffrey Martel, of the castle that had never been stormed, and of the Abbey relics. He must too have heard something of Ronsard, the most celebrated Vendômois of all, since one of his ancestors married a sister of the Cassandre Ronsard immortalized. In the eighteenth century Ronsard's reputation did not stand as high as it does today, but even so Rochambeau must have known about him even if he did not read him as carefully as a French schoolboy would today. We can assume that his education, like that of most sons of the gentry, was largely restricted to Latin and history. While one of his older brothers was still alive, Rochambeau won a prize in Latin. This aptitude for the classics was enough to convince his parents that since he was a younger son and not particularly robust, he would do better in the church than in the Army. He could never look forward to a successful career in the church if he finished his studies in an institution tainted with Jansenism, and with this in mind his father took him out of the College of the Oratorians and sent him to Blois, where the Jesuits were more likely to put him in line for a bishopric. The Bishop of Blois took to him and called him his *petit grand-vicaire.* The real *grand-vicaire,* the Abbé de Beaumont, later Archbishop of Paris, was equally impressed with his talents, and he was just about to be tonsured, the first step in preparation for the priesthood, when word was received of the sudden death of his brother. Rochambeau does not enlarge on the event, though it changed his whole life. He merely tells us that the good Bishop came to him one morning and, with typical Languedoc frankness, bade him forget all that he had said to him up to that time, that he had suddenly become the only son, and that henceforth he must serve his country with the same zeal he would have devoted to God. The boy then stepped into the Bishop's carriage and was driven off to Vendôme to finish his studies in the same College from which he had been withdrawn only six months before.

Whenever he came home he read, to the great delight of his parents, the military histories and memoirs—Philippe de Commines, Brantôme, and Sully among others—with which the library was well stocked. His father, who had been so eager for him to become a priest and to forge ahead in the church, was even more determined that his only son, now the Chevalier de Saint-Georges, should follow in the footsteps of his war-loving forefathers. Not much persuasion was necessary. In the dining room of the château, portraits of the kings of France and of Admiral Coligny, the great Huguenot leader who had been one of the chief victims of St. Bartholomew's Eve—there were Rochambeaus on both sides in the religious wars—stared down at him night and day, and reminded him that he belonged to a family who had made history. In the medieval castle overshadowing the town, where his father held sway as Governor, he must have seen the tombs of Antoine de Bourbon and of his fanatically Protestant wife, Jeanne d'Albret, father and mother of Henry IV, and in a manuscript which his father had carefully preserved he doubtless read how Jeanne d'Albret had plundered the treasury of the chapel, stolen the silver candlesticks, and thrown the relics of St. George into the river Loir.

Whichever way he turned there was no escape from history, nor was he ever inclined to look for one. *"Vivre en preux, y mourir"* (To live and die as a gallant knight) was the motto inscribed on the Rochambeau crest, and the young Chevalier de Saint-Georges accepted it without heroics, as a matter of course. At fifteen his father gave him his blessing; he said good-by to the pleasant surroundings of Vendôme, and climbed on the coach for Paris to be enrolled there in the Academy for officers, the famous school soon to be rechristened by Napoleon and to become better known to the world as the École St.-Cyr. Hardly did he have time to settle down to his studies before war broke out between Prussia and Austria, a war destined to engulf all Europe. The would-be seminarist transformed into a cornet of horse dropped his books and rode off, as so many young Frenchmen have done since, to join the Army of the Rhine. So began the fifty years of active campaigning that was to lead the future victor of Yorktown from the Rhine and the Danube to the Hudson and the Chesapeake, back again to the Low Countries, and finally to bring him full circle home to Vendôme.

Notes

1. For the details of this story see the *Voyage à la Sainte-Larme de Vendôme* by the Marquis Achille de Rochambeau (Vendôme, 1874). This story is also mentioned by J. J. Jusserand in *The School for Ambassadors and Other Essays* (New York, 1925), pp. 173, 174.

Two

THE WAR of the Austrian Succession has been described by a French historian as being as unreasonable in its object as it was disastrous in its consequences, a description which might be applied to a good many other wars as well. Cardinal Fleury in France and Sir Robert Walpole in England, both eager to maintain peace at almost any price, were forced into a declaration of war against their will. "They are ringing their bells now," said Walpole as the bells pealed at the announcement of hostilities; "they will be wringing their hands soon." For the first time in the history of either France or England, public opinion in each country had compelled the government to yield. Instead of resigning as they would today, the two ministers stayed on in office to conduct a war with which they were not in sympathy.

The war broke out over the possession of Silesia, one of the outlying provinces of the Austrian Empire which Prussia coveted, but the real question, as always, was the domination of Europe. Was not the balance of power tipping too much in the direction of Austria? Cardinal Fleury did not consider that Austria presented any threat to France, and he advised the King to that effect, but he was an old man now and not sufficiently vigorous to enforce his views.

In October 1740 the Emperor Charles VI had died after a short illness, leaving no son. The great object of his policy had always been to bequeath his whole Austrian dominions to his daughter Maria Theresa and to obtain for her husband, the Duke of Tuscany, the Imperial crown. With this end in view he had promulgated the law regulating the succession known as the Pragmatic Sanction. He had even taken the precaution of obtaining the assent to that law of all the great powers. England, Holland, Russia, Pope Benedict XIV, and the Republic of Venice acknowledged Maria Theresa the lawful heiress of the Habsburg dominions. The French ministers made a verbal declaration to the same effect. Best of all, the new King of Prussia, King Frederick II, wrote her the most friendly letters containing not merely a formal recognition of her claims but an unsolicited offer of help in case of need. With so distinct and so recent a recognition of her title by all the principal parties concerned the young archduchess, it was hoped, would have no difficulty in assuming the throne as Queen of Hungary and of the other dominions of her father, particularly since she did so with the warm assent of her subjects.

Everything, Maria Theresa must have felt, pointed to an easy accession. Though she was young and inexperienced she was as intelligent as she was beautiful, and she knew how to address her people with passionate eloquence. The story may be apocryphal that when she appeared before the Hungarian magnates with her infant son in her arms she so worked on their feelings that they shouted *"Moriamur pro rege nostro Maria Theresa"* (Let us die for our king Maria Theresa), but there was nothing apocryphal about her popularity. If Maria Theresa galvanized her people into action it was not merely because she was a queen, and a very lovely one, but because she was at the same time a woman of hard practical common sense.

The sudden decision of Frederick the Great to invade Silesia, and to add that rich province to his kingdom, cannot easily be defended, even by Frederick's great apologist Carlyle. The Elector of Bavaria had refused to acknowledge the title of the Empress, but the first blow was struck by Frederick. The falseness of his friendly letters to Maria Theresa had barely been suspected before it was published to the world by the invasion of Silesia by Prussian troops, thirty thousand of whom crossed the frontier on December

16, 1740. They found the province quite unprepared to meet this unexpected attack. The troops quartered in it were quite below even peacetime establishment, and could only throw themselves into a few fortresses, leaving the Prussians to overrun the rest of the province. That Frederick was moved to act as he did simply by the consciousness of his own military might and by the weakness and disorganization of the Empire are facts he never bothered to dispute. His own words, describing the motives of his first war, have often been cited: "Ambition, interest, the desire of making men talk about me, carried the day, and I decided for war."

He must also have been aware that in invading Silesia he was applying a torch to a powder magazine. As Macaulay reminds us, the consequences of his reckless ambition "were felt in lands where the name of Prussia was unknown; and, in order that he might rob a neighbor whom he had promised to defend, black men fought on the coast of Coromandel, and red men scalped each other by the Great Lakes of North America."[1]

The immediate result of the invasion of Silesia was to bring France into the war. Louis XV and Cardinal Fleury had been anxious to keep out of it. "All we need do," said the King, "is to stay quietly on Mount Pagnotte." Pagnotte was the name of a little hill in the forest of Chantilly where game was often found, and to stay on Mount Pagnotte meant to watch others do the fighting without entering into the conflict oneself. This was the policy of the peace-loving Cardinal, but unfortunately the King had other counselors. One of these was the Marshal de Belle-Isle, who saw in the weakness of the young Queen a chance of putting a finishing touch to the work of Richelieu and Louis XIV. Thanks to their firm policy, Austria had become a second-class power; it remained for Louis XV to destroy it altogether. The Marshal persuaded the King to support the Elector of Bavaria, who had refused to ratify the Pragmatic Sanction and was in fact claiming the throne of Austria for himself. Belle-Isle was eager to appear in the role of statesman, and if that should fail, in the role of military hero. Like his grandfather Fouquet, the all-powerful superintendent of finance under Louis XIV, who had overreached himself and finally been imprisoned for embezzlement, Belle-Isle was a man whose ability never quite kept pace with his ambition. Belle-Isle was too discreet to advocate an immediate invasion of the Austrian dominions. First of all, he must negotiate an alliance with Frederick the Great, as a result of which Frederick's Silesian adventure became transformed into the War of the Austrian Succession. Once that had been signed, France would be ready to invade Austria—ostensibly to enforce the Elector of Bavaria's flimsy claim to Maria Theresa's throne, actually to dismember the Austrian empire. In the spring of 1741 Belle-Isle led an army of forty thousand men up to the walls of Vienna, and from there on into Bohemia (Czechoslovakia today), where French troops under the Marshal de Broglie occupied Prague.

Among those who took part in the campaign was the sixteen-year-old cornet of horse who had only recently been reading the history of earlier French wars in his father's library. Presumably the young man pondered the rights and wrongs of this new war as he rode from Paris to Strasbourg and on to Nuremberg, where he joined his regiment. There he learned that the Elector, riding behind French troops, had made a triumphant entry into Prague and been proclaimed King of Bohemia. Until then the campaign had gone according to plan, but the French Army was soon to find itself in difficulties. Frederick the Great proved as cavalier in his relations with France as he had been with Austria. Having broken his word to Maria Theresa, it was easy enough to break it to Louis XV. Now that he had his hands on Silesia he had no further quarrel with Austria. Common sense dictated that he should withdraw from the conflict altogether. The day he signed a peace treaty with Austria, Frederick sent off one of his typical poetic effusions to Voltaire, glorifying the blessings of peace. It was not much of a poem, but Voltaire, who loved kings as much as he hated priests, wrote back immediately acknowledging *"les très jolis vers de mon adorable roi."* At the same time he pointed out that though as a philosopher he himself was in favor of peace, the rather sudden understanding Frederick had come to with Austria was not likely to be popular in Paris.

Frederick's treachery, involving as it did the collapse of the anti-Austrian policy devised by Belle-Isle, proved even more disastrous for the French armies than Voltaire had supposed. Maria Theresa, relieved of any further threat from Prussia, was now able to concentrate all her forces against the French. Instead of the steady succession of victories he anticipated, Rochambeau found himself shepherding the retreat of the Army which only a few months before had believed itself invincible. After penetrating deep into Austrian territory and occupying Prague, it was all Belle-Isle could do to extricate himself from the city, fight his way through the encircling Austrian armies, and lead a remnant of his exhausted troops back to the Rhine. Rochambeau's initiation into war could hardly have been more disillusioning. A retreat in the middle of winter of a starved, ill-equipped army, commanded by generals known to be at cross-purposes with each other, through a country-side inhabited by roving bands of guerrillas who massacred out-posts and vanished before the main body of troops could catch up with them, only sharpened his appetite for war. So eager was he for action that on one occasion his colonel placed him under arrest for taking part in an attack when his company was being held in reserve. It was the only time in his career that he was ever repri-manded.

The Army as a whole was so demoralized that many of the officers deserted. By the end of the campaign, Rochambeau was the only standard-bearer fit for active duty left in the regiment. Between Ingolstadt and Ratisbon, where the Army was to go into rest for a few days, he finally succumbed to a malignant fever. The regiment was ordered to move just when the fever was at its worst, and he was bundled into a cart in which he lay, shivering, during the week's journey to their new quarters. So intense was the cold

that the Danube froze, and the regiment marched across the river
with Rochambeau jolting along in the rear in a supply wagon;
feeling, he tells us, "as if he were being cooked in the hottest
oven." Youth and an indomitable spirit were on his side, and he
rejoined his regiment before the end of the retreat only to find
that the baggage, including his own few belongings, had been
stolen in one of the enemy's periodic raids. Fortunately he was
able to borrow twenty-five louis from the French minister at
Ratisbon, with which he bought himself a miserable packhorse, a
bearskin, and four shirts—sufficient, he calculated, for the outpost
duty to which he was assigned.

Altogether it was an inglorious campaign and, though there was
a good deal of talk about the splendid retreat from Prague, Rochambeau was too honest to see it as anything but a mistake from
beginning to end. Belle-Isle and Broglie were always bickering,
and Marshal Maillebois, who commanded the army that was to
have relieved Prague, proved grossly incompetent. Rochambeau
noted that the general incompetence of the commanding officers
was public knowledge. Maillebois' army was sarcastically referred
to as the Army of Mathurins, an allusion to an order of monks
founded for the redemption of Christian captives in the hands
of Barbary pirates. In this case the Mathurins accomplished
nothing. Forty years later, when it was his turn to command one of
the King's armies, Rochambeau may well have recalled the mis-
management of this, his first campaign. There would be no such
misunderstanding between him and General Washington.

The retreat from Prague was all the more discouraging in that
Frenchmen were sacrificed merely to thwart Maria Theresa, in
pursuit of an anti-Austrian policy inaugurated by Richelieu which
no longer fitted French needs. Of Belle-Isle's army of fifty thousand fewer than half, according to Rochambeau, fought their way
back to the Rhine. Michelet, who wrote his history to prove the
iniquity of kings and priests, describes the campaign as a miniature
retreat from Moscow, equally heroic and equally unnecessary.

Among the casualties of this unhappy campaign one of the most tragic was the young moralist-philosopher Vauvenargues who, less fortunate than Rochambeau, never recovered from the fever he developed during the retreat. He died shortly after his return to Paris. His death was not only a sad blow to his friends but also, as Voltaire recognized, an incalculable loss to French literature.

Rochambeau passed the next two years doing garrison duty on the Rhine. As so often happens in war, the pendulum swung from danger and discomfort to idleness and boredom. Evidently his superiors spotted him as an unusually capable young officer, for he was promoted to captain in 1743, just after his eighteenth birthday. At the same time they must have noticed that the fever had undermined his health and that he recuperated very slowly. His request for leave appears to have been granted without question. Most of this leave was spent not at home in the family château, which no doubt he would have preferred, but at Court where his mother had accepted a position as lady-in-waiting to the Duchesse d'Orléans. An idle life at Court either in the Palais Royal or at St. Cloud, depending on the King's mood at the moment, was not the kind of life to suit an ambitious cavalry officer. Rochambeau was essentially a countryman and never at home in the highly artificial life of the Court.

His mother had left Vendôme temporarily, not because she enjoyed Court society any more than her son, but because she wanted to plead the case of her husband's uncle, a naval officer who had fallen under the King's displeasure. By this time all Europe, not to mention America and India, had been sucked into the War of the Austrian Succession. Spain, as her share of the spoils, hoped to recover Gibraltar, which had been ceded to Great Britain by the Treaty of Utrecht. The Chevalier de Rochambeau was one of the small cogs in the vast, unwieldy mechanism which every nation was trying to operate to its own advantage. He commanded the squadron detailed to blockade Gibraltar and so prevent the British Navy from resupplying the garrison, which was supposed to be on the point of surrender. Somehow a few British ships had evaded Rochambeau's squadron, slipped through the blockade, and landed the necessary supplies. To mollify the Spanish authorities, disgusted at being balked of their prey, the commodore of the blockading squadron, responsible or not, had to be sacrificed. Accordingly, in spite of years of faithful service, the Chevalier de Rochambeau had been summarily dismissed.

Rochambeau's mother, an old friend of the Duchesse d'Orléans, hoped that by entering the household of a family so closely connected with the King she might have a chance to put in a word for the unlucky commodore. As it turned out, she could do nothing for him, but with her son she was more successful. Without ever seeking anything for herself, Madame de Rochambeau never hesitated about asking favors for her family. Her son was the last man in the world to covet an ornamental staff position, but when the Duc d'Orléans invited him to become one of his aides he was wise enough to accept.

However uncongenial the duties of aide to a royal prince, Rochambeau guessed quite rightly that they might well prove a steppingstone to something better. In the spring of 1746 the war on the Rhine, where his regiment was stationed, was at a standstill, but in Flanders the amazing Marshal Saxe was winning one victory after another. As long as the Duc d'Orléans was bound for the headquarters of the greatest soldier in Europe, Rochambeau would gladly go along with him.

The War of the Austrian Succession was fought in a peculiarly haphazard fashion. No nation defined its objectives, and nations supposed to be allies signed separate treaties with the enemy without troubling to inform one another what they were doing. Maurice de Saxe, illegitimate son of August I, Elector of Hanover (later King of Poland), and of Countess Maria Aurora von Konigsmarck, was the first man to grasp the fact that Flanders, then as always the cockpit of Europe, was the only theater of operations where France could hope to win the war. As a young man Maurice de Saxe had arrived in Paris to learn the business of soldiering. His father was flattered at the idea of having a son in the French Army, and the young man soon justified his hopes. Gambler and rake though he was, with no more respect for marriage vows than his father and mother, or indeed than his great-granddaughter George Sand was to have, Maurice was also a hard-working student who devoted himself to mathematics and to the science of fortification with a zeal that his scatterbrained companions could never understand.

In 1744, Maurice de Saxe at forty-seven was one of the most important men in France. To the great disgust of the French nobility, this foreign adventurer—a bastard, a German, and worst of all a Lutheran—had been raised to the dignity of Marshal of France. Louis XV, whatever his failings, was no fool. He was shrewd enough to detect ability in men or charm in women wherever he found it, and to commandeer it for his personal use. France needed a general who could win victories, and Maurice de Saxe was the man. It is a curious feature of this war that Ligonier, the ablest general in the English Army, was a French refugee, while on the French side Maurice de Saxe was a German and Lowendahl, his principal lieutenant, a Dane.

Early in the year, Louis XV had commissioned Marshal Saxe to undertake the invasion of England on behalf of Bonnie Prince Charlie, the Stuart Pretender. The impossibility of mounting this long-awaited invasion, so dear to Jacobite hearts, was so obvious that even before the troops had begun to arrive at Dunkirk, the port of embarkation, the King announced that the invasion had been postponed. As the new Marshal of France well knew, there was more to be gained by fighting King George in Flanders than by risking disaster in the Channel. His victory at Fontenoy, in which the French Army defeated a combined force of British, Dutch, and Hanoverians, proved once again, if further proof were necessary, that the King had made no mistake in picking a foreigner to lead his armies. Fontenoy was followed by further successes until finally the whole of the Austrian Netherlands (today's Belgium) had fallen into French hands.

It was an exasperating campaign for Marshal Saxe in spite of the results achieved. The King, the Dauphin, the Duc d'Orléans, and an enormous retinue—including the Duchesse de Chateauroux, the reigning mistress—set out from Versailles just before the Battle of Fontenoy to make a triumphant progress through Flanders in the wake of the victorious army. Maurice's burdens were not lightened by their arrival. In battle or on the march, the King's presence was anything but an asset. There was always the danger that some quick-witted cavalry captain might swoop down on the King's camp, strung out interminably behind the army, scatter the bevy of courtiers and courtesans, and capture the royal person. The Army was responsible for the King's safety, and Marshal Saxe must have been infinitely relieved when the King returned to Versailles to await the birth of his first grandchild. With him went the Duc d'Orléans.

Rochambeau remained with the army. At his request the Duke passed him on to the Comte de Clermont, who had been picked by Marshal Saxe to conduct the siege of Namur. Here at last was the opportunity for which Rochambeau had been waiting. The role of aide to a royal prince had paid off. Having trailed through Flanders in the royal entourage, he was now to be given a chance to prove himself.

Namur, situated as it is at the fork of the Sambre and the Meuse, is one of those picturesque old towns that pays a high price for its setting. As the last fortress on the Meuse route into France, it has always magnetized the invader. In World War I it relied for its defense, unsuccessfully, on a ring of outlying forts, but in the seventeenth century the key to the city was the rocky promontory between the two rivers. During the reign of Louis XIV Vauban, charged with the defense of the frontiers, a man with an unerring eye for a strong point, had built a citadel at the top of this promontory. It fell to the lot of Rochambeau, the newly arrived aide at the Duc de Clermont's headquarters, to reconnoiter the citadel and find out if it was really as impregnable as it was supposed to be. Rochambeau's *Mémoires*[2] are relieved by only an occasional gleam of humor, but in relating this incident he tells how he stumbled on a cleft in the rock, climbed up to the top on all fours, and discovered two sentinels peacefully smoking their pipes "who were good enough not to disturb me while I finished my reconnaissance."

Following the information Rochambeau brought back, Clermont launched an attack on the citadel which paved the way for the capture of the city itself. Even then Rochambeau's difficulties were not over. The citadel had surrendered only because the magazine was on fire, and unless the powder barrels were taken out at once there was bound to be an explosion which would prove as disastrous for the victors as for the vanquished. Again the General called on Rochambeau, this time to see to it that the powder barrels, some of them already smoking, were moved out of the castle to a place of safety.

Evidently Rochambeau's *sang-froid* on this occasion, as well as his resourcefulness, made an impression on his commanding officers. Here was a young man who could cope with any emergency. Clermont inquired about his plans for the future. Not being a rich man, Rochambeau could aspire to nothing more than an adjutancy in the King's *Gardes du Corps*. Clermont was not satisfied. His family must scrape up enough money to buy him a regiment. He himself would recommend him for it. Without waiting for Rochambeau's reply he dispatched a letter at once to Madame de Pompadour, who appears to have been the channel through which all recommendations for promotion had to pass. *"Elle jouoit déjà,"* says Rochambeau, *"le rôle de premier ministre."* The fact that a regiment had to be bought and that the approval of the King's mistress was, if not essential, at least very desirable did not strike Rochambeau as in any way extraordinary. He states the fact without comment in his memoirs, but perhaps it explains why it was that when the Revolution broke out after his return from America, where promotions were handled differently, he was sympathetic with the demand for reform.

As it turned out, Madame de Pompadour never received the letter, which eventually found its way back to Rochambeau, but he did get his regiment. How much his family had to pay for it we do not know, but judging by what Maurice de Saxe as a young man had had to pay for a similar command, it was not less than twelve thousand livres. (Any attempt to convert livres into dollars is at best a rough-and-ready approximation. Nominally a livre was worth a fraction less than the pre-1914 franc, but a study of the prices of common commodities in France at the end of the eighteenth century indicates that a livre purchased rather more than twice as much as the franc at the end of the nineteenth century.) At any rate, it was a substantial sum, and if the Rochambeaus had not been able to raise it their son would not have made his way in the Army, he would not have commanded the King's forces in America, and there might well have been no battle at Yorktown.

Everything turns out for the best in this best of all possible worlds, and on March 3, 1747, Rochambeau—not yet twenty-two years old—was appointed colonel of the Régiment de la Marche. It was an infantry regiment, which was what he wanted as offering more likelihood of active service than the cavalry. Better still, his regiment was attached to the army of his friend the Comte de Clermont, by whom he was not likely to be overlooked. Rochambeau's appetite for combat was soon gratified. Marshal Saxe had taken advantage of the absence of the Duke of Cumberland, who had been summoned home to meet the challenge of the Young Pretender, to step up his attacks on the Austrians and the Dutch. After capturing Brussels in January—no one believed he would be so unorthodox as to start campaigning in the middle of winter—he had thrust his way into Louvain and Antwerp. Everywhere the Austrians and Dutch were in full retreat, nor did the arrival of a British force stem the tide of victory. The allies were defeated again at Rocoux, near Liége, a battle which made the French Army master of the Austrian Netherlands, and opened the way to the Dutch Republic. Marshal Saxe, in such agony from dropsy that he had to be clamped into the saddle, was indomitable. One more campaign along the Dutch frontier would retrieve the earlier disasters of the war and put France in a position to demand an honorable peace.

The battle of Laufeldt proved the accuracy of the Marshal's calculations. It was an expensive victory in which the French casualties (fourteen thousand dead and wounded) were far higher than the losses of the allies, but it led to the occupation of Maestricht, the last stronghold on the Dutch frontier, and the end of the war. Among the casualties was Colonel Rochambeau, who was wounded leading his regiment in a charge against the center of the enemy's line. He was hit by two pieces of grapeshot, one in the temple grazing the corner of his eye and the other, a more serious wound from which he suffered all his life, in the thigh. According to a letter of his mother's, his fever was so severe that he had to be bled eighteen times, a fact which perhaps explains the slowness of his recovery.

King Louis XV was so impressed by the battle of Laufeldt, which he himself watched from a distance, that he ordered a painting of it. The picture shows the King in a scarlet uniform embroidered with gold, and in the distance the French troops charging the enemy. "The painter in ordinary to the King" chosen to execute this picture happened to be a certain Pierre L'Enfant, whose son, a better-known man than his father, at least to Americans, drew up the plans for the city of Washington.

As soon as he had sufficiently recovered from his wounds Rochambeau's gallantry in action was suitably recognized. The King admitted him to the select circle of those who were permitted to ride with him in his coach and to dine with him in private. "It would be difficult," Rochambeau says, "to give any adequate reason for this elaborate etiquette," but again he does not seem to have chafed against it. Apparently it was one of the rules of the game, and as such he conformed to it.

Just at this moment of his life, when he had recovered from his wounds sufficiently to go back to the wars, in the spring of 1748, questions of etiquette were not bothering him. Even his beloved regiment did not engross all his attention. Peace had just been declared. The Pragmatic Sanction had again been guaranteed; France, Austria, and England had restored the territories each had captured from the other during the war, and Maurice de Saxe had dragged his way to the Château de Chambord, there to die, a gay, lascivious, unrepentant Lutheran to the end. But for the Comte de Rochambeau, colonel of the Régiment de la Marche, the best was yet to be. He had met Mademoiselle Telles d'Acosta, and he was engaged to be married.

Notes

1. Lord Macaulay, "Essay on Frederick the Great."
2. Rochambeau, *Mémoires,* I, 80.

Three

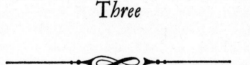

MADEMOISELLE JEANNE-THÉRÈSE D'ACOSTA was the daughter of Emmanuel Telles d'Acosta, a rich bourgeois of Portuguese origin who had made his money as a wholesale merchant in foods. Judging by the picture that hangs in the dining room of the Rochambeau château, a pastel attributed to Maurice Quentin de La Tour, Mlle d'Acosta was an unusually attractive young lady. The oval aristocratic face, the widely spaced eyes, and the ease and distinction with which she wears the anything-but-bourgeois dress hardly suggest the daughter of a grain merchant. Of the circumstances of the courtship Rochambeau tells us nothing. We only know that Mlle d'Acosta was not the first choice. Two other matches were considered, possibly by his mother, whom we know as something of a schemer, rather than by him, but fortunately they both fell through. Fortunately because, as Rochambeau tells us in his laconic language, the two women he might have married *"ont assez mal tourné,"* whereas the woman he did marry turned out to be everything, and more than everything, a man could desire. It was one of those perfect marriages that make the biographer groan with despair. All that can be said about it is that the couple lived happily ever afterward, or at least for nearly sixty years.

Madame Rochambeau brought her husband a dowry of some three hundred thousand livres, exclusive of laces and jewelry, a sum which even to Rochambeau's mother must have seemed more than adequate. He himself was not a rich man. The King had granted him a pension of two thousand livres from the royal treasury in recognition of his services at Laufeldt, to which he subsequently added another thousand, and his father gave him one of the estates in the family property. The Rochambeaus were not able to do as much for their son as the wholesale merchant had done for his daughter, but both families seem to have been satisfied with the match. The marriage took place in Paris on the twenty-second of December 1749.

With the declaration of peace the young couple might well have gravitated to Versailles, had they been so inclined. By the very fact of her marriage, the daughter of Emmanuel d'Acosta was to be presented at Court, since her husband "had been riding in the King's carriages" for the past two years and had dined at least once at His Majesty's table. Rochambeau's mother too was well established at Court, but the young couple shied away from palace life. A countryman by instinct and by upbringing, Rochambeau admits, or rather boasts, that he played a role *"fort médiocre à la cour."*

The first year of their married life was spent with his father at Vendôme. No doubt his health had something to do with the decision. Apparently he had been bled within an inch of his life, and it took him a long time to recover. The young wife caught smallpox and lost her first baby. The next child, Donatien-Marie-Joseph de Vimeur, was not born until 1755. Altogether it was a difficult first year, but they were young, they were in love, and Rochambeau was absorbed in his profession.

After a long convalescence he rejoined his regiment at Verdun and devoted himself to the regular routine of peacetime training. He was one of those dedicated professional soldiers, so essential to an army between wars, who actually enjoy the weary round of drills, inspections, and maneuvers. His attention to detail never flagged. Wherever the Regiment de la Marche was stationed during the few years of peace between the signing of the Treaty of Aix-la-Chapelle and the outbreak of the Seven Years' War, it stood out at once as the best-trained regiment in the garrison. The Marshal de

Belle-Isle, commanding the troops in Lorraine, noticed the young colonel who joined his troops on the parade ground at the first moment in spite of his poor health. He welcomed him into his house and encouraged his son, a colonel even younger than Rochambeau, to take the colonel of the Régiment de la Marche as a model. Rochambeau for his part could not help but be drawn to the old marshal, the man whom the King of Prussia himself had once regarded as another Alexander the Great. Whatever mistakes he had made as a diplomat, the retreat from Prague showed that he knew how to lead troops. Admittedly there was something of the charlatan about him, just as there had been about his grandfather Fouquet, but he had played such an important part in the history of the times that there was always something to be learned from his conversation.

Unfortunately for the prestige of the French monarchy, the death of Maurice de Saxe in 1750 left France with no general of his stature to lead her armies. The nation was soon to be plunged into war again, one of the most disastrous wars of French history, culminating in the loss of practically all the French possessions overseas. It was all very well for Voltaire to insist that France could be happy without Quebec, that Canada was a country covered with snow and ice for eight months of the year, a country inhabited only by barbarians, bears, and beavers, but the humiliating peace Great Britain inflicted on France at the end of the war was something that French statesmen and French soldiers could never forget. The statesmen consoled themselves for the Peace of Paris by the reflection that the loss of Canada was a sure prelude to the independence of the colonies. Vergennes, at that time the French ambassador at Constantinople, who was to become one of the principal architects of American independence, predicted to an English traveler, with striking accuracy, the events that would occur. "England," he said, "will soon repent of having removed the only check that could keep her colonies in awe. They stand no longer in need of her protection. She will call on them to contribute towards supporting the burdens they have helped to bring on her, and they will answer by striking off all dependence."[1]

The emotional La Fayette expressed himself less philosophically. The driving force behind his love affair with America was an unquenchable hatred of England. As he wrote to Vergennes in the summer of 1779, at a moment when France was contemplating an invasion of England, "the idea of seeing England humiliated and crushed makes me tremble with joy."[2] Rochambeau, a far more level-headed man than La Fayette, was equally convinced that there could be no durable peace in Europe until the balance of power was restored. As a result of the Seven Years' War the scales were weighted too heavily against France. For the moment England was the enemy, and England must be, if not destroyed at least so crippled that she would no longer constitute a threat to French prosperity and French prestige.

The origins of the Seven Years' War are difficult to determine. According to French historians the chief culprit was Admiral Boscawen, who deliberately attacked a French convoy off the banks of Newfoundland and captured two frigates, while the two nations were still at peace. The British claim that the French really started the war when Duquesne, governor of New France, sent a formal message to the governors of New York and Pennsylvania announcing that the French would not allow English settlements on the Ohio River. Under these conditions it was inevitable that hostilities should break out. The Peace of Aix-la-Chapelle had left the respective frontiers of the English and French colonies in America almost undefined. The limits of immense provinces, largely uninhabited and even unexplored, were necessarily vague, and as the colonists of both countries were always jealous of encroachments on what they considered their domain, it was inevitable that they should come to blows long before London and Paris knew what they were fighting about. A project of erecting an English fort near the point where the Monongahela flows into the Ohio was defeated by the quickness of the French, who had already

erected a fort, named after Duquesne de Menneville, the governor
of New France, on the spot selected by the British.

The name of George Washington, then twenty-two, the son of a
planter of Westmoreland County on the Potomac, now appears for
the first time in history. In 1753 he had been sent out by Governor
Dinwiddie of Virginia on a futile mission to negotiate a boundary
dispute with the French, and the following year he was dispatched
to the headwaters of the Ohio with a force of a hundred and fifty
men to enforce the Virginian claim. In May 1754 a skirmish took
place in which the French commander was killed, but soon afterward Washington was surrounded by a superior force and compelled to capitulate. The British ambassador in Paris lodged the
usual complaint, but nothing came of it.

In spite of these clashes in their American colonies, France and
England did not declare war for another two years. When war did
break out it was on account of a shift of alliances in Europe rather
than because of any boundary dispute on the American frontier.
Once again Frederick the Great anticipated matters by invading
Saxony, just as he had invaded Silesia in the War of the Austrian
Succession. Austria now came over to the side of France and, with
Spain and most of the German states, declared war against England, Portugal, and Prussia. Before the war was over it had extended to all parts of the world. British and French sea captains
sought each other out in the Atlantic, the Mediterranean, the West
Indies, and the Indian Ocean, and in many of these clashes the
French naval heroes Suffren and La Motte-Picquet, if they had
been properly supported at home, might well have turned the tide
of the war. The first years of the war were particularly disastrous
for England. In one of those periodic outbursts of self-abasement
which have always marked English history, John Brown, author of
the once-popular *Estimate of the Manners and Principles of the
Times* (1757), maintained that the nation was suffering from a
decay of religion, honor, and public spirit. "We are rolling," said
Brown, "to the brink of an abyss that must destroy us."[3] The

increase of national wealth had sapped the vigor of the nation. Luxury (or, as we should put it, "our high standard of living") "seems to have fitted us for a prey to the insults and invasions of our most powerful enemy," France. Such were the gloomy speculations, readily believed in all quarters, at the beginning of the most successful war in which England had ever engaged.

The fact was that the feverish French activity in Dunkirk and Brest, apparently with a view to invasion, entirely misled the British government. "The nation," said Burke, "trembled under a shameful panic too public to be concealed." The real object of the movement of troops in Picardy, Normandy, and Brittany was to divert the attention of the British Navy from an expedition that was fitting out at Toulon for an attack upon Minorca. This island with its splendid harbor, as important for the control of the Mediterranean as Gibraltar, would be an invaluable asset at the peace table. It could either be offered to Spain as a reward for her alliance, or it could be returned to England in exchange for such conquests as she might make in America.

At the beginning of the war, Rochambeau's friend the Marshal de Belle-Isle was in command of all troops in the north; Rochambeau, stationed at Besançon, did everything in his power to get himself and his regiment transferred to what he supposed would be the scene of action. Fortunately for his career, his efforts were not successful, which led him to reflect that it is just as well in the Army not to chafe against one's fate. Instead of being transferred to the north of France where he would have done nothing but train troops for an invasion which would never take place, he found his regiment had been attached to the army of the Duc de Richelieu, commanding the forces in the Mediterranean.

The Duc de Richelieu is described by Macaulay as "an old fop who had passed his life from sixteen to sixty in seducing women for whom he cared not a straw," but he was more than that. An old fop would never have captured Minorca. The Duc de Richelieu may not have been as brilliant a statesman as his great-uncle, the

Cardinal, who made the French monarchy the monolithic structure it was, but he was a man of considerable intelligence, utterly fearless, and as indefatigable in war as he was in love. The Minorca secret was well guarded. Colonel Rochambeau still did not know the destination of his regiment even after they had reached Toulon. So completely in the dark was he that when the commandant of the port asked him what rumors he had heard about the attack on Port Mahon he could only answer that a naval officer should be better informed on maritime affairs than a colonel of infantry. The Commandant protested in good faith that he had received no orders about provisioning or equipping the ships. Not until Richelieu himself arrived at Toulon was the destination disclosed. Thanks to his energy and to the ready cooperation of the Marquis de la Galissonière, formerly governor of Canada and one of the best sailors of his time, the expedition sailed from Toulon early in April 1756.

The convoy was hardly out of the harbor before a storm blew up, forcing La Galissonière to take shelter in the roadstead of the Hyères Islands. Rochambeau, eager for news, took the opportunity to visit the Admiral's flagship where he found Richelieu playing whist, while La Galissonière stood by the window watching the movement of a feather that served as a weathervane. "How long do you expect this wind to last?" grumbled Richelieu, knowing that sooner or later a British fleet was bound to discover them. "Monsieur le Maréchal," replied La Galissonière, "I once took three months to get to Gibraltar, and three days to get back. That will give you an idea of how impossible it is for us in the Navy to draw up a definite schedule."[4] The next day, however, the wind did change and the Admiral gave the signal for hoisting sail. No one was more delighted than Rochambeau when his transport dropped anchor off the port of Ciudadella at the northwest end of Minorca. Seasickness had brought on the old complaint of blood-vomiting from which he had been suffering off and on since the battle of Laufeldt, but he admits the voyage did him good, as he very rarely suffered from vomiting again until the last years of his life.

He would always treasure the memory of that landing on Minorca in the early dawn. What a spectacle it was—173 transports and twelve ships of the line riding peacefully at anchor under the shadow of Mount Moro! He would remember too, the eager welcome of the civilian population, the women in particular helping to unload the ships and pressing forward to kiss the hands of the villainous-looking Franciscan friar he had taken on at Toulon as chaplain. Minorca was an intensely Catholic country and the people had not taken kindly to the Protestant English garrison. Here was war waged as it should be, with a friendly population hailing the French as liberators, and the enemy nowhere in sight.

Richelieu had no difficulty in overrunning the island and within five days he had entered Port Mahon, the principal town. General Blakeney, the eighty-year-old British governor, realizing that he could not defend the 260 square miles of Minorca, most of it lowland, with the meager forces at his disposal, had withdrawn to Fort St. Philip, which commanded the town and harbor of Mahon. Until that fort was reduced, the French had not conquered Minorca. Fort St. Philip was a difficult nut to crack, far more difficult than the French Ministry for War had given Richelieu to understand. At Versailles, when he received his orders, he had been handed an old map which showed the fortress as it used to be in the time of the Spanish. With the British occupation it had been immensely strengthened so that it was now one of the most formidable strongpoints in Europe, defended not only by the usual redoubts and ravelins but also by a number of subterranean mines and galleries, cut with incredible labor out of the solid rock and affording unusual protection to the defenders. For a man who was considered an old fop, Marshal Richelieu set about the siege of this fortress in a thoroughly workmanlike way.

Rochambeau's regiment was detailed to transport the artillery and ammunitions from Ciudadella by sea to the little Bay of Ravale,

about a mile from Mahon. It was the first opportunity he had had
of exercising his talent for organization. First of all in feluccas
propelled by oars, then with oxen and mules, the guns, mortars,
bombs and gabions, and all the rest of the equipment necessary for
a siege were brought into place on time. Indeed, as he cannot help
telling us with pardonable pride, instead of bringing up two thirds
of the equipment by May 14, which was about all Richelieu
thought he could manage, everything was delivered by that date
without the loss of a single mule or wagon.

As soon as this task was completed, the Régiment de la Marche,
with Rochambeau at its head, took its turn in the trenches. The
siege, as everyone realized, was a race against time. The British
government had at last realized that the activity in the Channel
ports was merely a bluff, but that the French were threatening
Minorca in deadly earnest.

On April 7 Admiral Byng sailed from Spithead with ten ships of
the line. He had orders to touch at Gibraltar and embark another
battalion as a further reinforcement for the garrison at Fort St.
Philip. The only question was would he get there in time. The
French were bringing new batteries into position every day in the
hope of reducing the fort before Admiral Byng got there. When
finally the white sails of the British ships hove into view, Richelieu
knew it was touch and go. Either La Galissonière would scatter the
British ships and drive them back to Gibraltar, in which case
Richelieu would capture the fort and be hailed as a hero, or Admiral Byng would fight his way into the harbor, the garrison would
be relieved, and he would be sent home in disgrace.

Rochambeau, who was with Richelieu watching the action
through a telescope, describes his commander-in-chief's comments
on this nerve-racking occasion as being *très chevaleresque*. "Gentlemen," remarked Richelieu to the three or four colonels who
were with him, "you are watching a very interesting game; if
Monsieur de la Galissonière defeats the enemy, we shall continue
the siege at our ease [*en pantoufles*]; but if he is beaten, we shall

have to set about scaling the fortress as our last resort. There is no one in the Army who does not think as I do, that it would be better to become a monk on the top of Mount Moro than to go back to France without having taken Fort St. Philip."[5]

As it turned out, Richelieu and his colonels did not have to become monks. Instead of pressing the attack home, Admiral Byng fought a half-hearted engagement and then, frightened of sustaining further casualties, withdrew his fleet altogether. For a few days the garrison comforted themselves with the idea that he would be back with reinforcements, but it was not to be. The Admiral was a conscientious man but he was not a fighter. His ships were undermanned, and he was not willing to risk defeat at the hands of a more powerful squadron. On his return home he was court-martialed and found guilty of neglect of duty. The court accompanied its verdict with a recommendation for mercy, but the failure to relieve Minorca caused such a savage outburst of indignation throughout the country that King George II did not have the courage to stand up to it. Byng was accordingly shot at Portsmouth on March 14, 1757. As Voltaire put it in a memorable phrase, the Admiral was shot *"pour encourager les autres."* The execution reflected more discredit on the British people than had the military disaster that provoked it. Voltaire acted with characteristic humanity in sending to the court a letter he had received from Richelieu stating that Byng had done everything that could be expected from an able sailor and a brave man.

Richelieu was boasting when he said that if Byng were defeated he would capture the fort at his slippered ease. Byng was defeated, or rather he turned tail and sailed away before he could be defeated, but the garrison, discouraged though they must have been, showed no signs of surrendering. The sheer walls of the fortress gave them an uninterrupted field of fire, while the underground galleries in the rock sheltered them from the fire of their opponents. Until Richelieu could construct battery positions near the fort, he suffered heavier casualties than the besieged. He drove his

men night and day. As Rochambeau puts it, "Monsieur le
Maréchal was always in a hurry, in war as well as in love." As
soon as a battery got into position it began firing. Finally the whole
fort was ringed. With every battery firing at once, opening up
breaches in the walls at different points, the besieged could not
know where the main assault would be delivered.

On the night the fortress was stormed, Rochambeau was lying
flat on his back awaiting the signal for assault, but instead of the
signal he heard the voices of the stretcherbearers. From them he
learned that the Queen's redoubt, the strongest of the defenses,
had been captured, that Colonel Jeffries, the ablest officer of the
garrison, was a prisoner and that parleys for surrender were under
way. The grenadiers of the Royal Italian Regiment, who had been
selected for this operation, finding their scaling ladders too short to
reach to the top of the ramparts, which were twenty-two feet high,
drove their bayonets between the chinks of the stones and mounted
on the shoulders of their comrades.

Richelieu was too delighted at having at last overcome the stubborn resistance of the garrison, who had held out for another
month after Byng's failure to relieve them, and too much in dread
of the reappearance of the Squadron, to haggle over the terms of
surrender. The garrison, therefore, was permitted to march out
with all the honors of war and shipped to Gibraltar. "The noble
defense which the British have made," wrote Richelieu, "having
merited all the marks of esteem and veneration that every soldier
ought to show for such actions, and the Maréchal de Richelieu
being very desirous to testify to General Blakeney the admiration
due to the defense he has made, accords to the garrison all the
honors of war that they can enjoy under the circumstances of
their marching out for embarkation, namely, firelocks on their
shoulders, drums beating, colors flying, twenty cartridges per man,
and also lighted matches."[6]

In thinking about the Minorcan campaign afterward, Rochambeau came to the conclusion that the French would never have

captured the fortress of Port Mahon if they had known how strong it was, and that the British lost it only because they knew its strength too well—an interesting reflection from which the builders of the Maginot Line might well have profited. From the Minorcan campaign Rochambeau learned also how much success in the field depends upon the commander-in-chief's solicitude for the comfort of his men and upon his awareness of their morale. In a country where the wine was so cheap it was difficult to prevent the soldiers from drinking too much. Instead of forbidding the sale of wine altogether, he hit on a method of stamping out drunkenness which was later adopted throughout the Army. He issued an order that no man would be permitted to take part in an assault who had been drunk the day before. From the day that order was published drunkenness ceased to be a problem. An officer today, in the French Army, or any other, might be skeptical of the effect of such an order, but under the *ancien régime* when war still had a certain "style," the disgrace of not being allowed to risk one's life with one's comrades was something that a private in Rochambeau's regiment did not care to face.

Notes

1. George Bancroft, *History of the United States* (10 vols., Boston, 1834–1874), IV, 461.

2. Henri Doniol, *Histoire de la Participation de la France à l'Établissement des États-Unis d'Amérique,* IV, 291.

3. John Brown, *An Estimate of the Manners and Principles of the Times* (2 vols., London, 1757), II, 26.

4. Rochambeau, *Mémoires,* I, 70.

5. Rochambeau, *Mémoires,* I, 76.

6. H. Noel Williams, *The Fascinating Duc de Richelieu* (New York, 1910), p. 251.

Four

ON HIS RETURN to France after the capture of Minorca, Richelieu was everywhere hailed as a conquering hero. At Toulon, out of which he had sailed three months before, and at Marseilles, the city authorities decreed public celebrations in his honor, and at the opera house in Montpellier he was awarded a wreath of laurel, which he plucked apart so as to be able to distribute the leaves among his officers. Rochambeau shared these honors. In addition to the sprig of laurel he was appointed brigadier general and a Chevalier of St. Louis. It is perhaps worth noting that Rochambeau won this promotion in 1756, the year before La Fayette was born. Already, at the age of thirty-one, he had spent more than half his life in the Army. The new brigadier general was assigned again to active service sooner than he had expected.

During the Minorcan campaign France, at the bidding of Madame de Pompadour, had taken the first step on the road that was to lead to the death of Montcalm on the Plains of Abraham, to defeat in India and to the loss of her colonial empire. On May 17, 1756, France and Austria signed the first Treaty of Versailles, by the terms of which the contracting parties bound themselves to guarantee and defend each other's possessions in Europe. A year later a second Treaty of Versailles was signed which condemned France to a war against Prussia until Frederick agreed to disgorge the province of Silesia. In return for the enormous sacrifices she was called upon to make on behalf of Austria, France was to get possession of a few frontier towns in the Austrian Netherlands, and a promise that Austria would use her good offices in preserving Minorca for France when the contestants came to the peace table. The advantages of this treaty were wholly on the side of Austria. Austria remained neutral in the Anglo-French quarrel, but France was obliged to go to the assistance of the Empire, whoever attacked it. While France was squandering her manpower in Germany so that Maria Theresa might win back her beloved Silesia, the demands of the French Navy were being ignored and the overseas possessions left to fend for themselves.

Rochambeau was under no illusions about this *"malheureuse guerre."* He pinned the responsibility for it on Madame de Pompadour. It was under her auspices that the French armies invaded Germany, and under her orders that ministers were forced out of the cabinet. Yet Rochambeau does not inveigh against her. She was a gentle, kindly woman by nature, but the King's infatuation for her combined with his almost pathological indifference to public affairs induced her to assume a role for which she was not qualified. Whether Rochambeau was right in thinking of it as her war, a war that she prodded the King into declaring, is open to question, but it was certainly a view widely held among his contemporaries. On the other hand, the loss of the colonies, which Rochambeau deplored, was not felt so keenly by his fellow countrymen. Whatever the Establishment may have thought about it, public opinion was not particularly aroused. In this respect public opinion sided with the intellectuals, who have always been skeptical about colonies, in the eighteenth century no less than in the twentieth. "An empire is like a tree," said Montesquieu, "if the branches spread too far they drain the sap from the trunk. Men should stay where they are; transplanted to another climate their health will suffer."[1] In the *Supplément au voyage de Bougainville* Diderot strikes an even more modern note when he makes a Tahitian launch forth on a diatribe against the vices of Europeans, and ends up by demanding that these wicked men should take themselves off as quickly as possible.

Madame de Pompadour, not content with reconstructing cabinets and negotiating treaties, now undertook to pick the generals who should command the French armies. Belle-Isle and Richelieu were both seriously considered, but Belle-Isle's failing health was against him, and Richelieu—though his success in Minorca had made him a popular favorite—was believed to disapprove of the alliance with the Court of Vienna. The choice therefore fell on Marshal d'Estrées, not a military genius but at least as capable as anybody else. The King grumbled, with truth, that he no longer had any generals, only a few captains.

Among the royal princes serving under the command of Marshal d'Estrées was Rochambeau's patron the Duc d'Orléans. They had lost track of each other since the end of the last war as a result of Rochambeau's refusal to mingle in Versailles society, but with the outbreak of new hostilities the Duke sought him out again. The young brigadier was just the man he needed. Royal princes were always given important commands at the beginning of a campaign, regardless of their qualifications, and the Duc d'Orléans was wise enough to delegate authority to a professional.

The vanguard of the French Army, commanded by the Duc d'Orléans with Rochambeau at his elbow, crossed the Rhine near Wesel early in April 1757. There they waited for a few weeks until D'Estrées had arrived to assume command of the whole army, after which they advanced in a leisurely fashion across Westphalia, while a motley army of British, Hanoverian, Hessian, and Prussian troops, commanded by the Duke of Cumberland, fell back in front of them. Having made a name for himself by defeating Bonny Prince Charlie and his Highlanders on Culloden Moor, the Duke of Cumberland was not willing to risk his reputation by engaging the better-trained French troops in a pitched battle. The memories of Fontenoy, where Marshal Saxe had defeated him in the moment of what he thought was victory, may well have made him hesitate to commit himself. The King of Prussia was so disgusted with the Duke's cautious tactics that he withdrew the Prussian contingent

from his command. He himself, in characteristic fashion, had fore-
stalled his adversaries by invading Saxony, occupying Bohemia,
and laying siege to Prague before any of the generals opposed to
him were ready to take their places on the stage. Rochambeau
suggests that the Court of Versailles was just as impatient with
Marshal d'Estrées for not coming to grips with the enemy as Frederick was with the Duke of Cumberland.

The fact was that all the French generals, D'Estrées, Belle-Isle,
Richelieu, and Broglie, were jealous of each other, and these jealousies did not make for close cooperation. Marshal d'Estrées' chief
of staff, Marshal Maillebois, had served under Richelieu in
Minorca, and was suspected of conspiring in favor of his former
chief, whereupon Belle-Isle, realizing that an intrigue to replace
D'Estrées was afoot, sent him a secret message that he had better
have a decisive victory to report very soon if he did not want to be
recalled. Spurred on by this warning, D'Estrées attacked the Duke
of Cumberland and won the battle of Hastenbeck. Unfortunately
for D'Estrées, the victory was not as complete as it should have
been. There were ugly rumors afloat afterward that Maillebois had
deliberately allowed the enemy to escape, and though Rochambeau could not bring himself to believe that Maillebois was guilty
of such an act of perfidy, D'Estrées was relieved of his command
immediately after the battle.

Richelieu, who had been superseded by D'Estrées after his capture of Minorca, now found himself back in command. Each man
had been relieved by the other immediately after winning a victory.
Rochambeau's fortunes were affected by the change in command
in a way that was unexpected and not entirely agreeable. First of
all, Richelieu asked for his services, which was in itself complimentary. From having been a brigadier general under a royal
prince he now became a major-general under the eye of the
commander-in-chief. Hardly had he settled into his new duties
when the blow fell. The Duc d'Orléans, who had been second in
command to D'Estrées, indignant at Richelieu having been pre-

ferred to him, threw up his command and returned to France. With
the amalgamation of the two armies, Richelieu was saddled with a
number of staff officers he did not need but for each of whom a
suitable position had to be found. One of the superfluous officers
happened to be senior to Rochambeau and therefore had to be
appointed in his place. Going back to command a brigade which
included his old regiment was no great disappointment to Rochambeau, although it meant a loss in rank, but there was a financial question involved which caused him serious embarrassment.
His brief appointment to Richelieu's staff had cost him a considerable outlay, which he could ill afford. In a letter to the Secretary of
War he complains that in order to furnish a house and to live in a
style suitable to the position with which he had been honored, he
had had to spend twenty-five thousand francs of his wife's money
besides drawing heavily on his own salary. He respectfully requested that the King compensate him for these expenses, which
had been incurred by his zeal for the service and not by his own
wish.[2]

Rochambeau was not a rich man and was constantly in the
position of having to request compensation for extra expenses he
had been forced to incur.

History does not relate whether the King ever heard of this
request, or deigned to notice it if he did. As soon as he returned to
service with troops, Richelieu picked him for a task requiring qualities that so far the serious-minded young brigadier had given no
indication of possessing. By this time the French Army had advanced deep into Hanover, still without meeting any serious resistance. Richelieu, goaded by Versailles, had so far outdistanced his
supplies that he was forced to live off the country, the rich farming
land between Halberstadt and Magdeburg serving him as a gran-
ary. One fortress, Regenstein, on the borders of the Harz Moun-
tains, still held out, from which the French foraging parties were
continually being threatened. So impregnable was this fortress that,
according to legend, the devil himself could not set foot in it

without the Governor's permission. Knowing that it would be difficult and costly, if not actually impossible, to storm the fortress, Rochambeau bluffed his way to victory by announcing that the whole French Army, of which he was only the vanguard, would soon be battering their way into Regenstein, and that the commandant would be well advised to surrender under the generous terms he offered. To this exploit, more suggestive of one of Napoleon's marshals than of any of the generals of the Seven Years' War, Rochambeau added a further touch of artistry. He made sure that his victory should redound to the credit of his immediate superior, the Duc de Noailles. Obviously Rochambeau was becoming a man of the world. At least he understood enough about the Army not to steal the thunder of his superior officers.

The capture of Regenstein enabled Richelieu to occupy all Hanover and bottle up the Duke of Cumberland's army in the estuary of the Elbe. The Duke, penned in between the Elbe, the sea, and the French Army, proposed a suspension of arms "to permit the two courts to arrange what I cannot call a peace, since I am not aware that war has been declared between France and the Elector of Hanover." Richelieu replied that "the King had placed him at the head of his armies to fight the enemies of his allies, and not to negotiate."[3]

On second thought, Richelieu abandoned this uncompromising attitude and decided on his own authority, without informing the French government of his intentions, to sign an armistice with the Duke known as the Convention of Closterseven. By the terms of this convention, the French were to remain in occupation of Hanover and Bremen, while the Hessians, Brunswickers, Hanoverians, and English were to be sent home on the understanding they would not fight against France again while the war lasted. Richelieu was enchanted with his handling of the situation, but the Convention was badly received by all the governments concerned. Instead of insisting on a capitulation of the Duke of Cumberland's army, as he should have done, he had allowed the enemy to sign a convention which would not be binding unless ratified by all the respective governments. Neither George II nor Frederick of Prussia would have anything to do with the Convention. George II even went so far as to tell the Duke of Cumberland, his own son, when he arrived home, that he had ruined his father and disgraced himself. Richelieu, always an optimist—he had already withdrawn his troops from Closterseven, thinking the war was over—awoke to find his insubstantial pageant faded and himself in disgrace. As Rochambeau put it, he had made the mistake of the huntsman who courses two hares without catching either of them.[4]

Here at Closterseven in October 1757, if Richelieu had been a little more skeptical of his own talents, France might well have won the Seven Years' War, but by the end of the year it was too late. The tide turned at the battle of Rossbach, where Frederick routed the larger but far less cohesive army of French regulars and German auxiliaries commanded by Madame de Pompadour's favorite, the Duc de Soubise, a brave enough man, according to Rochambeau, but one totally unfitted to command an army. Prussia had long been administered like a great camp, and the King of Prussia, now since the death of Maurice de Saxe the ablest general in Europe, had brought his army to the highest pitch of efficiency. Exactly one month after Rossbach, on December 5, he fought another decisive battle at Leuthen, in which he destroyed a great army commanded by Prince Charles of Lorraine and put an end forever to Maria Theresa's dream of recovering Silesia.

After the easy successes of the first year the French armies were now engaged in heavy fighting from which nothing was to be gained. Frederick was outnumbered, but disunity among the French generals fought his battles for him. Once again Rochambeau speaks of the *"malheureuse guerre"* in which France paid the inevitable price for allowing the King's favorite to decide who should command the armies and where the war was to be fought. *Malheureuse* for France though the war was, for Rochambeau it proved an admirable training ground for his command in America.

The perfect cooperation between himself and Washington can be traced in large part to his observation of the disastrous effect upon an army of jealousy and bickering in the high command.

This lesson was strikingly brought home to him by a petty quarrel, between the Duc de Belle-Isle and the Duc de Broglie, in which he happened to be involved. After the battle of Crefeld in 1759, in which the French had been driven back across the Rhine, Rochambeau was appointed to the command of the Régiment d'Auvergne, one of the crack regiments of the French Army. As a result of the constant advancing and retreating to which the French force was being subjected, as one general after another evolved a new plan of campaign, Rochambeau came to appreciate the importance of light infantry. The armies of the eighteenth century moved slowly. Sometimes, even after they had reached the field of battle, it took them a whole day to get into position. As soon as he took command of the Auvergne, Rochambeau organized a company of *chasseurs* for each battalion, and placed it under the command of the best officers. These companies of *chasseurs,* which Napoleon subsequently used to such good effect, acted as a screen for the other battalions in the regiment. By the formation of these companies Rochambeau accomplished two objectives. He built up an *esprit de corps* among the recruits of smaller stature and at the same time took advantage of their quickness and agility, qualities the grenadier under heavy marching order too often lacked.

The Duc de Belle-Isle, who was Minister of War at the time, approved of Rochambeau's *chasseurs* and accepted his recommendation that they be recognized as special troops and paid accordingly. The Duc de Broglie, who had been appointed to command the Army against the wishes of Belle-Isle, was even more enthusiastic. He ordered that companies of *chasseurs* should be formed in every regiment, whereupon Belle-Isle changed his mind, took an aversion to the whole scheme, and refused to authorize the extra pay demanded. All of which proves, comments Rochambeau, that the Minister of War allowed his judgment to be clouded by private likes and dislikes. Under such conditions it would be increasingly difficult for France to win the war.

Of all the generals who came and went during the Seven Years' War the Duc de Broglie was probably the ablest. He was also a peppery character and so outspoken that on one occasion he argued with the King, who promptly relieved him of his command and exiled him to his country estate, thus depriving his armies of the one general in whom the troops had full confidence. Rochambeau was not blind to the faults of the Duc de Broglie but admired him as one professional admires another. In one particular engagement the General's complete indifference to danger endeared him not only to Rochambeau himself but to the whole Auvergne regiment. The Duke had stationed himself near Rochambeau's regiment to watch the progress of an attack he had ordered on the Crown Prince of Brunswick. Seeing that he was exhausted, Rochambeau offered him some bread and a glass of wine. At that moment an enemy shell exploded an ammunition wagon nearby. As soon as the smoke had cleared, Rochambeau saw that the Duke had not moved. He was still sitting in the same spot, glass in hand. Rochambeau could not help congratulating him on the fact that the explosion had not disturbed him. Broglie brushed off the compliment. "Monsieur," he replied, "I am dumfounded to see a regiment, after such an explosion, take up its position again with such order and such *sang-froid*."[5]

The Duc de Broglie had another opportunity to observe the gallant conduct of the Auvergne regiment at the Battle of Clostercamp. On this occasion, thanks to Rochambeau's regiment, the Duc was able to turn a near-defeat into victory. One incident of this battle, of which Rochambeau gives us a spirited description, has passed into the folklore of the French Army. During the night before the Battle of Clostercamp a *chasseur* of the Auvergne regiment, a certain Captain d'Assas, lost contact with his patrol and stumbled into a detachment of the enemy. He was quickly overpowered and warned, at the point of the bayonet, not to make a sound. Waiting for a moment until he could get his breath, the dauntless captain shouted at the top of his lungs, *"Tirez, chasseurs, ce sont les ennemis!"* The shout that cost him his life saved the French Army from a surprise attack which might well have proved disastrous.[6] As it was, the enemy were forced to give up the siege of Wesel and shortly afterward to retire across the Rhine, but though the French may be said to have won the battle, it was not the kind of victory that could be repeated often. The Auvergne lost fifty-eight of the eighty officers serving with the regiment at the time and more than eight hundred men. Among the casualties was Rochambeau himself. Though severely wounded in the thigh in the early stages of the battle, he insisted on being supported by two of his *chasseurs* so that he could conduct the operations of his regiment until the enemy broke off the engagement.

The Battle of Clostercamp played an important part in Rochambeau's career; it again brought him to the attention of the Duc de Broglie, through whose good offices he was promoted to the rank of *Maréchal de camp*.

In addition to his promotion Rochambeau was promised still more important favors. The King was so impressed by the account of his courage, his brilliant handling of troops on the battlefield, and his utterly selfless devotion to duty that he fully intended to reward him with a governorship of one of the towns of France as soon as one became vacant. These governorships were more or less sinecures, but because of the revenue that came with them they were very much in demand. Unfortunately for Rochambeau, either the King forgot about his promise or the governors were exceptionally long-lived, for it was fifteen years before he heard anything more about his governorship. Finally, on the sixteenth of April 1776, the King remembered the *fidèle conduite* of the Comte de Rochambeau and appointed him governor of Villefranche en Roussillon, a post that carried with it a revenue of eight thousand francs. Rochambeau's expenses in connection with his profession were always a source of worry to him, and the long-awaited governorship with its additional eight thousand francs a year must have been most welcome.

Considering that he would never have anything to do with the Court of Versailles and that he deliberately ignored Madame de Pompadour, Rochambeau scaled the ladder of promotion more rapidly than might have been expected. Hardly a month after his promotion to *Maréchal de camp* he was appointed inspector-general of infantry, a position he had coveted for a long time. Nor was he passed over in the list for decorations, though he did not receive the Grand Croix of the Order of St. Louis, to which his services entitled him, until 1771, eight years after the end of the war.

Another tribute, one that must have given him great satisfaction, came to him from an unexpected source. It came in the form of a letter from Lord Granby, the officer commanding the British cavalry in the Crown Prince of Brunswick's army, such a letter as adversaries in war no longer write each other. After the Battle of Wilhelmstal, in which Rochambeau had had to cover the retreat of the French Army, a thankless task which fell his lot more often than he liked, Granby wrote to thank Rochambeau for the excellent care he had taken of the prisoners he had captured, and to inform him about the condition of the French wounded in British hands. At the same time he congratulated Rochambeau on the brilliant manner in which he had extricated his army from the encircling German and British troops. "The bravery of your troops has not surprised me," says Lord Granby, "since learning from your officers of the great respect every one in the corps has for their general, and for the confidence they so rightly place in his judgment."[7] Rochambeau, who had no love for the British, was deeply touched. His most intimate friend could not have written him in a more complimentary way.[8]

Immediately after the engagement at Wilhelmstal, Rochambeau wrote to the Duc de Soubise, who had succeeded Broglie in command of the Army, demanding that he take the offensive. Granby's

troopers were exhausted. Now was the time to launch a counter-
attack. "If we content ourselves with parrying blows without giving
any," he writes, "we shall be like the strongest breastplate which
ends by being pierced." This remark was significant in view of the
fact that Rochambeau was later to be accused, particularly by La
Fayette, of being overcautious, a man wedded to the defensive. No
accusation could have been more false. Again and again during
these campaigns Rochambeau complains that the various marshals
under whom he served allowed opportunities for victory to
slip through their fingers, either through jealousy of each other
or indifference to the King's interests. In America he would be
fighting side by side with a man who was absolutely single-minded,
a man who never envisaged any outcome of the war except victory.
The Seven Years' War was different. The French people did not
feel themselves involved. For the armies it was a prolonged exercise in the art of war, rather than a life-and-death struggle in which
the fate of the nation was at stake.

The general mood of discouragement is well reflected in Voltaire's history of the period. Voltaire speaks of the utter useless-
ness of the bloodshed. As a result of the war France had lost her
marine, her commerce, her credit, and—worst of all—the flower
of her youth.[9] On the Prussian side the story was the same. "According to Friedrich's computation," says Carlyle, "there had perished of actual fighters, on the various fields, of all the nations,
853,000; of which above the fifth part, or 180,000, is his own
share: and, by misery and ravage, the general population of Prussia finds itself 500,000 fewer; nearly the ninth man missing."[10]

Rochambeau, who saw things more from the point of view of a
professional soldier than that of a philosopher or a historian, was
discouraged by the haphazard way in which the war was fought. If
the generals failed to make the most of their opportunities, it was
because no one in Paris or in Vienna was capable of long-range
planning. In a rare moment of bitterness he speaks of his last
campaign in Germany, just before the end of hostilities, as one of
the saddest of his life. By that time everything had been lost.

Canada, as Pitt expressed it, had been conquered in Germany. Great Britain had subsidized the King of Prussia and had sent a contingent of British troops to serve under the King's brother-in-law, Ferdinand of Brunswick, in order to divert the energies of France to the Continent, but Pitt never forgot that the war would be won or lost at sea. Aided by Madame de Pompadour's determination to have her own way and the general incompetence of Louis XV and his ministers, Pitt gave the English admirals an overpowering superiority which they used to such good effect that the French Navy was practically destroyed and the French possessions overseas almost all conquered.

These were lessons Rochambeau did not forget. Twenty years later, when he was being criticized at home and in America for keeping his four precious regiments bottled up in Rhode Island, he wisely dissuaded Washington from taking the offensive until they had convinced themselves that the sea lines of communication were secure.

Meanwhile in England the glittering prizes of the Seven Years' War had blinded all but a very few to the dangers that lay ahead. Acute observers had already predicted that the triumph of England would soon be followed by the revolt of her colonies. The destruction of the French power in America removed the one ever-pressing danger which secured the dependence of the English colonies on the mother country. By the time the victory celebrations were over the British people were beginning to realize that some of their conquests were splendid rather than useful. Furthermore, victories had to be paid for, and the burden of debts England had incurred revived schemes for the taxation of America which the colonists had hoped were never going to be mentioned again. France watched the train of events in America with the keenest attention. While the British ambassador in Paris could not put his finger on any specific breach of the peace, there was a general feeling in the air that the humiliating treaty of 1763 had left the French government highly receptive to the appeals for help from any nation, or would-be nation, ready to challenge the might of her age-old rival.

Notes

1. Montesquieu, *Lettres Persanes*, Letter 121.

2. "Le zèle dans mon métier fait tout mon bien, j'ay mangé vingt cinq mille francs de celuy de ma femme pour me faire un équipage et monter une maison telle qu'elle convenait à la place dont vous m'aviez honoré et dont je n'ai pas joui huit jours." *Archives de la Guerre*, Vol. 3462.

3. Williams, *The Fascinating Duc de Richelieu*, p. 265.

4. Rochambeau, *Mémoires*, I, 99.

5. *Ibid.*, I, 149.

6. *Ibid.*, I, 163. This story will also be found in Voltaire's *Précis du Siècle de Louis XV*.

7. *Archives de la Guerre*, Dossier of the Comte de Rochambeau, No. 1797.

8. "Mon ami intime ne m'auroit pas écrit d'un style plus honnête sur la vigueur et la précision des mouvements qu'il avait vu faire au corps de troupes françaises que je commandois, pour échapper à la triple supériorité de ses forces." Rochambeau, *Mémoires*, I, 200.

9. Voltaire, *Précis du Siècle de Louis XV*, chaps. 33 and 34.

10. Thomas Carlyle, *Frederick the Great*, book XX, ch. 13.

Five

Rochambeau's appointment as inspector-general of infantry brought him into close contact with the Duc de Choiseul, the new Secretary of War. It was a relationship from which both men profited. Choiseul, though he owed his position to Madame de Pompadour, happened to be a man of great ability. He has been described as being "very much like Sir Winston Churchill, with bright red hair, bright blue eyes, a turned-up nose, and an expression of humorous pugnacity. A *dogue* [mastiff], said his contemporaries."[1] Rochambeau nevertheless found the Duke a good man to work for, easily accessible, and open-minded enough to be willing to try out the reforms his inspector-general had so much at heart. Rochambeau was a born instructor. As soon as the peace was ratified he devoted himself to organizing training camps. Garrison duty in peacetime had always been a stultifying experience for everybody concerned. Instead of the old routine of guard duty and the manual of arms he instituted a series of tactical exercises and maneuvers, in which everyone in the Army, from the humblest trooper to the general, studied the lessons of the last war. During this period he himself began to show a talent for clear, forcible speaking on tactics and military affairs in general, of which, as he tells us in a moment of rare self-satisfaction, he had not previously been aware.

One aspect of Rochambeau's character which surprised Choiseul at first because he had never met it before, but which he soon learned to respect, was his complete indifference to intrigue. One of the men Rochambeau admired was the Duc de Broglie, who had been relieved of his command and confined to his own estate, largely at Choiseul's instigation. It was well known that Choiseul did not take kindly to requests to visit the old marshal in his exile, but Rochambeau, who never paid any attention to who was in or who was out, did not hesitate to demand permission to spend a few days with his old chief, for whom, as he told Choiseul, he had the greatest admiration. No one else talked to the all-powerful Choiseul quite so bluntly. It took him a moment, but only a moment, to recover from his surprise. Yes, Rochambeau should visit the Duc de Broglie whenever he wanted.

Even the King had to learn that Rochambeau was not a man to be trifled with. On one occasion His Majesty sent a messenger to Rochambeau's headquarters with special instructions, containing presumably some criticism of what Rochambeau was supposed to have said or done. Rochambeau received the officer in his tent in the presence of several colonels, and replied to the royal message in a way that must have endeared him to his staff. "Go tell the King that I have nothing to explain about so-called facts that never existed. Rochambeau is a loyal servant of France and of the King. I request the King to make a public statement assuring me of his confidence, otherwise I shall resign from the army and retire to Vendôme, there to grumble at my ease."[2] The King backed down without a word, and Rochambeau got his letter assuring him royal favor. Evidently Choiseul had advised the King that this outspoken soldier was too valuable a man to lose.

So long as Choiseul was in power Rochambeau knew that he had a friend at Court who would always back him up in his reforms, but with the death of Madame de Pompadour, Choiseul's enemies, led by the new favorite, Madame du Barry, were too much for him. Rochambeau remarks that the Minister usually had no difficulty in getting on with pretty women, but Madame du Barry was the exception. Whether he insulted her, as Rochambeau suggests, or whether she took an immediate dislike to him as the friend of her predecessor, Choiseul was relieved of his office and ordered to retire to his estate at Chanteloup. The new Minister began by revoking all the changes Choiseul had initiated, but Rochambeau stood his ground, and the reforms in Army administration he had advocated were later adopted.

With the death of the old King and the accession to the throne of Louis XVI, the prospects of the French Army and the Navy began to brighten. Under the new King, the royal mistresses disappeared and the general tone of public life improved. Though the ministers still followed each other in rapid succession—Rochambeau himself was offered the post of Minister of War at one moment, but he refused it—there was no question but that the fresh air he had pumped into Army administration was beginning to tell. Two of his pamphlets, the *"Mémoire sur l'Infanterie"* and the *"Mémoires sur les recrues et la désertion"* show how widely his mind ranged over every aspect of Army life. One of the principal tenets of his belief was that the King should be served by the best-trained troops in Europe, and that his troops should be given not only the best training but the best equipment available. No detail was too trivial for him. He even goes into the question of the material of the uniforms. It should be good enough to last two years, if it were turned the second year; at the end of which time it could be used as an undergarment.[3]

This close attention to the physical well-being of the Army as well as to economy did not preclude an intense awareness of the spiritual element in discipline. The recruit must be taught that the basis of all discipline is his duty to God and to the church. Officers must therefore form the habit of attending mass with their troops. Only religious training can safeguard a recruit from the temptations to which all soldiers are subject, and in particular from the crowning sin of desertion. Ever since the Battle of Rossbach, which France lost, partly at least because five thousand men were absent without leave on the day of the battle, Rochambeau had decided that the victories of Frederick the Great were due not so much to superior strategy as to superior morale.

The motive underlying all Rochambeau's reforms was his deep sense of justice. The soldier who felt that his superiors regarded him only as cannon fodder was not likely to give a good account of himself on the battlefield. Rochambeau was quick to forestall grievances. At a time when almost every officer came from the noble or ecclesiastical class, he championed the rights of the few commoners who had found their way into the Army. No sooner was peace declared than he discovered in the province of Dauphiné, where he was stationed, that some thirty-three of these officers were slated for discharge. Rochambeau promptly took up their case with Choiseul and convinced him that twenty-seven out of the thirty-three had earned the right to be kept on as commissioned officers in spite of their humble origins. A few years later such a decision might well have been attributed to the gathering forces of democracy, but there is nothing to indicate that Rochambeau was affected by any of the new social doctrines. It was merely that he knew a good officer when he saw one, and he hated to have the Army deliberately discriminate against the very men it needed. In his scheme of things there was no place for either the snob or the demagogue. He was not impressed by a man because he had a title before his name, nor was he prejudiced against him. The Revolution was to ride roughshod over men of his independent spirit, but when the storm had passed, the people woke up to find that many of these loyal servants of the old monarchy had a more genuine understanding of the rights of man than the self-styled patriots who had denounced them as aristocrats.

This sturdy independence, or obstinacy as some of his fellow officers were more inclined to call it, involved him on one occasion in an unfortunate misunderstanding with the Marshal de Broglie, the man to whom he owed his promotion and for whom he felt an almost filial affection. After the death of Louis XV, Broglie had been reinstated in favor and placed in command of the camp at Vaussieux in Normandy where, under Rochambeau's direction, troops were being trained for the inevitable war with England. To

Rochambeau was assigned the delicate task of testing out certain new tactics which he had initiated but of which Broglie strongly disapproved since they had been adopted by the man who had taken his place. One of the questions at issue was whether troops should be drawn up on the field of battle on a thin front or on a deep front. Rochambeau advocated *l'ordre mince* as opposed to the massed formations favored by the Marshal. The lightly held front offered less of a target to the enemy artillery. At the same time he pointed out that success on the field of battle did not depend on such-and-such a system laid down in the textbooks, but on the quick judgment of the man on the spot and the flexibility of his maneuvers. The Duc de Broglie was not convinced. The handbook on tactics had been written under his direction, and he resented any changes. In the field exercises that followed the discussion, Rochambeau found himself in the difficult position of proving to his commanding officer that he had been mistaken. He concluded magnanimously that the Marshal was a great tactician, and that if he had been led astray in this one instance it was because he had concerned himself with details that were not in his province and that were below his dignity.

Having demonstrated almost against his will that the new Army regulations he had drawn up were an improvement on the old, Rochambeau tactfully requested and was immediately granted three months' leave. At home with his wife in the Château of Rochambeau, he could indulge in the illusion shared by so many men of action that he wanted above all things to escape from the turmoil of life. He said good-by to the old marshal with tears in his eyes, but at the end of his three months, he was more than glad to be back at Vaussieux in command of the advance guard of the army being trained for the invasion. With him also at this time was his son, the Vicomte de Rochambeau, now twenty-four, who was serving his father as aide de camp. As a fighting soldier who had won his promotion on the battlefield and as a student of war who had devoted all his energies since the end of the Seven Years' War to questions of training, equipment, and administration, Rochambeau, if he had had sufficient rank, might himself have been chosen to command the expedition. Unfortunately, since he had no friends at Court, promotion had come to him slowly. He was still only a *Maréchal de camp,* a rank approximately equal to that of *Général de division* in the French Army of today.

As it turned out, the command of the invasion force was given not to Rochambeau or to the Duc de Broglie, who had every reason to expect it, but to the Comte de Vaux. Broglie, as his custom was, had quarreled with the Minister of War, who thereupon passed him over in favor of a man with whom he knew he would have no difficulties. The Comte de Vaux was something of a popular hero as the man who had defeated Paoli, the Corsican patriot, a victory which had led to the annexation of Corsica to France. He was selected, however, not so much for that reason as because he could be counted upon to obey orders without questioning them. As Rochambeau said, he was *"plus souple à suivre des ordres"*—he never asked the reason why.[4]

Whether or not Vaux was qualified for the command, Rochambeau was more than satisfied with the five battalions of *chasseurs* and grenadiers assigned to him for the advance guard. As soon as the landing was made, other troops were to be put at his disposal, so that ultimately he would be in command of seven thousand men. At last he was coming into his own. After fifteen years of administration, inspection, and training, he welcomed the prospect of active service and the opportunity it gave him of putting his new theories on tactics to the test.

Ever since the humiliating treaty of 1763, France had been casting about to find some way of retrieving her position. The expedition entrusted to Vaux and Rochambeau was born in the brain of Choiseul, and though Choiseul was no longer in power, the idea of making a direct attack on the English coast, instead of frittering away the Army and Navy in sporadic attacks on British possessions overseas, appealed to the Comte de Vergennes, the

new Minister of Foreign Affairs, no less than it had to his predecessor. Vergennes was a less brilliant but a more patient man than
Choiseul. As ambassador in Constantinople, Choiseul noted that
he had often found reasons for not doing what was proposed, but
when the decision was made he never found any difficulty in carrying it out. If Vergennes had been asked for the head of the Vizier
he would have grumbled, but he would have sent it. Jefferson, who
knew him only at the end of his career, considered him "a great
minister in European affairs but," says Jefferson, "he has very
imperfect ideas of our institutions, and no confidence in them. His
devotion to the principles of pure despotism renders him unaffec-
tionate to our governments. But his fear of England makes him
value us as a make weight. . . . It is impossible to have a clearer,
better organized head; but age has chilled his heart."[5] With this
realistic and utterly dedicated man Louis XVI felt perfectly at
home. The young King was intelligent enough to know that he
could rely completely on the judgment of his Foreign Minister.
Indeed, if Vergennes had lived a few years longer, and if he had
been at the King's side in the early days of the Revolution, the
course of French history might have been very different.

In 1779 Vergennes was not yet ready to throw in his lot with
the American colonies. Without quite knowing their resources, he
had already signed a treaty of commerce with them, a virtual
recognition of their autonomy, and he had secretly dispatched a
naval squadron to America under Vice-Admiral d'Estaing, but he
was more interested in waging war against England than in helping
the colonists win their independence. In his relations with America Vergennes was guided by the attitude of Spain. Early in April,
France and Spain had signed a secret convention which was in fact
a treaty of alliance against England. The one object of their policy
was to seize the moment of England's quarrel with her colonies to
avenge the defeats of previous wars, to cripple the commerce of
their hereditary enemy and, in the case of Spain, to win back the
rock of Gibraltar.[6] While ready enough to fish in troubled waters,

Spain was naturally reluctant to champion the cause of the colonists, whose rebellion against the mother country set a dangerous example to the inhabitants of her own immensely valuable dependencies in the New World. In view of the attitude of Spain, Vergennes and Count Florida Blanca, the Foreign Minister of His Catholic Majesty King Charles the Third, decided to aid the colonists indirectly by making a direct thrust at the heart of England's power.

Vergennes conceived a design of landing troops on the Isle of Wight and destroying the dockyards and arsenals of Portsmouth. By crippling the British Navy he would restore the balance of power in Europe. The success of this operation depended on the ability of the combined French and Spanish fleets to get control of the Channel, either by defeating or containing the British squadron on guard, and to hold control long enough to allow the safe passage of the French expeditionary force and its supplies. The army was to be provided by France, while Spain contributed half of the necessary shipping and a sum of money calculated on the expense of the regiments she would otherwise have been under obligation to supply. If the Spaniards had been more punctual at the rendezvous, the plan might well have succeeded. The British knew that a force of fifty thousand men had been assembled in the neighborhood of Havre and St. Malo, and that four hundred vessels were prepared for their transport, but the exact intentions of the enemy were unknown. Only one thing was certain. The combined French and Spanish fleet was superior to any force that could be collected to bar their way if they came up the Channel.

From the point of view of Vergennes the conditions for a successful raid on the south coast had never seemed more favorable. The bulk of the British Navy, under the incompetent direction of Lord Sandwich, had been sent across the Atlantic, leaving the Channel ports practically defenseless. A squadron of thirty-five ships, scraped together from every available quarter, under the command of Sir Charles Hardy, a retired veteran who for the last

nine years had been Governor of the Greenwich Hospital, was no
match for the great armada of sixty-six ships of the line that was
supposed to be bearing down on them. Rochambeau and the
Comte de Vaux had every reason for confidence. Their army was
ready for embarkation, well-equipped and well-trained, but as the
summer wore on and the mighty fleet never appeared, the confidence gave way to disappointment and finally to disgust. Once
again the difficulty of combining operations with allies was brought
home to Rochambeau, and presumably filed away for future reference.

The troubles began in the office of M. de Sartine, the Minister of
Marine, who was so intent on getting his ships to sea that, ignoring the pleas of Admiral d'Orvilliers, the most experienced tactician in the French Navy, he sent them off badly manned and short
of provisions and water. D'Orvilliers arrived at the rendezvous off
Corunna on the eleventh of June, but not until the twenty-third of
July did the Spanish fleet join him. By that time he was running
short of water and provisions, sickness was spreading among his
crews, and the fair-weather period was coming to an end. Even
after the Spanish admiral joined him, more time was wasted in
agreeing upon a common code of signals and in teaching it to the
fleet. D'Orvilliers must have had his forebodings, for he warned
Sartine not to expect skillful maneuvering from vessels of different
navies that had had no experience working together.

Finally at the end of July, the combined fleets headed northward. They were already six weeks late, and they loitered for a
while in front of Brest, exchanging messages with the Ministry at
Versailles, but by the middle of August they were at the mouth of
Plymouth Sound without having seen a British ship. In spite of his
difficulties, D'Orvilliers seemed on the verge of success. No one
knew the whereabouts of Sir Charles Hardy or what disaster might
have befallen him. Actually he was cruising sixty miles west of the
Scillies, "as the most proper station for the security of the trade
expected from the East and West Indies, and for meeting with the

fleets of the enemy should they attempt to come up Channel."[7] Nothing was certain except that D'Orvilliers had thrust himself between the British fleet and the British arsenals and dockyards. The seriousness of the situation was brought home to the naval commandant at Plymouth when the *Ardent,* a fine ship of sixty-four guns, was cut off and captured within sight of the ramparts.

At this critical moment sickness in the French ships, the interference of the French authorities in Paris, and a change in the weather combined to avert a British catastrophe. The French ships had set out on their voyage with smallpox on board. So serious was the epidemic that five hundred of the worst cases were put ashore at Corunna, but by that time the whole fleet was infected. One captain reported that those of his men who still had strength to go aloft were too few to make sail, and that if he encountered the enemy he would be unable to muster sufficient hands to prepare his ship for action.

While D'Orvilliers was lying becalmed outside Plymouth, wondering how long he could remain at sea, a frigate brought him new instructions. The project for invasion had been entirely altered. The idea of a landing on the Isle of Wight had been abandoned. The new plan was to land the troops, or at any rate that part of the Comte de Vaux's army that was at St. Malo, in Falmouth Bay on the south coast of Cornwall. D'Orvilliers was further informed that it was the King's intention that the fleet should remain at sea for several months, and that a supply convoy was about to leave Brest to join him. The day after these instructions reached him, August 17, an easterly wind sprang up and D'Orvilliers was compelled to weigh anchor and give his attention to the safety of the fleet instead of to invasion plans. The wind gradually increased to a gale, and by the twentieth the combined fleet was driven fifty miles west of the Lizard. The same wind blew Hardy's squadron to the westward so that the two fleets were still fifty miles apart.

In view of the increase in disease, the change of plans, and the impossibility of ferrying the French army across the Channel

owing to the lateness of the season, D'Orvilliers, after chasing the
British squadron and not catching up with it, anchored in Brest
Harbor on the fourteenth of September. The Spanish squadrons,
having parted company offshore, returned to their own ports.
D'Orvilliers came back to France a broken-hearted man. He had
failed in his mission and he had lost his son, a fine young naval
officer who was serving on one of his fever-stricken ships and who,
like so many others, had fallen victim to smallpox.

The complete failure of the Vergennes plan for a descent upon
the coast of England is one of the forgotten incidents of naval
history, forgotten because it does not reflect credit on any of the
nations involved. As an English historian has aptly expressed it:

"The story of the Armada of the sixteenth century is familiar,
but the story of the insolent threat to the British flag when the
French and Spanish fleets sailed unchallenged up Channel in 1779
fills a comparatively obscure page in English history. Never were
these shores in greater peril from an invader. Fortunately no leader
appeared among the allies possessing the rare talent of command
or the inspired gift of naval daring who was capable of turning the
situation to the decisive advantage of their arms."[8]

Of all those involved in the plans for invasion, no one was more
disillusioned than Rochambeau. He had worn himself out in
maneuvers and in training his *chasseurs* and his grenadiers so that
they would be able to cope with every conceivable contingency.
His friend the Duc de Lauzun, who took life more lightheartedly,
complained that M. de Rochambeau could talk of nothing but
troop movements. He was always maneuvering troops, in the field,
on the beaches, on the table in his room, or if you offered him a
pinch of snuff on the cover of the snuff box. Rochambeau did not
quarrel with the decision of the Council of War, held at Brest late
in September, that the attempt to land a force on the south coast of
England must be given up, at least for that year. At the same time
he had no hesitation in describing the abortive campaign against
England as the most extravagant and badly planned operation he

had ever known. After thirty-seven years in the Army, much of it spent in trying to rectify the mistakes of other men, he was thinking more seriously than ever of retiring to private life. He was married to a wife he adored, and they were both weary of separation. In the last list of promotions he had finally been appointed lieutenant-general, which represented a fitting climax to his career. This promotion, the last he could expect, coupled with the death of his father, which necessitated his presence at home, plus the fact that he was suffering from inflammatory rheumatism, decided the question for him. True, certain rumors had reached him that an expeditionary force was to be sent to America and that he was being spoken of for the command, but since the Minister of War had approved his request for indefinite leave, he paid no attention to what must have seemed to him idle gossip.

The post horses were actually at the door of his house in Paris, in the rue du Cherche-Midi, ready to start for Vendôme, when a courier from Versailles ordered him to report to the King at once. Visions of a comfortable old age evaporated as Rochambeau clattered out to Versailles to receive His Majesty's instructions. The details of the interview are unknown, but whatever was said touched off a train of events that led not merely to the independence of the thirteen colonies, but beyond that to the creation of the United States and the downfall of the French monarchy.

Notes

1. Nancy Mitford, *Madame de Pompadour* (London, 1953), p. 240.
2. "Allez dire à sa Majesté que je n'ai pas à m'expliquer sur des faits qui n'ont pas existé. Rochambeau sert loyalement la France et le Roy. Je prie notamment le Roy de me donner publiquement des preuves de sa confiance, ou j'abandonnerai le service et rentrerai dans Vendôme pour y grogner à mon aise." *Nouvelle Revue,* Vol. XVI (n.s.), 319.
3. "Il doit être d'une étoffe à durer deux ans, en la retournant la seconde

année . . . le manteau peut etre destiné à faire le gilet ou la veste de dessous."
Rochambeau, "Mémoire sur l'Infanterie," *Archives de la Guerre.*

4. Rochambeau, *Mémoires,* I, 233.

5. *Jefferson Papers,* edited by Julian P. Boyd (Princeton, 1955), XI, 95.

6. In a letter to the French ambassador to Spain, September 21, 1779, Vergennes states his foreign policy very clearly:

"Remember that I have always laid down the principle that while devoting our efforts to humbling England, we must carefully avoid giving any impression that we are seeking her destruction. She is necessary to the balance of Europe, wherein she occupies a considerable place. . . . We shall be feared less if we content ourselves with cutting off our enemy's arms than if we insist on running him through the heart."

Quoted by A. Temple Patterson in *The Other Armada* (Manchester, 1960). The letter will be found in the Archives du Ministère des Affaires Etrangères.

7. Captain W. M. James, *The British Navy in Adversity* (London, 1933), p. 179.

8. Captain W. M. James, *The British Navy in Adversity* (London, 1933), p. vi.

Six

THE KING'S ORDERS were explicit. Rochambeau at age fifty-five had been chosen to head an expeditionary force of four thousand men which the government had decided to send to America to aid the colonists in their struggle for independence. The expedition was to set sail as soon as possible, not later than the beginning of April. The selection of the commander-in-chief appears to have been made by the Prince de Montbarey, the Secretary of the Army, who was wise enough to see that Rochambeau was better fitted for this difficult command than anybody else. Not that he was particularly friendly with Rochambeau; indeed Montbarey's references to him in his memoirs are anything but complimentary,[1] but of the other two generals considered, the Duc de Broglie was too quarrelsome and the Comte de Vaux too easy-going. Rochambeau had their virtues without their defects. He never quarreled with anybody, he was not an intriguer, he was firm without being truculent, and above all he was a man in whom the Army had the greatest confidence. Rochambeau knew his métier. It was a popular appointment.

Whether Rochambeau coveted this honor or whether he approved of the war we do not know, but it is interesting to note that Montbarey was definitely out of sympathy with the idea of sending troops to America. As a good public servant, he accepted the decision of the Cabinet. At the same time he makes it thoroughly clear in his memoirs that whatever success might be achieved would never compensate the nation for the staggering expenses involved. France was being ruined for interests that were not her own.[2] Rochambeau does not seem to have been aware of these opinions. At any rate he does not mention them, and though he is critical of the staffwork of the Secretary of the Navy he has no fault to find with Montbarey.

Rochambeau, who is usually reticent when we want him to be expansive, has little to say about the circumstances of his appointment. He tells us only that he had been thinking of retiring. In the eighteenth century a man of fifty-five was considered elderly, particularly a man who had been wounded as repeatedly and as seriously as Rochambeau. At the same time, whether he felt tired or not, he could hardly fail to have been elated by this long-delayed recognition of his talents. At long last, after forty years' service, he was to be given an independent command. The French troops were to serve as a separate unit, but with that proviso in mind he was to accommodate himself in every way to the wishes of General Washington. Those who care for historical parallels may be interested to note that, in the first world war, President Wilson issued the same instructions to General Pershing. American units were not to be broken up, otherwise they were to be at the disposal of Marshal Foch. The instructions to Rochambeau made it clear that the French troops were serving as auxiliaries and that therefore they must always yield the place of honor to the Americans. Not the least important part of his instructions was the emphasis on maintaining good relations with the Americans. The French were determined to do their part, and in return the King was confident that a man of General Washington's well-known humanity would not risk carelessly the lives of the brave men who were being sent more than a thousand leagues to the rescue of his country.[3]

Since in war all eventualities must be considered, Rochambeau was told that, in the event of the American Army being overwhelmed by the British, he was to withdraw the expeditionary force to Santo Domingo, where he would find good wintering.

In his first interview with the King, before these instructions were issued, Rochambeau had respectfully pointed out that a force of four thousand men was hardly adequate for the task in hand. At the battles of Laufeldt and Clostercamp he had lost two thirds of the troops under his command. If the same casualties were to occur in America, as was quite possible, he would need a minimum of six thousand men. A corps of twelve battalions or six thousand men would enable him to keep one third in reserve, to strike a decisive blow in the event of victory, or to protect the retreat in the case of a reverse. Rochambeau felt so strongly on this point that he would probably not have accepted the command if the King had not let him have his way. As it was the King, presumably on the advice of Vergennes, who drafted the instructions, made no difficulties. His heart was set on this expedition and the commander-in-chief he had selected should have what he wanted. On the understanding that he was to have his six thousand men, and that a second contingent would follow later, Rochambeau forgot his inflammatory rheumatism and plunged into all the problems that such an expedition involved.

Louis XVI, so timid and ineffective in tackling abuses at home under his very eyes, had no difficulty in making up his mind on the American question. It is hard to believe that the grievances of the colonists can have seemed very distressing to so absolute a monarch, but believing as he did that England had always been the enemy of his house and that she was always ready to make war on France when it suited her convenience, common sense dictated that he should step up the aid France was already giving England's rebellious colonies. Having failed in an effort to strike a blow at British naval installations by landing a force on the Isle of Wight, he was ready to listen to, and eager to believe, those like Vergennes who told him that the ancient enemy who had wrested away her colonial empire from her was herself more vulnerable overseas than at home.

Vergennes, who had been trying all through the year 1779 to align his policy with Spain, was now almost against his will falling under the influence of the Marquis de La Fayette, to whom the

Spanish connection meant nothing. At the age of nineteen this glittering young man, a captain in the Dragoons, had made his way to America, been wounded at the Battle of the Brandywine, endeared himself to Washington, and established himself before the world as the connecting link between France and the United States. After two years' service in the field Congress had granted him a furlough, and he had returned to his own country to plead the cause of the "insurgents." The unexpected and triumphant return of the Marquis de La Fayette, still only a captain in the French Army but a major-general in the service of the United States, rekindled enthusiasm in Paris for the American cause. The French had begun to tire of this long-drawn-out conflict to which there seemed to be no issue, and here was La Fayette back again, talking of liberty and independence in a way that made the gilded young men of Versailles tremble with excitement. All kinds of rumors about his prowess had been spread abroad. As one biographer puts it, "he was the crusader back from the Holy Land— and if the Holy Land was not quite as holy as it ought to be, that was, after all, quite consistent with the story of the Crusades."[4]

After a week under technical arrest in Paris, for in going to America in 1777 without the King's permission he had committed an offense which the King had to appear to punish, La Fayette was free to visit Versailles and present himself to the sovereign. The jail happened to be the very comfortable house in Paris (now the Hotel St. James et d'Albany) belonging to his wife's grandfather, the Duc de Noailles. Since he was allowed to see friends and relations, and since all Paris was at his feet, the "punishment" was actually the gentlest of reprimands.

La Fayette had returned from the United States with two objects in view. One was to persuade the French government to champion the American cause, which he now referred to as "our cause," more vigorously. He already thought of himself as a citizen of two worlds. In his letters to Washington he writes as an American, and when he writes to Vergennes he resumes his French nationality.

The other object he had in view was to bring about the discomfiture of Great Britain in any and every way possible. His fertile brain was teeming with schemes whereby these two desirable objects might be accomplished simultaneously. He wanted to invade Canada, stir up a revolution in Ireland, and sail around England and Scotland with John Paul Jones, attacking important seaports, seizing prominent citizens and holding them for ransom. The French government raised John Paul Jones to the rank of commodore and put him at the head of a squadron of five ships, including an old East Indiaman which he renamed the *Bonhomme Richard*. With this squadron he did great damage to British shipping and captured a number of prizes, among them the *Serapis,* but by that time La Fayette was occupied with other and bigger schemes. Much that he suggested was foolish and ill-considered, yet as he went the rounds of the French ministers, pleading the cause of his adopted country and proposing one plan after another for squaring accounts with Great Britain, some of his enthusiasm may have rubbed off. Franklin listened attentively to the breathless young schemer, though he did not always agree with him, and even the cautious, slow-moving Vergennes seemed to feel something of the political foresight and the boyish charm that had won the respect as well as the affection of George Washington. Only Choiseul, Louis XV's old minister, refused to be impressed. Gilles le Grand he called him, after Gilles, the fool's part on the French stage, but Choiseul was no longer a factor in French politics.

As soon as he heard there was a plan on foot to invade England, La Fayette bombarded Vergennes with letters begging that he be given a command in the expedition. Let him land in England at the head of two thousand grenadiers, which was after all only a third of the number he had often commanded in America. Vergennes must know how eager he was to land on English soil and plant the first French flag in the midst of that "insolent nation."[5]

La Fayette was finally assigned to the expedition as an assistant quartermaster-general, which was not at all what he wanted, but it gave him an opportunity to write patronizing letters about the Comte de Vaux, whose disciplinary measures he found very satisfactory. Having been a major-general himself, he knew the value of discipline. He was probably not disappointed when the whole plan of invasion, in which he was to play such a minor role, was called off. Now at last he was free to concentrate on the project of sending an army to America, which was even closer to his heart than the invasion of England.

Others besides La Fayette had broached this matter of an expeditionary force, but he was the first man to speak about it with any authority. He knew there were many American patriots, John Adams among them, who were not in favor of the French sending troops to America. Adams was confident that the colonials could handle the British troops themselves, provided France kept the ports open and supplied Congress with the necessary funds. The American government had asked for a great deal from France, but neither Washington nor Franklin had formally requested aid in the form of the manpower La Fayette was so anxious to bring them. The world must not be allowed to think that the colonists were at the end of their rope, as they actually were, and that without the stiffening of the French Army, as well as that of the French Navy and Treasury, they could never hope to win their independence. There were many other prejudices and obstacles to be overcome. The French were not popular in America. Earlier in the war the French government had sent a powerful fleet to America under command of Admiral d'Estaing with instructions to perform "some action advantageous to the Americans, glorious for the arms of the King, and fitted to show the protection which His Majesty extends to his allies."[6] D'Estaing had been repulsed at Savannah and he had again failed, largely through misunderstandings with General Sullivan, in an attempt to capture Newport. The bad feeling, skillfully fomented by the Tories, resulting from this abortive campaign had not encouraged Americans to think well of the French Navy or of the French Army.

In spite of these and many other objections, La Fayette kept hammering away at his pet project. Certainly there would be jealousies between the French and the Americans, but if the right man were chosen to lead the expedition, a man who understood the Americans and had already won their confidence, he was confident these jealousies could easily be overcome. In his letters to the Comte de Maurepas, whom Louis XVI had selected as his chief minister, and Vergennes, the foreign minister, with whom he was more intimate, La Fayette reminded them that Franklin, for whom they had the greatest respect, was very much in favor of his plans, and that France stood to gain as much from American independence as the Americans themselves. As British power declined, French prestige would rise. British commerce would suffer an irreparable loss by the separation of the colonies, from which France would surely profit.

How La Fayette at twenty-two can have so impressed himself on these elder statesmen is one of the mysteries of the Revolution, yet if he had not pleaded the cause of the colonists so eloquently Rochambeau and his four regiments would never have been sent to America. Not that Rochambeau was the leader La Fayette would have selected. La Fayette made it abundantly clear that he considered himself the obvious choice. Who else could handle the different elements in Congress so well as he? Who else could distinguish between an officer from Boston and one from New York? Such knowledge was essential.[7]

There was certainly plenty of egoism in La Fayette, plenty of talk about his own amazing popularity with the Americans. It is all the more to his credit therefore that when he was passed over in favor of Rochambeau, who did not speak English and knew nothing about America, he did not sulk in his tent. Louis XVI and his ministers recognized his undoubted abilities and were influenced by his arguments, but they could not give the command of an expeditionary force to a young man who was totally unknown to the French Army, however brilliant he might be. The other officers would have refused to serve under him.

Evidently La Fayette suspected that someone else might be

chosen, for he recommended that if he were not given the command, even though he was ideally suited for it, he should be sent to
America at once to pave the way for the arrival of the French
troops. To this suggestion Vergennes readily agreed, and everything was done to satisfy his wounded pride. On the morning of
February 29, 1780, instead of dodging a *lettre de cachet* as he had
done on his first visit to America, La Fayette, dressed in the uniform of an American major-general, paid a formal visit to Versailles to take leave of the King and Queen. Marie Antoinette was
particularly friendly. The time was to come when she would hate
La Fayette with a fierce hatred, but for the moment he was in her
good graces. Was he not bound for America again to help those
charmingly homespun colonials, whose funny republicanism appealed to her just as the *petit Trianon* appealed to her, as representing an escape from the stuffy formalities of Versailles?

Before leaving Paris, La Fayette made a point of seeing Rochambeau and giving him the benefit of his experience. As an
American major-general and as France's accredited representative
to the American commander-in-chief, no one was better fitted to
give advice than La Fayette. In the assumption of these two very
different roles he managed to antagonize a good many of his countrymen, but Rochambeau was never one to stand on his dignity
where the service of the King was concerned. He listened attentively to the younger man and profited from everything he told
him. La Fayette warned him that his army must be entirely self-
sufficient. The Americans themselves were in want of everything.
Rochambeau must take with him not only such obvious things as
flints for the muskets, harness for the artillery horses, flour, bis-
cuits, bricks with which to build ovens—these could be brought
over as ballast—but also such unexpected items as needles and
thread, leather for shoes, tools of all kinds, and even beads with
which to win the friendship of the Indians. An expedition into
what used to be known as Darkest Africa could not have been
planned with more care.

As a result of his conferences with La Fayette, Rochambeau drew up two documents, one for Montbarey, the Minister of War, and the other for Sartine, the Minister of Marine, specifying the equipment he would need. The first sentence in the document addressed to the Minister of Marine is significant: *"Rien sans la marine prépondérante."* Without naval superiority Rochambeau knew he could achieve nothing. He had pondered the loss of Canada, and he had rightly interpreted the struggle in America, in which he was now to be engaged, as essentially a maritime war. Washington's army must be kept alive to take advantage of the opportunities offered by the Navy, but the ultimate success of the colonists depended on the issue of the fight between Great Britain and the triple forces of France, Spain, and Holland for the control of the sea along the American coast and for access to the West Indies and the Indian Ocean.

Fortunately for France, while England had allowed her sea forces to decay at the end of the Seven Years' War, the Duc de Choiseul and his cousin, the Duc de Choiseul-Praslin, who between them controlled the destinies of France from the end of the war to 1770, had gone to work to reconstruct the French Navy as well as to reorganize the French Army. In the dockyards of Bordeaux, St. Malo, and Brest ships had been built with feverish activity. French shipwrights turned out a three-decker in fourteen months compared to the three years required by the British.[8] Choiseul had breathed a new spirit into the personnel of the service, and his reforms had touched every branch of naval administration. At the same time he made his countrymen understand that it was their duty to contribute to the rebuilding of the Navy, since the very existence of their country depended upon it. The citizens of Paris gave the money for the building of the great three-decker, the *Ville de Paris* which was to become the flagship of Admiral de Grasse and as such played an important part in the victory at Yorktown. Other French provinces were equally patriotic.

By the end of March 1780, six regiments quartered near Brest were ready to embark, the Bourbonnais, Saintonge, Soissonnais, Royal Deux-Ponts, Anhalt, and Neustrie, plus the Lauzun Legion. The Legion was a "proprietary" corps owned by the Duc de Lauzun and raised by him for colonial service under authority of the Minister of Marine. Rochambeau had not lost an hour's time, but the Navy had not been able to keep pace with him. Under M. de Sartine, the new Minister of Marine, the admirable efficiency established by the Duc de Choiseul had lapsed into neglect. As Rochambeau noted, the watch of the Minister of Marine was very apt to be slow. Having been in too much of a hurry the year before, when he sent D'Orvilliers' squadron out to sea before the ships were properly equipped, Sartine now went to the other extreme. This time he would not be hurried. Six ships of the line were riding at anchor in Brest Harbor ready to safeguard the convoy across the Atlantic, but there were no transports available. The departure of another fleet for the West Indies had stripped Brest of all its troopships. The Chevalier de Ternay, who had been appointed to command the squadron, was in despair. Orders for troopships were sent to Bordeaux and St. Malo, but when they finally hove into view Rochambeau and Ternay discovered to their disgust that there were not enough of them. Instead of waiting for the missing transports they were ordered to embark as many men as possible in the vessels available and to put out to sea immediately. Two regiments, the Anhalt and the Neustrie, had to be left behind, on the understanding that they would follow in the next convoy. Rochambeau had intended embarking horses for his cavalry, but these too would have to wait for the second division. So short of space were they that Rochambeau could not even take his own two horses with him; they would have taken up the place of twenty men.

By crowding the troops together in what today would be considered disgustingly unsanitary conditions, Ternay managed to embark about fifty-five hundred men. The convoy was ready to sail by the middle of April, but there was a tedious delay of another two weeks while they waited for the wind to shift to the right quarter. Finally, on May 2, they got under way. Rochambeau wrote the last of his many letters to Montbarey, the Minister of War, recommending the fortunes of the expedition to the friendship of an old comrade and the zeal of a faithful Minister of the State. He may well have feared, and if so his fears were only too well grounded, that the government would leave him to shift for himself as soon as he got to America. Meanwhile he could take satisfaction in the knowledge that he had been given some of the best regiments in the French Army. The corps was still too small for his liking, but the officers were competent and the morale unusually high.

Men and officers alike were eager to see the New World and to strike a blow for American liberty. It may seem strange that French aristocrats, whose peasants were far more downtrodden than any American colonist, should have been so captivated by the vision of political liberty three thousand miles away. La Fayette, one of the greatest landowners in France, with estates in Brittany, Touraine, and the Auvergne, did not even know whether his peasants were serfs or not. Everything was left in the hands of his agent, and as long as his agent produced substantial revenues, which La Fayette spent on equipping American soldiers, no questions were asked. The King had recently freed all serfs in the royal domains, hoping that the big landowners of France would follow his example, but whether they did or not was their affair.[9]

Strange it may have been, but the fact is that the war in America to give men rights they had not yet won in France fired the imagination of all kinds and conditions of men. Distance lent enchantment to the view. "All France," we read in the Grimm and Diderot correspondence, "was filled with an unbounded love for humanity," and felt a passion for "those maxims which rouse the enthusiasm of young men and would cause them to run to the world's end to help a Laplander or a Hottentot." No doubt, to the younger generation of today these feelings will not seem as absurd as they did to Grimm and Diderot.

The whole expeditionary force seems to have been equipped with rose-colored spectacles. Many of those who sailed had read their Rousseau and were determined to find a new Arcady in America. Noble savages, romantic scenery, social equality, and a struggle for liberty under the banner of a leader who might well have stepped out of the pages of Plutarch—surely a golden age was in the making!

The senior officers included many of the best-known names in French history. The Duc de Lauzun, the Chevalier de Chastellux, the Vicomte de Noailles, the Comte de Charlus and the Comte de Custine—these men and many others like them were as eager to risk their lives for American independence as their ancestors had been to fight for the Holy Sepulchre. In America they were all united in a common cause, but the French Revolution drove them into different camps. The colonel of the Soissonnais, the Comte de Saint-Maime, remained faithful to the Bourbons, while his second in command, the Vicomte de Noailles, influenced no doubt by his observation of society in the New World, gave an impetus to the French Revolution by proposing in the National Assembly the abolition of feudal rights. Later he became a general in the Revolutionary Armies and was killed in a battle with the British in West Indian waters. The Saintonge was commanded by the Comte de Custine, who also rose to the rank of general in the Revolutionary armies. Successful at first, he was finally defeated and, along with many other aristocrats who held high commands and failed, he was suspected of treason and marked for the guillotine. The colonel of the Bourbonnais was a Laval Montmorency who emigrated during the Revolution and returned to France with the Bourbons in 1815. His second in command, the Vicomte de Rochambeau, the general's son, was not so fortunate. Captured in the West Indies during the Napoleonic wars, he spent seven years in a British prison. He was exchanged, unfortunately, in time to take part in the 1813 campaign and was killed at the Battle of Leipsic.

The fourth regiment in Rochambeau's corps, the Royal Deux-

Ponts, was a proprietary regiment under the command of Count Christian Forbach des Deux-Ponts, ruler of the Duchy of Deux-Ponts, also known as the Duchy of Saarbruck-Zweibrucken. This regiment, which was recruited out of the dominions of the Bishop of Liége, was entirely German-speaking. While the rulers of Hesse and Anspach hired out their troops to the British, the Dukes of Deux-Ponts remained fiercely loyal to France.

Rochambeau was particularly fortunate in his three *Maréchaux de camp*,[10] the Baron de Vioménil, his brother the Vicomte, and the Chevalier de Chastellux. According to one Newport admirer, the Vioménil brothers were the best-looking men in the world. The Baron, Antoine Charles de Houx, who commanded the corps after Rochambeau went home, was a hot-tempered man who did not get on with the Americans as well as Rochambeau or Chastellux, but there was no question about his ability or his courage. As soon as the Revolution broke out in France he became an unquestioning supporter of the royal family, and he fell mortally wounded in their defense during the attack on the Tuilleries, August 10, 1792.

The Chevalier de Chastellux should be better known to posterity than any other of Rochambeau's officers, as he recorded his impressions of America in a lively book of travels.[11] No one has given us a more spirited picture of the American scene during the Revolutionary period. As his recent editor has pointed out, Chastellux's book is not a soldier's report on the military events in which he played an important part, but rather an account of journeys made between campaigns, when he was freed from the active duties of his command. As soon as the French Army had dug itself in at Newport and Rochambeau had satisfied himself that the British Army had no intention of attacking him, Chastellux seems to have been given an indefinite leave of absence in which to explore the country and indulge his passion for sightseeing. His first journey took him through New England, across the Hudson to Washington's headquarters in New Jersey, and on down to Philadelphia, where to his great delight he was elected a member of the American Philosophical Society. The pleasure over his election was considerably enhanced by the fact that it was unanimous, whereas La Fayette, who was elected at the same time, received one blackball. He returned to Newport via Albany and Boston, having been away for three months.

Chastellux certainly made the most of his opportunities. A professional soldier who had distinguished himself in the Seven Years' War, he was also a literary man of some importance, a friend of the Encyclopedists, and the author of a two-volume work on public welfare, *De la Félicité Publique,* which Franklin said showed him to be a real friend of humanity. Without being a profound thinker, he applied his mind to everything. He found the pageantry of life endlessly fascinating, and he was always flinging open windows to get a more extensive view. As one keenly interested in the new frontiers of knowledge he was the first to plunge into the scientific, or pseudo-scientific, sensation of the moment. When Mesmer, the Austrian doctor who gave his name to mesmerism, arrived in Paris, Chastellux attended his lectures and immediately rushed into print with an article on animal magnetism. For us the remarkable thing about Chastellux is that he was willing to forgo the infinite variety of Paris as soon as he found there was a chance of getting to America. The liveliness of his book of travels proves that he was not disappointed.

The most famous, or at least the most notorious, of the officers who sailed with Rochambeau was the Duc de Lauzun. Armand Louis de Gontaut, Duc de Lauzun, later known as the Duc de Biron, was the epitome of everything that was extravagant, self-indulgent, reckless, gallant, and charming in the *ancien régime*. The list of the Duc de Lauzun's conquests, as he reports them in his memoirs, grows wearisome, but there was another side to him which was more admirable. In between his facile love affairs he devoted himself to the Army. As a reward for his exploits in Senegal, which he captured from the British, Louis XVI made him not only the colonel but also the owner of the regiment bearing his name. In one of her wonderful letters to Horace Walpole, Madame du Deffand says that the garrison captured by the Duc de Lauzun in Senegal consisted of four men, three of whom were sick, and that he would have done a good deal better if he had found a few gold mines with which to pay his debts. However that may be, he was sufficiently in favor at Court to be given a command in Rochambeau's army. Owing to the lack of space only half of the Légion Lauzun could be taken aboard, but the Duke was promised that the remaining six hundred would be sent over with the second division. Lauzun bitterly resented that his legion was not kept intact and that they had to leave their horses behind, but with the limited space available there was no question of shipping over horses.

During his stay in Newport, this *romanesque* character was billeted in the house of Mrs. Hunter, a widowed lady to whom he was much devoted, as he was to her three daughters, but for once in his life there was no scandal. The man who had the reputation of being the greatest rake in Europe behaved with great circumspection during his two years in America. Maybe he found the easy cameraderie between the sexes, noted by Chastellux, a refreshing change from the grand passions in which he had always been involved in Europe. At any rate, Lauzun thoroughly enjoyed life at the charming house at 264 Thames Street, where he regaled the Hunter ladies with anecdotes of life in London, in Poland, Corsica, Senegal, not forgetting of course Paris and Versailles. Had they been his own sisters, said Lauzun, he could not have been more devoted to them.

Rochambeau picked Lauzun to carry back to France the news of Cornwallis' capitulation, but in spite of this gesture of friendship the two men did not get on well together. Lauzun was not the type of man to appeal to Rochambeau, and no doubt he was conscious of it. He complains in his memoirs that Rochambeau never mentioned in his dispatches Washington's letter of commendation about him. In contrast, Rochambeau's aides were devoted to him. The position of aide de camp was one much in demand. Since the needs of the aristocracy determined the size of its officer corps, the French Army of the period had a large surplus of officers. Many of these could be carried only *à la suite*— attached to some unit which they were usually not encouraged to annoy with their presence. Unless these surplus officers could be taken on as aides they were left behind when their regiments went on active service. Among those selected as aides by Rochambeau were a certain Count Axel de Fersen, devoted to Marie Antoinette, who within a few years would be organizing the flight of the royal family to Varennes, and a friend of his, Mathieu Dumas, a young officer in the engineers who, by a strange quirk of fortune, was the man who guarded the royal coach on the return from Varennes to Paris. Others included the Chevalier Charles de Lameth, later one of the liberal deputies in the National Assembly in the early days of the French Revolution. Charles de Lameth, who was badly wounded at Yorktown, was one of three brothers who fought for liberty in America. Like so many of their friends who hoped to graft American ideas of liberty on to the French monarchy, they were eventually forced to fly their country to escape the guillotine. Finally there was Baron Ludwig von Closen, an inquiring young German whose journal is one of the main sources of information about the French expeditionary corps.

These eager young men and many others had flocked to Brest to win a place in the expedition. The ships (the wretched *sabots,* Closen called them) were so tightly packed that not everyone could be taken on board. Among those left behind, though he did get to America later, was Captain Alexandre Berthier, one day to be Napoleon's chief of staff, who clung to the rope ladder of the flagship and begged to be taken on as one of the crew.

One of the most controversial figures in the expedition was the Chevalier de Ternay, the admiral in command of the squadron. Rochambeau speaks well of him but he was not generally popular, either with the Navy or the Army. Ternay was of the school who

thought the whole expedition was becoming too elaborate. He
complained of all the paraphernalia he was called upon to find
room for in his already overloaded ships.[12] Like so many of those
who insist on keeping to the letter of the law, Ternay was not
enterprising by nature. He demanded precise instructions, which
he observed meticulously but would not venture one inch beyond.
The issue came up as to whether he should engage British ships
they came across on the way over, or whether he should devote his
whole attention to getting his convoy to its destination as quickly
and as safely as possible. Much to the disgust of the young gallants
on board, he decided to play for safety.

Before sailing Ternay had received word that Rear-Admiral
Thomas Graves of the British Navy would be racing him across
the Atlantic, hoping to intercept his convoy before they reached
their destination. The long delay at Brest that resulted from the
lack of transports and the unfavorable weather had been a source
of great anxiety, but Rochambeau comforted himself with the reflection that it was raining in Portsmouth too. The two fleets sailed
almost simultaneously, Graves being favored by the same wind
that first carried the French vessels out of Brest. The storm
stopped him before he got out of the Channel and forced him to
return to port. The French convoy therefore got ahead of the
English. Graves could have arrived in New York much sooner had
he not wasted time in taking prizes and towing an East Indiaman.
Once again the desire for prize money seriously affected the course
of events, as it had so often done before.

After the storm in the Bay of Biscay the Chevalier de Ternay
decided to take the southern route which, though it was longer,
gave him the advantage of the trade winds. The southern winds
which usually prevail during the summer along the Atlantic coast
would bring the expedition northward to Cape Henry in Virginia
or to Rhode Island, wherever they might choose to disembark.
There was also less likelihood of meeting the enemy than on the
shorter but more dangerous western route. On June 11 they captured an English sloop laden with codfish and herring, sailing from

Halifax to St. Eustatius. Rochambeau had the codfish and herring distributed to the troops. On the eighteenth they overhauled a cutter, with no cod but with the unwelcome news that the British had captured Charleston and taken four thousand prisoners. A few days later, south of Bermuda, the frigates of the vanguard signaled that six vessels under full sail were bearing down upon the convoy. Ternay put his vessels in line of battle, and the enemy, astonished to see seven ships of the line come out of a group of merchantmen, stopped. In the engagement that followed, Ternay, if he had been more adventurous, might have cut off one of the English ships which had dropped to leeward, but he allowed her to escape and proceeded on his way. "He preferred," says Rochambeau, "the preservation of his convoy to the personal glory of having captured a hostile vessel."[13]

From another prize captured off the coast of Virginia it was learned that, following his victory at Charleston, General Clinton had returned to New York. Ternay and Rochambeau both realized that they could be of no use in the South and that they had better make for Rhode Island. After another week of skirting the coast through heavy fog, they reached Martha's Vineyard, and from there American pilots steered the convoy into Newport Harbor. The *Duc de Bourgogne,* flagship of the fleet, dropped anchor early in the morning of July 11, 1780, and the troops disembarked as peacefully as if they had been landing at Brest. The crossing had taken seventy days. Ternay had accomplished his mission.[14]

Notes

1. Prince de Montbarey, *Mémoires Autographes* (3 vols., Paris, 1826), II, 78.
2. *Ibid.,* II, 339.
3. Doniol, IV, 285.

ROCHAMBEAU

In his picture of the "Surrender of Cornwallis" Trumbull seems to have caught Rochambeau as he really was. This ruddy-faced, stocky figure, friendly, unassuming and obviously competent, quickly dispelled the popular prejudice against Frenchmen.

The death of the gallant Chevalier d'Assas, a captain in the Auvergne
Regiment, has become one of the legends of French history. On the eve
of the battle of Clostercamp, 1760, the Chevalier was making a reconnaissance of the enemy position when he was surrounded and captured.
Threatened with death if he made a sound, he shouted at the top of his
lungs, *"A moi, Auvergne, ce sont les ennemis!"* The shout cost him his
life, but it saved the French army from a surprise attack that might
have proved disastrous. Rochambeau was in command of the Auvergne
at the time.

Once he had decided that it was in the interest of France to support the American cause, Louis XVI's Minister of Foreign Affairs proved an invaluable ally. While he could hardly be called an enthusiast for independence, he seized on the revolt of the colonies as a means of redressing the balance of power in Europe.

THE CHATEAU
DE ROCHAMBEAU

One of the many beautiful chateaux in the old province of Touraine. Rochambeau also owned a house in Paris, in the Rue Cherche-Midi, but he was essentially a country lover and he was really happy only in the peaceful surroundings of the family home overlooking the little river Loir, four miles west of Vendôme.

ROCHAMBEAU'S HEADQUARTERS IN NEWPORT

Thanks to the Preservation Society of Newport, the house where Rochambeau established his headquarters, on the corner of Mary and Clarke Streets, is in excellent repair. It belonged to William Vernon, a prominent Whig and one of the first citizens of Newport. Mr. Vernon charged no rent for the house, but before the French left he presented a bill for 135 pounds, which was duly paid.

The statue of Rochambeau in Newport was unveiled in 1934. It is a replica of the one that stood outside the Abbaye de la Trinité in Vendôme and which was destroyed by the Germans in World War II.

MAJOR ANDRÉ

This portrait sketch was made by André himself on the eve of his execution. André seems to have endeared himself to everybody, including his captors. Washington wrote to Rochambeau, "While we yielded to the necessity of rigor, we could not but lament it."

WASHINGTON

Trumbull painted several portraits of Washington, of which he considered this one which he called "Washington at Trenton," the best. It was painted in 1792 for the City of Charleston, but the city fathers were not satisfied with it. According to Trumbull, they would have preferred "a more matter-of-fact likeness." The portrait remained in Trumbull's possession and was subsequently bought by Yale College for $500.

LA FAYETTE

La Fayette has always appealed to posterity as the first of the great aristocrats to embrace the cause of popular liberty. By the end of the Revolution
he was probably, next to Washington, the most popular man in America.
Jefferson, though he admired La Fayette as everybody else did, speaks of
his "canine appetite for popularity and fame."

ADMIRAL DE GRASSE

From a drawing in the *London Magazine,* August 1782. By defeating the British fleet off the Virginia Capes, in the early days of September 1781, De Grasse sealed the fate of Cornwallis. He was a big, hot-tempered man, standing six feet two on ordinary days, but, according to his sailors, six feet six on battle days.

THE DUC DE LAUZUN

Armand Louis de Gontaut, Duc de Lauzun, later known as the Duc de Biron, was the epitome of everything that was extravagant, self-indulgent, reckless, gallant and charming in the French aristocracy of the day. He commanded the allied cavalry at Yorktown. Washington thought highly of him.

Vignon del.   Frédéric Lignon sculp.

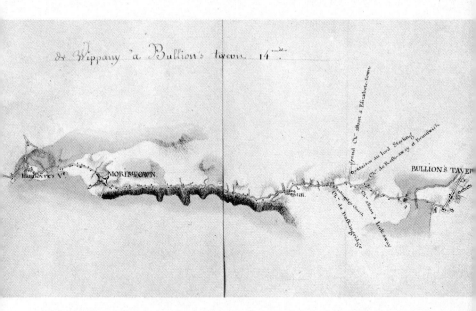

One of Berthier's maps depicting the route of Rochambeau's army through New Jersey in August 1781 when it was on its way from the Hudson to the Yorktown peninsula. From Suffern the route led through the Ramapo Valley to Pompton Plains, to Whippany and past Morristown to Bullion's Tavern (now Liberty Corner).

ALEXANDRE BERTHIER

Later a marshal of France and Napoleon's chief of staff, Berthier learned his trade as a staff officer at Rochambeau's side. His special talent was map making, and the maps with which he supplied Rochambeau are still in existence. Sketches made on the spot during the march were later made up into finished maps, designed to serve as an official record of the campaign.

THE SURRENDER OF CORNWALLIS

Like many of Trumbull's battle pieces, this picture was painted in Benjamin West's studio in London. Trumbull left out the heads, hoping to fill them in later from life. The French officers, including Rochambeau, sat for him in Jefferson's house in Paris, in the autumn of 1787.

KEY TO SURRENDER OF CORNWALLIS

The central figure on horseback is called General Lincoln, but a comparison of portraits of Lincoln and Cornwallis leaves little doubt but that the figure originally represented Cornwallis. Trumbull was probably not too familiar with the details of the capitulation. When the portrait of Cornwallis in the scene of surrender was criticized by the public as being inaccurate, the change was made. Lincoln received the surrender from O'Hara, who does not figure in the picture at all.

Key to Surrender of Lord Cornwallis

by John Trumbull

1. Count Deuxponts, Colonel of French Infantry.
2. Duke de Laval Montmorency, Colonel of French Infantry.
3. Count Custine, Colonel of French Infantry.
4. Duke de Lauzun, Colonel of French Cavalry.
5. General Choizy.
6. Viscount Viomenil.
7. Marquis de St. Simon.
8. Count Fersen, Aide-de-Camp of Count Rochambeau.
9. Count Charles Damas, Aide-de-Camp of Count Rochambeau.
10. Marquis Chastellux.
11. Baron Viomenil.
12. Count de Barras, Admiral.
13. Count de Grasse, Admiral.

14. Count Rochambeau, General in chief of the French.
15. General Lincoln.
16. Colonel Ebenezer Stevens, of the American Artillery.
17. General Washington, Commander in Chief.
18. Thomas Nelson, Governor of Virginia.
19. Marquis de La Fayette.
20. Baron Steuben.
21. Colonel Cobb, Aide-de-Camp to General Washington.
22. Colonel Trumbull, Secretary to General Washington.
23. Major General James Clinton, New York.
24. General Gist, Maryland.
25. General Anthony Wayne, Pennsylvania.

26. General Hand, Adjutant General, Pennsylvania.
27. General Peter Muhlenberg, Pennsylvania.
28. Major General Henry Knox, Commander of Artillery.
29. Lieutenant Colonel E. Huntington, Acting Aide-de-Camp of General Lincoln.
30. Colonel Timothy Pickering, Quartermaster General.
31. Colonel Alexander Hamilton, Commanding Light Infantry.
32. Colonel John Laurens, South Carolina.
33. Colonel Walter Stuart, Philadelphia.
34. Colonel Nicholas Fish, New York.

Citoyen

Rochambeau's letter requesting his release from the Conciergerie.

(This letter was presumably addressed either to Leblois, the public prosecutor, who had replaced Fouquier-Tinville, or to Garnier de l'Aube, who signed the decree authorizing Rochambeau's release.)

Citoyen
permet moy de te rapeller que je te
remis icy il y a 15 jours dans ta visite de l'hospice
détenu et traduit au tribunal révolutionnaire par
un ordre du comité de sûreté générale du 16 pluviôse
je crois que je suis le dernier général dans le prison
de la Conciergerie ... après un patriotisme aussi constamment
soutenu dans les deux hémisphères, couvert de blessures
et d'infirmités dans ma 70ième année, j'ose espérer que
ma position intéresse ta justice et ta probité pour
finir une détention aussi longue et aussi peu
meritée.
    julienne remplace chauveau mon déffenseur
officieux, et en son absence est chargé de mes
pièces.   Rochambeau.
à l'hospice de la Conciergerie
le 3 Sans Culotte.

TRANSLATION:
Citizen,
    Permit me to remind you of the memorandum I gave you 15 days ago during your visit to the hospital. [In this memorandum I stated that I had been] detained and brought before the revolutionary tribunal on an order of the committee of the Committee of General Security of the 16th pluviose [Feb. 4]. I think I am the last general [to be detained] in the Conciergerie. After [a career in which my] patriotism has been clearly demonstrated in two hemispheres, crippled with wounds and infirmities, [now] in my 70th year, I am bold enough to hope that my plight will appeal to your sense of justice and honor, and that [you will put an end] to my long and unmerited imprisonment.
    Julienne is replacing Chauveau, my regular lawyer, and in his absence he has charge of all the documents in the case.
                        Rochambeau

The hospital of the Conciergerie
3 Sans Culotte

4. Michael de La Bedoyere, *Lafayette, a Revolutionary Gentleman* (New York, 1934), p. 55.

5. Doniol, IV, 291.

6. *Ibid.*, III, 238.

7. "Si le commandant françois ne sait pas ménager les esprits de Congres et les esprits différents de chaque État, s'il ne connoit ni les préjugés du peuple, ni les partis formés dans le gouvernement, ni la manière de plaire à l'armee, ni la conduite à tenir avec le pouvoir civil; s'il parle à un officier de Boston comme à celui de Newyork; à un membre de l'assemblée de Pookepsie comme à celui du soi-disant État de Vermont, il est bien sûr de déplaire, bien sûr de manquer le but de son voyage." *La Fayette to Maurepas, January 25, 1780,* Doniol, IV, 310, 311.

8. Geoffrey Callender, *Sea Kings of Britain* (3 vols., London, 1907–11), III, 5, 6.

9. Louis R. Gottschalk, *Lafayette and the Close of the American Revolution* (Chicago, 1942), pp. 50–51.

10. The rank of *maréchal de camp* no longer exists in the French Army. It would correspond today to a *général de division*. In Rochambeau's time, brigadier generals could command only forces of their respective arms, while a *maréchal de camp* was assigned to the command of combined forces of infantry and cavalry.

11. *Voyages de M. le Marquis de Chastellux dans L'Amérique Septentrionale dans les Années 1780, 1781 & 1782* (Paris, 1786).

12. "Je crois que nous agissons trop méthodiquement. La guerre dans le nouveau monde ne se fait pas avec cet attirail immense que je traîne après moi. M. de Rochambeau en verra un jour toutes les inutilités." Comte de Charlus, unpublished memoirs (Archives Nationales).

13. Rochambeau, *Mémoires,* I, 242.

14. Ternay's fleet consisted of seven ships of the line: the *Duc de Bourgogne,* 80 guns; the *Neptune* and the *Conquérant,* 74 guns; the *Éveille, Provence, Jason,* and *Ardent,* 64 guns; three frigates, the *Surveillante, Amazone,* and *Gentille*; a cutter, the *Guêpe,* and a supply ship, the *Fantasque,* which was fitted out as a hospital ship. In addition to the fighting ships there were thirty-two transports.

Seven

———◦⟨∞⟩◦———

ROCHAMBEAU'S FIRST impressions of America were not favorable. This is hardly surprising. The inhabitants did not greet him with the enthusiasm he had expected, the windows were not lighted, and no one came out in the streets to welcome him. Tories, of whom there seemed to be a great number, had spread the rumor that the French squadron was stopping in Newport only for supplies and would be gone in a few days. The fact was that the French were not popular in America. So far, though the French government had been secretly supporting the American cause with money and munitions, the only thing the average colonial knew about France was that the French fleet commanded by Admiral d'Estaing had failed to drive the British out of Newport in 1778, that the following year D'Estaing had failed to relieve Savannah, and that in 1780 he had sailed back to France having accomplished nothing.

Luckily Rochambeau was a man not easily ruffled. The people of Newport were puzzled by him. This ruddy-faced, stocky figure did not fit in with their previous conception of a mincing, frog-eating Frenchman. The air of quiet self-possession, the friendly blue eyes, the unmistakable competence of the man were something new in foreigners. As he went about his business, dressed in a sensible blue coat, with waistcoat and trousers of white cotton, nodding to the people he met in the street, the prejudices against him began to melt. Rochambeau let it be known that, contrary to the Tory rumors, he was not merely passing through. His Majesty King Louis XVI had cast in his fortunes with the Americans, and

[87]

the five thousand troops just landed were merely the advance guard of a much more powerful army. Within forty-eight hours the Tory propaganda was silenced. Flags were hung out and the church steeples illuminated. The Town Council of Newport did its best to welcome the French army in style. It announced that houses in the main streets were to be illuminated until ten o'clock at night, and it further resolved "that the Treasurer shall furnish a box of candles at the expense of the town, and that the same be distributed to such of the inhabitants who reside in the streets heretofore ordered to be illuminated, and who are not of ability to furnish the same."[1]

Newport, like every other town along the seaboard, was feeling the pinch of war. In a letter to Montbarey, written only a few days after landing, Rochambeau paints a grim picture of the desperate straits in which the colonists found themselves. Paper money stood at sixty to one, and every recruit for Washington's army cost Congress a hundred piastres in hard money. The American Army fluctuated between fifteen thousand and three thousand men, and at the moment it was nearer three thousand. American soldiers, Rochambeau discovered would fight gallantly in defense of their homes, but when the immediate danger was averted the army melted away. No one understood the seriousness of the situation more clearly than Washington himself. Savannah and Charleston had both fallen. The British were in control of three states, and in the other ten the will to win showed dangerous signs of cracking. Washington talked of "the totally deranged situation of our affairs" and "of the utter impracticability of availing ourselves of the generous aid [i.e., Rochambeau's army] unless the States would rouse from the torpor that had seized them."[2]

The return of La Fayette, who always exuded confidence and who brought news this time of substantial French aid, had raised men's spirits, but though the Whigs were delighted to see him they did not think that the aid the French King had sent them was substantial enough. He should have sent them twenty thousand men and twenty ships of the line to enable them to drive the British out of New York. From such comments Rochambeau concluded that American independence was bound to depend more and more upon French efforts. Send us troops, ships, and money, and do not count on these people or on their resources. Such is the refrain that runs through all his letters to the authorities at home. Rochambeau was particularly insistent on the importance of his being supplied hard money. If the spirit of the revolution is to be kept alive he must have funds, *"de l'argent comptant, s'il vous plaît,"* not only for his own use but also for Washington's army. America was bankrupt, *"sans un écu et sans crédit."* France had been generous; she must be more generous still.[3]

While Rochambeau assured his government that he would make every possible economy, he warned them of expenses he could not control. There was no question of living off the country, as he had done in Germany. Among allies one paid for everything down to the campsites his troops occupied. Having discharged his duty by giving the Minister of War a none-too-rosy picture of the American prospects, Rochambeau turned to the more congenial and more strictly military task of establishing his troops ashore in anticipation of a British attack. Admiral Graves had reached Sandy Hook only two days after he had arrived off Newport, and there was every reason to suppose that General Clinton and Admiral Arbuthnot, the senior naval officer in New York, reinforced by the six ships of the line brought over by Graves, would make a combined attack on Newport before the French had had a chance to fortify their position. Had they done so, the French expeditionary force might well have been annihilated. It was three weeks at least before Rochambeau was ready to repel an attack. As always happened in the eighteenth century after a long voyage, the troops were suffering from scurvy. Claude Blanchard, the commissary officer who helped establish the hospitals, reported eight hundred sick in the land forces and a further fifteen hundred sick in the fleet. So serious were the conditions at the end of the voyage that

Blanchard wondered whether a naval action could be more murderous than another week at sea.

The failure of the British forces in America to attack the French troops in Newport before they had dug themselves in can be attributed only to the incompetence of Admiral Arbuthnot and to his unwillingness to cooperate with Sir Henry Clinton. With the strong garrison of New York at his disposal, Clinton was ready to make the effort, but Arbuthnot, who could always produce cogent reasons for doing nothing, advised against it. The delay in the appearance of Admiral Graves was another factor. His reinforcements too arrived in a sickly state, necessitating a change in crews in New York, so that it was not until July 22 that the British ships were sighted off Newport. A reconnaissance showed Ternay's fleet anchored in a defensive position across the harbor and a number of guns mounted on shore. "The great and small artillery," says the Newport *Mercury,* "landed by our generous allies, and disposed of in different parts of this town and island, exceed anything of the kind ever seen here. They have brass cannon, from four to forty-eight pounders, and in great plenty."[4]

It was a hard nut to crack, and the two admirals decided to await the arrival of Clinton. Owing to a misunderstanding between the Army and the Navy, transports were not immediately available, and not until the twenty-seventh was Clinton able to embark his troops. He had actually embarked six thousand men at Throg's Neck when the alarming news reached him that an American army of fifteen thousand men had appeared at Kingsbridge. Clinton thereupon changed his mind, abandoned the whole enterprise, and turned back to defend New York. It was a fatal decision on his part, for it meant that the initiative had passed out of his hands. Until then it was always Clinton and Cornwallis who planned offensive operations, while Washington and his generals did their best to hamper the execution of their projects, yielding here, advancing there, attacking with guerrilla bands. Neither was definitely imposing his will on the other. The introduction of Rocham-

beau and Ternay on the scene changed the whole situation. Merely
by threatening an attack on New York, Washington had set the
British commanders at loggerheads. Clinton and Arbuthnot had
done nothing while a French army entrenched itself on Rhode
Island. Even more serious was the potential threat to British sea
communications represented by a French squadron riding peacefully at anchor in Newport Harbor. The control of American
waters that the Royal Navy had exercised almost unchallenged for
nearly five years was now in jeopardy.

Nothing could be more damning than Clinton's own admission
of the failure of the British high command to prevent these all
important reinforcements from reaching their destination:

. . . I am unwilling to ascribe the failure of this enterprise to any particular cause, though I must acknowledge it to have been my firm
opinion that we should scarcely have been disappointed of success had
Mr. Graves fortunately reached New York six days sooner than he did,
or even had Admiral Arbuthnot contrived by his frigates to have obtained timely information of the French fleet's arrival, and his transports had been ready as promised for the immediate reception of troops.
But let what will have been the cause, this nation will ever surely have
reason to lament that anything intervened to prevent either attack, as
there is little doubt that our not being able to crush this reinforcement
immediately on its arrival gave additional animation to the spirit of
rebellion, whose almost expiring embers began to blaze afresh on its
appearance.[5]

While Clinton, Arbuthnot, and Graves were fumbling over their
plans, Rochambeau was girding himself for battle. If they had
attacked him immediately, before he had had a chance to fortify
his position, and while a quarter of his effectives were still in the
hospital recovering from scurvy, it would have gone hard for him.
But by the beginning of August, instead of dreading an attack he
was looking forward to it. Thanks to Washington's foresight General Heath, commanding the militia of Massachusetts and Rhode
Island, had been ordered to greet the French troops on their arrival

and to offer them any assistance necessary. With the help of
Heath's five thousand militiamen the French troops were soon
ready for any eventuality. The lines the British army had laid out
during its stay in Rhode Island, and which it had evacuated during
the previous year, were repaired and perfected. The French were
soon strongly entrenched across the island, protected from sea
attack by the floating "castles" of the fleet and on the land side by
the heavy artillery brought from France. Batteries flanked with
earthworks were erected in all the commanding positions. An entry
in the diary of Rochambeau's aide, Baron von Closen, shows that
by the end of July the situation was well in hand:

On the 30th we had the very pleasant news that the [English] transports
that were carrying the army of disembarkation, commanded by Sir
Henry Clinton, had been sent to Long Island, where the troops were
going ashore. This reassured us completely!! If the enemy had been able
to land in the first six days after the appearance of his fleet, we would
not have been able to put up a very strong opposition, and our army
would have risked a good deal. But with these endeavors, as with the
fair sex, if the first moments of surprise are lost, all is over: the favorable
moments never return.

Rochambeau acknowledged the services of the militia in a
cordial letter to Samuel Huntingdon, the President of Congress. At
the same time he was anxious not to demand too much of them.
The militia was composed largely of farmers, and as a countryman
himself Rochambeau knew how important it was for them to get in
the harvest. With this in mind he let most of them go by the
beginning of August. Much as he appreciated their willingness,
Rochambeau could not help noting that they looked to the French
for everything in the way of equipment. They arrived badly armed,
without tents or provisions. The only commodity with which they
were well supplied was cattle. At least the French did not have to
feed them. La Fayette, as a major-general in the American Army,
was afraid that the unsoldierly bearing of the American militia

would make a bad impression on the French. He even warned General Heath not to speak of uniforms "as a novelty in our army," but he need not have had any such fears. The French soldiers were not inclined to scoff at the privations of their allies.[6]

While the spick-and-span French regiments, well-equipped and well-disciplined, and the ragged American militia were eyeing each other with mutual interest, Rochambeau and his officers, as soon as they were satisfied they could repel any attack, found time to savor the friendliness of American life and to enjoy such hospitality as Newport had to offer. Rochambeau also saw to it that his men, as well as his officers, should enjoy as many comforts as possible. General Heath seconded all his efforts, and it was not long before the two armies were living together in what Geneal Heath called "the most happy fraternity." It is a tribute to the perspicacity of the two generals that, though they could communicate only through an interpreter, each recognized the ability of the other. Rochambeau was fully aware of the handicaps under which the Americans were struggling, and in all his dealings with them he was tact itself. No doubt the good relations between the two armies were largely due to the amazing discipline of the French troops and to the fact that they paid for everything in hard money. On the very day he landed Rochambeau had assured Washington that the King's army would maintain as strict a discipline in America as though they were encamped under the walls of Paris.[7] He was as good as his word. The people of Newport, accustomed to the depredations of their own troops as well as of the British, rubbed their eyes in astonishment when they saw chickens and pigs walking between the French lines without being disturbed and the apple trees laden with fruit overhanging the tents, untouched.

An inactive army is usually a discontented army, and the long period of inaction to which the French expeditionary force was condemned by force of circumstances, lasting from July 1780 to June 1781, subjected Rochambeau more than anybody else to a severe strain. The living conditions were agreeable enough. During the winter the troops were housed in buildings which had been partially destroyed by the British and which the French army repaired at their own expense. The officers were billeted among the townspeople, and with the exception of Count Fersen (who complained of the dullness of Newport and the selfishness of the inhabitants) they agreed with the Prince de Broglie and young Berthier in finding Newport itself a charming place. As for the ladies of Newport, they were all, owing to the simplicity of their life, *"jolies et fraîches."*

Rochambeau and his son occupied the beautiful Vernon house, still standing and recently restored to its original condition. Ternay chose the home of Colonel Walton on Water Street. Baron de Vioménil, Rochambeau's second in command, appears to have lived a secluded life, but the Chevalier de Chastellux entertained at the Mawdsley house on Spring Street in what would today be considered the grand style. Ezra Stiles, the president of Yale College, in whose invaluable diary are recorded his impressions of the French troops in Newport, speaks of dining "at General Chastellux in a Splendid manner on thirty five dishes. He is a Capital Literary Character, a member of the French Academy. He is the glory of the Army." He also dined with Rochambeau. "I conversed with the General in Latin," says Dr. Stiles. "He speaks it tolerably."[8]

Certainly no one could have done more than Rochambeau to maintain the morale of the army and to combat the boredom and the weariness of the long months of waiting. Many of the French officers acquired horses as soon as they arrived, and according to some accounts they were often seen riding about the island in gay cavalcades, sometimes accompanied by "running footmen," which was said to be "an ancient custom of the old nobility." "The exercise," says one of the observers, "was severe, and drew heavily on the reserved powers of muscles and sinews. On their return they took hot potions, and retired immediately to bed, to recover, by free perspiration and rest, ability to repeat those demands upon their endurance."[9]

Rochambeau encouraged all such activities. He also built for his officers an assembly hall, which served as a club where they could entertain their friends and play cards—Rochambeau insisted that the stakes should be low—and occasionally give balls. Commissary[10] Blanchard, who belonged to a different social class from Rochambeau's other young men and whose journal is all the more interesting for that reason, refers to the assembly hall rather contemptuously as a place where the officers held their minuets and *"contredanses."* The aides, particularly Berthier, who had finally got himself to America via the West Indies and had been attached to Rochambeau's staff, took a very different view. According to him the assembly hall was a godsend to the whole army. It did honor to M. de Rochambeau who, wherever he was, made himself the father of the family.

In spite of the amenities of Newport and the pleasant relations he had established with the local population; in spite, too, of the extraordinary failure of Sir Henry Clinton to interfere with his landing operations, for which he was thankful, Rochambeau soon found himself involved in difficulties he could never have anticipated. The chief source of his difficulties was La Fayette. Instead of smoothing the way for him as might have been expected, La Fayette in his eagerness to serve the cause put Rochambeau in the awkward position of seeming reluctant to fight. On the arrival of the French troops in America Washington, not being at home in the language, made the mistake at first of leaving communications between himself and Rochambeau entirely in La Fayette's hands. No doubt he did not realize that this eager young Frenchman, in whom he had the greatest confidence, had no particular standing in the French Army. He might be a major-general in the American Army, but as far as the French were concerned he was merely a captain in the reserve. His courage, his headlong enthusiasm for the cause, his charming manners, and his great wealth, by means of which he was able to provide the men under his command the best equipment, had endeared him to every

American patriot. They did not necessarily endear him to his own countrymen.

La Fayette had arrived in Boston April 28 and made his way from there to Washington's headquarters at Morristown, where he conferred with members of Congress and with La Luzerne, the new French minister plenipotentiary. La Luzerne had come from the Army into diplomacy. Being an extraordinarily likable man, as well as a skillful diplomat, he was always listened to respectfully. He was probably the one man who had the full confidence of Washington, La Fayette, Rochambeau, and Congress. No one was more adept at pouring oil on troubled waters.

From the information he had received before leaving France, La Fayette believed that Ternay's armada included twelve ships of the line, and on the strength of that rumor he drafted a letter for Rochambeau urging an immediate attack on New York. Washington, not being willing to seem to dictate to his new ally until he had heard from him, toned down the letter so that by the time it reached Rochambeau it merely suggested that, provided Ternay's forces were superior to the British Navy in and around New York Harbor, a joint attack by French and American land forces might be carried out sometime in August. Even so, Rochambeau was not prepared to embark on any large-scale offensive until the second division of his expeditionary force, which he was expecting momentarily, had arrived, or until Ternay's squadron was reinforced —La Fayette was quite wrong about the number of ships in the squadron—or until Clinton, by going to the aid of Cornwallis, had so reduced the garrison of New York that the French could march away from their base in Rhode Island without risking its recapture.

One of the redeeming byproducts of D'Estaing's failure at Savannah had been the British evacuation of Newport. Fearful that D'Estaing, having failed at Savannah, might attack New York, Clinton had recalled the troops and vessels stationed in Rhode Island. All the subsequent British reverses were due, according to Admiral Rodney, to the abandonment of that island. It was, he said, "the most fatal measure that could have been adopted."[11]

La Fayette thought that the French occupation of Rhode Island was of no use to the Americans, but as Rochambeau pointed out to him, it had had the effect of confining Clinton to New York and of immobilizing the British fleet, thereby enabling American privateers to roam the coastline at will and to capture a number of important prizes. Believing as he did that the presence of French troops at Newport was a genuine asset to the cause, he would have to be very sure that it was Washington himself and not just La Fayette who was urging him to commit all his forces in an attack which, according to the information at his disposal, was not likely to succeed. He had seen enough Savannahs in his military career without wanting to risk another. In any case he was determined to meet Washington face to face instead of having to communicate with him in writing via La Fayette. "In an hour of conversation," he told La Fayette, "we shall be able to settle things far more definitely than in volumes of writing."[12]

Washington was no less anxious to meet Rochambeau, but the five-day journey from his headquarters at Preakness (Paterson), New Jersey, to Newport presented many difficulties. He could hardly hope to obtain the men, money, and munitions he so desperately needed for the next campaign unless he was on hand to answer the questions of the congressional committee about the preparations that were already under way. Under the circumstances Washington's decision to use La Fayette as his liaison officer was perfectly natural, but, had Rochambeau not been as even-tempered as he was, La Fayette's attempt to dictate the plan of campaign might easily have had a disastrous effect on the cooperation of the two armies. As it was, he contented himself with writing two letters, one to La Luzerne complaining that La Fayette, after seeming to agree with him, had proposed such extravagant things as taking Long Island and New York without the assistance of the Navy. To this letter La Luzerne replied in his characteristically tactful way that whatever La Fayette had said was the result of his zeal and his high courage, implying that his opinions on military tactics must not be taken too seriously.

Rochambeau's second letter, addressed to La Fayette himself, shows that he had taken this hint to heart. It was a friendly letter, a letter from Age to Youth, in which the younger man was very gently put in his place:

Newport, August 27, 1780.
Permit an old father, my dear Marquis, to reply to you as to a son who is very dear to him. You know me well enough to realize that I do not need to be spurred into action, and furthermore that at my age, once I have taken all the military and political factors into account and reached a decision, under the hard compulsion of circumstances, nothing can make me change that decision unless it be a direct order from my superior officer. Such is not the case here. On the contrary, I am delighted that General Washington's dispatches indicate that my ideas are substantially in accord with his. . . .

It is always well, my dear fellow, to think that Frenchmen are invincible, but let me tell you a great secret which I have learned after forty years of experience. There are no troops more easily beaten when they have lost confidence in their leaders, and they lose confidence as soon as they see that their lives are being risked to satisfy somebody's personal ambition. . . .

Rest assured of my very real friendship for you. If I have brought to your attention, as gently as possible, the things that displeased me in your last letter, it was because I judged that the warmth of your heart and spirit had for the moment gotten the better of your sober judgment. Keep this last quality for the council chamber, and reserve your warmth and fire for the moment when plans are to be put into execution. And please remember that it is always old papa Rochambeau who is talking to his dear son La Fayette, whom he loves, and will continue to love and esteem to his last breath.

It speaks well for La Fayette that this letter did not rankle. He must have known that Rochambeau was right, and yet at the same time he may well have felt that Rochambeau did not quite appreciate the importance of bolstering American morale and of counteracting Tory propaganda which had given it out that the French were doing nothing. He had hoped to take some of the weight off Washington's shoulders by conveying to the French what he knew the commander-in-chief had in mind, but he had made a mess of it by overstating the case. Obviously the conference Rochambeau wanted could not be delayed. Washington, torn in a dozen directions, would have preferred not to meet Rochambeau until he could tell him definitely how many men he would have under his command. Rochambeau, master in his own house, could present him with an exact table of information—so many regiments, so many guns, so many men per regiment, so many rounds of ammunition per man. Unfortunately Washington could not reciprocate. When he met Rochambeau to discuss his plans for the next campaign he would have to reveal to him that the American Army was in desperate straits for food, ammunition, and clothing, and that he did not know at any given moment what his effectives would be.

It was under these circumstances that Washington finally yielded to Rochambeau's persistent requests for an interview. By the beginning of September, being free for the moment of congressional committees and having dismissed his three-month militia and given up all hope of an immediate offensive, he felt he could afford to leave his army for a few days. Clinton, idling in New York, showed no signs of crossing the Hudson. On September 8, accordingly, Washington wrote to Rochambeau and Ternay asking them to meet him at Hartford. "Our plans," he confided to them, "can only turn up possibilities; which is the more unfortunate, as the affairs of this country absolutely require activity, upon whichever side they are viewed."[13]

The conference took place on the twentieth of September at the house of Colonel Jeremiah Wadsworth. Washington reached the rendezvous, which was about equally distant from his headquarters and Rochambeau's, after two days of hard riding. He was accompanied by General Knox, his chief of artillery, La Fayette, M. de Gouvion, his chief of Engineers, a French officer who had joined the American Army early in the war, six aides including Alexander Hamilton, and an escort of dragoons. Rochambeau brought with him Ternay, Chastellux, his aides Fersen and Dumas, and his son the Vicomte de Rochambeau. He arrived at the conference late owing to an accident to his coach. Under ordinary circumstances he would have made the journey on horseback, but Ternay was sick and a coach had been provided for his convenience. A broken axle necessitated a wheelwright, and when Fersen finally located one, he turned out to be suffering from fever at the moment and would not leave his bed for a "hatful of guineas." With the help of Admiral Ternay, Fersen finally persuaded the shivering wheelwright to change his mind. The axle was mended, and the French party reached the conference without further mishap. On the way home the axle broke again, and again the village smithy had to be summoned from his bed. In commenting on this incident Rochambeau has a good word to say for the patriotism of this particular man, and of the Connecticut farmers in general, but he did not want to give the impression that all Americans were like this good wheelwright.[14]

If the Hartford conference had served no other purpose than to acquaint the two generals and their staffs with each other, it still would have been abundantly worth while. The impression Washington made on the French officers would be hard to exaggerate. Everyone was anxious to meet him, and no one was disappointed. We know now, thanks to the more objective biographies of Rupert Hughes and Douglas Freeman, that Washington was a man of flesh and blood, far more human and likable than the spotless hero Parson Weems tried to inflict on posterity. We know that he often lost his temper, that he could be relentless as well as forgiving, that he sometimes blundered on the battlefield and had to be coerced into victory in spite of himself, but we know too that by the sheer force of his character he dominated men abler in many ways than himself. Certainly of all the Frenchmen who met Washington there was not one who did not feel that he had been in the presence of a very great man. The massive figure in the "buff vest, buff breeches, buckles at the knee, long spurred boots, white neck cloth and blue buff-lined coat"[15] represented something that Versailles could not produce—the unpretentious aristocracy of the New World.

To the Marquis de Chastellux, a member of the French Academy and very much a man of the world besides being one of Rochambeau's major-generals, Washington was "the greatest and the best of men. . . . General Washington has left on my mind," says Chastellux, "the idea of a perfect whole, that cannot be the product of enthusiasm, which rather would reject it, since the effect of proportion is to diminish the idea of greatness."[16] Count Axel de Fersen, who was more critical of Americans than the other young men on Rochambeau's staff, describes Washington as "illustrious, if not unique in our century. His handsome and majestic, while at the same time mild and open countenance perfectly reflects his moral qualities; he looks the hero; he is very cold; speaks little, but is courteous and frank. A shade of sadness overshadows his countenance, which is not unbecoming, and gives him an interesting air."[17]

Mathieu Dumas, another of Rochambeau's aides and, unlike Fersen, a great lover of all things American, was more outgoing. "We had been impatient to see the hero of liberty. His dignified address, his simplicity of manners, and mild gravity, surpassed our expectation and won every heart."[18]

Rochambeau was too exclusively the man of action to favor us with character sketches in his memoirs, but we know from the letters that passed between them after the war that his affection and admiration for Washington never wavered. In the last mention of his old comrade in arms he says that though "politics brought an end to our correspondence our hearts will remain united in life and in death." This uncharacteristic outburst of feeling will be found only in the manuscript of the memoirs. On the ground perhaps that it was too personal, Rochambeau deleted it from the printed text.

The results of the Hartford conference were not encouraging to those who, like La Fayette, demanded immediate action. Rocham-

beau had no difficulty in winning over Washington to his opinion
that no effective operations could be undertaken against the British
without assured and continuous naval superiority. This was the
conclusion he had arrived at in Paris, and everything he had seen
since his arrival in America confirmed it. The two generals also
agreed that the greatest blow they could inflict upon the British,
and the surest way of ending the war, would be to capture New
York. Rochambeau may well have had reservations about prefer-
ring an attack on New York to anything else, but he did not argue
the point. He did stipulate, however, that in the event of an attack
on New York, in addition to naval superiority, they must be able
to count on a force twice as great as that of the garrison. Clinton
was known to have fifteen thousand men at his disposal. Washington and Rochambeau therefore could not mount the attack with
less that thirty thousand. It was obvious from the discussions at
Hartford that the outcome of the war hinged on the French effort.
Not only must the French government redouble its stakes in the
way of ships and men, but it must also dig down once again into
the national purse.

The fact was the Americans were short of everything. The demand that Rochambeau was to hear so often for ships, men, and
money was embodied in a document written in French and drawn
up in two columns. The point of view of Rochambeau and Ternay
was stated in one column, and Washington's rejoinders in the
other.[19] For Washington it must have been a bitter blow to admit
his complete dependence on French help. Where Rochambeau
stated on one side of the page that he would need a corps of fifteen
thousand men, Washington commented on the other side that,
since he had no way of knowing how many men Congress would
allow him for the next campaign, he considered it very important
that His Christian Majesty should reinforce the French corps at
least to the number of men Rochambeau had demanded. In the
last article of the memorandum Rochambeau stated very clearly
that, in view of the extraordinary expenses of war in a country
where everything had to be paid for, even the fields where the men

were encamped, he would need a large discretionary fund. Otherwise he might find himself in the position of having to suspend operations before they were completed. Washington could only add it was all too true that war was more expensive in America than it was in Europe. Once again he hoped His Majesty would bear Rochambeau's request in mind.

After being closeted together for two days, the Generals separated mutually pleased with each other. "At least," says Fersen, who seems to have known something about international conferences, "they say so." It was agreed that Rochambeau should dispatch the appeal to Versailles in the hands of an officer capable of bringing home to the government the necessity of acting generously and quickly. The Duc de Lauzun thought that he should have been chosen for this mission since he knew Vergennes and Maurepas better than anybody else, but Rochambeau chose his own son instead. The young man was instructed to learn the contents of the document by heart in case he had to destroy it in the event of his ship being captured on the way over. So important was this mission considered that Ternay selected his fastest frigate to run the blockade, with his most enterprising captain to command it—the Comte de La Pérouse, later to become famous for his exploration of the northeast coasts of Asia. Washington resolved to send an emissary of his own, young John Laurens, to reinforce the demands already being made by Franklin as well as by Rochambeau's son, for further help from France. "Without a foreign loan," Washington told Laurens, "our present force which is but the remnant of an army cannot be kept together for this campaign, much less will it be increased and in readiness for another."[20]

Washington at one moment had hoped that the French West Indies fleet, now under the command of the Comte de Guichen, would join Ternay's squadron in Newport and so make the attack on New York feasible. He had written very frankly about the desperate situation of the country. Ternay had also joined in the cry for help, but Guichen had already sailed for France and the letters never reached him. Instead of Guichen it was the famous Admiral Rodney who appeared in New York with a squadron of thirteen vessels. The sudden appearance of Rodney, which the French officers heard of while they were on their way to Hartford, made them eager to get back to Newport as soon as possible. Vioménil, who had been left in command, evidently expected to be attacked at any moment. They set out on the return journey on Friday, September twenty-second. Presumably they were in good spirits in spite of the news about Rodney, as Governor Trumbull of Connecticut had done the handsome thing by them. He sent them off with a thirteen-gun salute and defrayed all the expenses of the conference. This unexpected generosity was probably even more welcome to the Americans than to the French. Washington had had to borrow all the money he could to pay the expenses of his staff, and even so all he had been able to raise was eight thousand paper dollars, the equivalent of perhaps a hundred forty in real money. There was general rejoicing when the bills were called for and they found there was nothing to pay.

Washington left Hartford the next day. As he jogged over the bad roads from Hartford to Litchfield, and on through Fishkill to West Point, he little realized the shock that was in store for him. He had planned to inspect the fortifications of West Point with the commander of the fort, General Benedict Arnold, but to Washington's great annoyance—he was not a patient man—no one could tell him where General Arnold was to be found.

Notes

1. Edwin M. Stone, *Our French Allies ... from 1778 to 1782* (Providence, 1884), p. 206.

2. George Washington, *The Writings of George Washington* (edited by John C. Fitzpatrick; 39 vols., Washington, D.C., 1931–1944), XIX, 226.

3. Doniol, V, 345.

4. Stone, *op. cit.,* p. 202.

5. Sir Henry Clinton, *The American Rebellion* . . . (New Haven, 1954), p. 208.

6. Letter from La Fayette to General William Heath, June 11, 1780. Massachusetts Historical Collections, Seventh Series, Vol. V.

7. Doniol V, 349.

8. Ezra Stiles, *Literary Diary* (3 vols., New York, 1901), II, 473.

9. Stone, *op. cit.,* p. 225.

10. The word *commissaire* is impossible to translate literally. Blanchard, who held the rank of *Commissaire-Général,* handled supply, evacuation, and transport. His immediate superior was the Chevalier de Tarlé, *Commissaire-Ordonnateur,* who was also responsible for all financial operations.

11. Alfred T. Mahan, *The Influence of Sea Power upon History, 1660-1783* (Boston, 1890), p. 530*n*.

12. Doniol, V, 350.

13. Washington, *Writings,* XX, 16.

14. Rochambeau, *Mémoires,* I, 251.

15. I. W. Stuart, *Life of Jonathan Trumbull* (Boston, 1849), p. 487.

16. Chastellux, I, 119.

17. *Magazine of American History,* III, 305.

18. Lt. Gen Comte Mathieu Dumas, *Memoirs of His Own Time* . . . (2 vols., Philadelphia and London, 1839), I, 29.

19. Doniol, IV, 104-7.

20. Washington, *Writings,* XXI, 438.

Eight

O F ALL THE BLOWS that rained down on Washington during seven years of war nothing can have plunged him deeper into the black depths of despair than the discovery that Benedict Arnold, the hero of Saratoga, the man he had championed in the face of Congress, had gone over to the enemy. It was only by luck that Arnold's treachery was discovered in time to prevent a disaster. As Washington put it, "Providence interposed in our favor."

As far back as June 1779 Arnold had been in secret correspondence with the British commander-in-chief in New York. He had persuaded Washington to appoint him to the command of West Point on the grounds that he had not yet sufficiently recovered from his wounded leg to take on the more active post Washington had offered him. In accordance with his wishes, he was assigned to direct the defenses of the Hudson, though Washington reminded him that this was not much of a command for a man of his temperament and that the garrison would consist chiefly of militia and invalids. This was exactly what Arnold wanted. After prolonged negotiations conducted in cipher with Major John André, Clinton's adjutant-general, Arnold had agreed to cut the chain that stretched across the Hudson and to distribute the garrison in such a way as to make it possible for the British to storm the supposedly impregnable defenses of West Point and to capture the fort itself. Had he succeeded in his treachery—and he came uncomfortably close to success—Clinton would have won control of the whole length of the Hudson River, thereby cutting the American

Confederation in two and separating the French forces from the Continental army. Under these conditions the small, starved American Army might well have been compelled to lay down its arms.

By the end of September, just at the time Washington and Rochambeau were conferring at Hartford, Arnold and Clinton had come to a substantial agreement. Arnold, who was in financial difficulties at the time, wanted cash in advance. He stipulated for £10,000 if the plan failed; £20,000 if he delivered the fort. To complete the arrangements Major André was conveyed up the Hudson by the *Vulture,* a British sloop of war. On the evening of Thursday, September 21, he met Arnold by appointment at a house near the landing place below West Point belonging to one Joshua Smith, a man of some local reputation who had succeeded in currying favor with both the Americans and the British. The two men fell to business quickly. A code of signals was arranged by which Arnold would be informed of the approach of the British ships, and the men in command of the expedition would in return be assured that the way had been paved for their reception within the fortress. Arnold then handed over to André documents in his own handwriting giving a comprehensive account of the defenses of the fortress and the composition and location of every unit in the garrison. The details of the business may have taken longer than was expected, for by the time they had finished, the *Vulture,* disturbed by a few shots fired at her by a patriot gunner on shore, had shifted her moorings and found a safer berth some miles downstream. No one was prepared to row André down the Hudson in the hope of catching up with the *Vulture.* He had to make his way south by land. Since he would be traveling through American-held territory until he reached the outskirts of New York, he would have to wear civilian clothes instead of his uniform.

The rest of the story is too familiar and too tragic to be retold in any detail. As everybody knows, André was caught and hanged as a spy, and Arnold escaped into the British lines. The verdict on André was inevitable. The discovery of the documents on his person, and the fact that he was not in uniform, made it impossible for the court to acquit him. At the same time his courage, his candor, and his extraordinary personal charm were such that the whole court shed tears on signing the report that sent him to the gallows. No spy was ever more popular with his executioners. Even Washington admitted André had met his fate "with that fortitude which was to be expected from an accomplished man and a gallant officer."[1]

While the British spy became almost the hero of the American camp, Benedict Arnold was being hanged in effigy in every town and village. In some other world where rewards and punishments are meted out more justly, Arnold would have been caught with the papers on him and André would have escaped. As it was, Arnold lived to invade Virginia, capture and burn Richmond, and later in the war, having eluded La Fayette's attempt to capture him, to harry the coast of New England and sack the town of New London, only thirteen miles from his own birthplace. After the war was over, he went to England, where he had to stomach some insults, but there is no indication that at any time he underwent agonies of remorse or that he died of a broken heart. On the contrary, he wrote to Washington immediately after his escape that his heart was "conscious of its own rectitude" and that he had acted as he did from a principle of love of country, and that though the world might find some inconsistency in his conduct, the world very seldom judges right of any man's actions. The letter did not happen to mention that he was to have received £20,000 for "the inconsistency of his conduct."

Arnold's carefully calculated act of treachery was such a shock to Washington that for a moment he wondered if there was anyone he could trust, but the mood of despair passed quickly and by the time he wrote an account of the event to Rochambeau he had recovered his usual composure. Evidently he had decided that, so far as his allies were concerned, the whole affair must be played down. The letter to Rochambeau sounds almost casual: "This is an event that occasions me equal regret and mortification; but traitors are the growth of every country and in a revolution of the present nature, it is more to be wondered at, that the catalogue is so small that there have been found a few."[2] Rochambeau took his cue from Washington. The timely discovery of Arnold's treachery proves to him too that "Providence is on our side." He had suspected as much for a long time.

One of the most regrettable results of Arnold's treason was the gloomy speculation it aroused in France. Vergennes, who heard the news from Rochambeau's son and from La Pérouse, wondered whether treason was not perhaps inevitable in a country where jealousy seemed to be the essence of government. Would the thirteen states ever be willing to sink their differences and work together?[3] He was disgusted with what he had heard of the bickering that went on in Congress between the different states and with what he had seen of the bickering of American agents in Paris. If he had had a chance to talk with Washington, his doubts would have been confirmed. Washington could have told him of the difficulty he was having with his generals. Those who were not jealous of each other were constantly warring with Congress. Nathanael Greene, the Quartermaster General and probably the ablest officer in the Army next to Washington, had resigned as head of his department in protest against the criticism in Congress, and it was with the greatest difficulty that Washington had prevented him from resigning from the Army altogether. General Knox was so outraged by the promotion of a younger man to the rank of major-general that Washington had to warn friends in Congress that if his artillery commander were passed over again he would be almost certain to resign, and that Washington would be unable to replace him. Gates, who for a long time had been trying to undermine Washington, had been court-martialed following his defeat at Camden; Schuyler and St. Clair had been superseded. General Sullivan had been sent off after his quarrel with Admiral d'Estaing to fight Indians in the western territory. Such reports of discontent among the generals, culminating in Arnold's treachery and soon to be followed by ugly rumors of mutiny among the troops, all contributed to the fall of American prestige in Europe. Though the relations between Franklin and Vergennes remained unimpaired, the French Cabinet were beginning to think they had done enough for the Americans, at least until they showed some disposition to do something for themselves.

Rochambeau continued to think that the second division he had been promised before he sailed would be arriving at any moment, but week after week went by and nothing was heard of it. His government left him completely in the dark as to its plans. He had dropped anchor in Newport Harbor on July 11, and when he finally met Washington in Hartford at the end of September he was still without any word from home. While Chastellux was touring the countryside and his younger officers were entertaining the ladies of Newport or visiting Washington's headquarters, as all of them looked forward to doing, Rochambeau, realizing that a long winter stretched ahead of him with no prospect of bringing the war to an end, must have looked back with some nostalgia to the campaigns in Germany. There at least he was in the center of things, but in America, pleasant as his surroundings were, he felt himself in a strange limbo, cut off from all news of the civilized world. During the Seven Years' War, whenever the army went into winter quarters, there was always a chance of his being sent home to his beloved Vendôme, there to recuperate from his wounds. The stalemate in America offered no such solace.

The monotony of camp life was relieved on one occasion at least by the arrival in Newport of nineteen Indian warriors. Most of them were members of the Oneida tribe, which had remained faithful to France after the loss of Canada. The visit of this delegation had been arranged by General Schuyler of New York to prove to the Indians that France and the United States were firmly united. "The savages," says Closen, "were treated with much distinction." On their arrival they asked to hear Mass, after which

Rochambeau entertained them at dinner and gave them blankets and medals representing the coronation of Louis XVI. In return they gave their hosts sandals, belts, and many other trinkets, "also some scalps."[4] Closen was disgusted with the oily appearance of the Indians, but Blanchard the commissary, perhaps less fastidious, says they behaved themselves well and ate cleanly enough.

During the entertainment one of the chiefs asked Rochambeau a question which surprised him: "How was it that the King of France, our father, sends his troops to protect the Americans against the King of England, their father?" Rochambeau answered that the French King protects the natural liberty God has given to man and that he had come to the aid of the Americans because they had been overloaded with burdens they were no longer able to bear. "In this way," he confides to his journal, "I extricated myself as best I could from a question I found very embarrassing."[5] He then exhorted them to maintain strict neutrality in the campaign which was about to begin. Whatever the Indians thought of the argument—and their people had suffered too much from the white man, French, English, and American, to think that any of them could be altruistic—they went back to their tribes thoroughly satisfied with the presents they had received. Washington congratulated Rochambeau on his treatment of "agreeable and respectable guests." He did not add that he himself had not always found the Indians either agreeable or respectable.

By the end of the year Rochambeau faced another, far more difficult, test of his diplomacy. The Hartford conference had settled that there could be no joint offensive until the spring of 1781 or until the French reinforcements arrived, but La Fayette had never been satisfied with the decision. The idea of a stalemate was anathema to him. When he heard, therefore, that the Spanish were contemplating an attack on Pensacola and St. Augustine, he goaded Washington into sounding out Rochambeau and Ternay on the possibility of making this a joint operation. If Ternay would join forces with the Spaniards, the allies would have achieved the naval supremacy that both Washington and Rochambeau believed essential. After completing the conquest of Florida they might even go on to recover Georgia and the Carolinas. Washington's letter to the two French commanders was expressed in the charmingly courteous language of the period, but he was clearly anxious that they should agree with him. The request for cooperation in what was really a sideshow put Rochambeau in a difficult position. He had already refused to be drawn into a premature attack on New York for reasons which Washington had grudgingly admitted were sound. Still he had refused, and to refuse again might lay him open to the charges circulated by the Tories that though the French made a great parade of their American alliance they were not prepared to fight. They had ensconced themselves comfortably in Rhode Island, and there they intended to remain.

Rochambeau was not at all attracted to the plan. Washington did not mention La Fayette's name, but Rochambeau may well have suspected that his restless young countryman was at the bottom of it. At Hartford they had come to a definite agreement to defer action until they had heard what further support they could expect from France, and here was a hastily conceived diversionary plan which ignored the resolutions of the Hartford conference altogether. Rochambeau was not a flexible man and he did not take kindly to the discarding of plans once they had been approved. While he knew nothing of the relations between Spain and the United States, he doubted very much whether the Spanish admiral, who must have received definite instructions from his own government, would be prepared to sail north to Rhode Island on his own authority and risk an engagement with the British fleet in order to convoy French troops down to Florida. By the time he reached Newport, supposing he could be persuaded to fall in with Washington's plan, Rochambeau hoped to have news from Brest about the second division he had so long been expecting. He had already heard indirectly that the Marquis de Castries, a man in whom he had the greatest confidence, had been appointed Minister of Marine in the place of Sartine. Under the more vigorous direction of Castries there was every reason to suppose that reinforcements would arrive in good time for the spring offensive.

There was still another objection that Rochambeau might have raised, though it was not one that gave him any satisfaction. Washington's original letter to Rochambeau had crossed one of his, in which he had told Washington of the sudden death of his great friend and colleague, the Chevalier de Ternay. The admiral, who had been ill for only a few days, died of some mysterious ailment officially described as a malignant fever. La Fayette spread it abroad that he had died of a broken heart at being held in disgraceful idleness in Newport. Opinion as to his ability was divided. Being a morose man he was not generally popular, particularly among the younger officers, who would have preferred a more dashing commander. Closen admitted his skill in maneuvering but thought him overcautious, which was probably pretty close to the truth. Rochambeau, however, would hear no criticism of him. He had brought the convoy safely across the Atlantic, avoiding the temptation to engage the enemy en route, and for that feat alone France and America would cherish his memory.

The Chevalier Des Touches, who took Ternay's place, was no more favorably inclined to the Spanish venture than Rochambeau. Under the circumstances, Washington bowed to the inevitable. He had come away from the conference at Hartford with the impression that his control of the French forces was more nominal than real, and though in this case he had only asked for an opinion, he wisely decided not to press the point.

The reluctance of the French to cooperate with him may have been discouraging, but with the beginning of 1781 (the year which, had he known it, was to bring him victory) Washington was faced with something far more ominous than the intransigence of his allies. On the morning of January 3 an officer drew up at his headquarters and handed him a letter from Brigadier General Anthony Wayne. Bad news was no newcomer at Washington's headquarters. He may have thought he had touched rock-bottom that evening at West Point when Alexander Hamilton brought him the dispatches confirming Arnold's treachery, but villainous though it was, Arnold's conspiracy began and ended with himself. The letter from General Wayne opened Washington's eyes to a danger far more difficult to combat. In unexpectedly matter-of-fact language, "Mad Anthony" Wayne, a fighting general who had always been popular with his troops, informed the commander-in-chief that a mutiny had broken out in the Pennsylvania line, and that a number of the men, with some artillery, were marching on Philadelphia.

Washington had always dreaded the possibility of mutiny. As he stated in his circular to the New England states, it was impossible to tell "at what point the defection will stop or how extensive it may prove God only knows . . . it is in vain to think an army can be kept together much longer under such variety of suffering as ours has experienced."[6] Once again the thirteen states stepped up to the edge of the precipice and then drew back. The men of the Pennsylvania line were not traitors. They were not going over to the British, nor was their quarrel with their officers, but rather with Congress and the Pennsylvania Council. They demanded the shirts and shoes they had been promised. Above all, they demanded to be paid. The President of the Pennsylvania Council, Joseph Reed, met with a committee of sergeants at Princeton and offered them generous terms, including back pay and the right to a discharge if they had served three years or more. Washington regretted the leniency of the terms, but in this case the policy of appeasement worked. Many of the men took the back pay, accepted the discharge, and then re-enlisted. A few weeks later the revolt spread to the New Jersey line, and the New Jersey legislature promptly appointed commissioners to discuss the men's grievances, but this time Washington handled the mutiny in his own way. Before there could be any negotiations, the rebellious detachment was surrounded and forced to surrender. Three ringleaders were tried by court-martial and sentenced to death. Two of them were executed, and the other reprieved. This swift action brought the mutinies to an end.

Washington was glad of the chance to strike a blow for discipline. He was always ready to plead with Congress and the state legislatures on behalf of his longsuffering soldiers, but whatever Congress did or did not do, discipline must be maintained. As he pointed out in General Orders, January 30, 1781: "We began a contest for liberty and independence, ill provided with the means of war, relying on our patriotism to supply the deficiency. We expected to encounter many wants and distresses, and we should neither shrink from them when they happen, nor fly in the face of law and government to procure redress." The thoughtful soldier listening to these Orders, as they were read out to him, was made to realize that by enlisting in the Army he had incurred tremendous obligations without at the same time acquiring any clearly defined rights. No general—not even Garibaldi who, seventy years later, after the fall of the Roman Republic, offered his soldiers hunger, thirst, forced marches, battles, and death, ever put patriotism on a loftier plane. Such a doctrine could not be imposed on free men indefinitely. The signs of cracking were only too evident. Everywhere, in England and in France even more than in America, there was talk of peace. After six years of fighting men were weary of pouring out blood and treasure in a struggle that seemed to lead nowhere.

Better than anyone else in America, Washington and Rochambeau both knew that independence could be won only with the help of France. Only with French money could Washington hope to pay his troops and provide them the equipment needed for the next campaign. Only with French ships could they break the strangling British blockade. Would the promised help ever come, and when it came would there be strings attached, or would Washington be free to use it as he wanted? His eyes were fixed on New York, but he had not yet succeeded in convincing Rochambeau that New York was the all-important objective. Rochambeau was more interested in Virginia, where La Fayette and General Greene were battling against Cornwallis and Benedict Arnold.

All through January and February 1781, while he was stamping out the fires of mutiny in the Pennsylvania and the New Jersey line, and when he was not wrangling with Congress over the unending problems of stores and provisions, Washington was wondering how to cope with the depredations of Benedict Arnold in Virginia. Not knowing what to do with his newly acquired ally, Sir Henry Clinton had sent Arnold down to Virginia at the head of sixteen hundred men with a roving commission to do as much damage as possible. Arnold carried out his instructions to the letter. He captured Richmond, destroyed the foundry and arsenal nearby, chased Governor Jefferson into hiding, and carted off or burned seven thousand hogsheads of tobacco. At the same time he made havoc of the shipping in the interior waterways of the state. In the course of a single expedition he captured or sank seven armed brigs or sloops without a man of his own being killed or wounded.

The lurid reports of Arnold ravaging the state of Virginia at will were almost more than Washington could bear. If he were to continue his activities unchecked he might soon make it impossible to move stores and provisions overland to General Greene's army in the Carolinas. The more Washington thought about it, the more eager he was not merely to put a stop to Arnold's maraudings but to capture and hang him as he had had to hang poor André. He could scrape up enough troops for the purpose, and La Fayette was just the man to lead the expedition, but he needed the cooperation of Rochambeau and Des Touches as well. If Des Touches could send a force up the Chesapeake strong enough to cut off Arnold from the sea, La Fayette might well corner him and starve him into surrender.

Washington had remained on excellent terms with Rochambeau in spite of his slight disappointment over Rochambeau's unwilling-

ness to join in the Spanish expedition to Florida. There had been
no secrets between them. Each knew the other's difficulties. Washington had confided in Rochambeau his anxiety over the mutinies,
and had explained to him that, serious though the situation was, at
least there was no treason involved. Clinton had tried to capitalize
on it, only to have his emissaries to the rebellious troops handed
over to the proper authorities and hanged. Rochambeau had been
equally frank with Washington. Even if there had been no other
objections to the Spanish venture, the fleet was so short of provisions at the moment that it would have been impossible for it to
sail. He too was beginning to wonder how long his army could
continue to exist without funds. It was more than six months since
he had had any communication from his government.

Under these very depressing circumstances when it seemed that
the French would once again have to refuse his call for help,
providence suddenly intervened in Washington's favor. On January
26, Rochambeau wrote him that in spite of a severe storm two
frigates and a transport bringing much-needed supplies for the fleet
had just put into Newport. The same storm, which the French
ships had weathered with the greatest difficulty, had struck the
British blockading squadron off Gardiner's Island and severely
crippled it. According to the first reports, one ninety-gun ship had
disappeared entirely, one "seventy-four" had been driven ashore
and wrecked, and two other ships of the line had been demasted.
Thanks to this heaven-sent storm, naval superiority had shifted at
least temporarily from the British to the French side. Rochambeau
was quick to capitalize on his good fortune. In answer to two
requests, a longstanding one from Washington and a more recent
one from Congress transmitted by the Chevalier de la Luzerne,
Des Touches immediately detached one ship of the line and two
frigates to operate off the Virginia coast in conjunction with La
Fayette. Washington would have preferred a more powerful
squadron including troop-bearing transports, but unfortunately,
owing to the slowness of the mails—the special courier service had

been discontinued for lack of funds—the little squadron had already sailed before his letter arrived. Congress and the Governor of Virginia had requested exactly what Des Touches sent. There had been no mention of troops or transports.

If only Washington's appeal for more effective help had arrived sooner, or if his original appeal had been more specific, Des Touches would perhaps have decided to go out with his whole fleet instead of sending two or three ships under a subordinate. Rochambeau would have been glad to supply the necessary infantry. The small French squadron, finding nothing could be done in the Chesapeake, as the ships drew more water than the British vessels supporting Arnold, returned to Newport. Captain de Tilly, in command of this squadron, did not consider his mission a failure since he had captured the *Romulus,* a British forty-four, off the capes, together with several merchantmen and some five hundred prisoners. In other words, he had conducted a good raid, but a good raid was not what Washington had asked for. Arnold, skilled in all the arts and practices of amphibious warfare, was still at large.

On the basis of Tilly's report and in response to Washington's demands, Rochambeau and Des Touches now decided to send a full-scale expedition down to Virginia, including troop-carrying transports. The expedition would be headed by Des Touches himself and by the Baron de Vioménil, who would be in command of the land forces, including twelve hundred grenadiers and *chasseurs* and a detachment of artillery. This time there was to be no mistake. Vioménil would cooperate with La Fayette in such a way as to ensure the destruction of Arnold's force. Certain very human difficulties remained to be resolved. The Marquis de Laval, commanding the Bourbonnais regiment, refused to take orders from La Fayette, and Baron de Vioménil made it equally clear that he would not serve under Washington's drillmaster, Baron von Steuben, who was in command of the Virginia militia. The two barons never got on together. The French officers asked for nothing better than a chance to serve under General Washington, but they had not traveled three thousand miles to take orders from any of his lieutenants, least of all from La Fayette. The only exception to this rule was the Duc de Lauzun, a born fire-eater and as such ready to fight under anyone, even La Fayette, who offered him a life of excitement.

How serious these jealousies would have proved will never be known; the troops never got ashore. Everything in this expedition depended on speed and Des Touches was a cautious man who was not to be hurried. If it were to succeed, the French ships would have had to slip out of Newport very quietly, preferably without Admiral Arbuthnot in Gardiner's Bay being aware of it, or at least before he was ready to put to sea himself. Such secrecy was out of the question, due to Washington's arrival in Newport on a long-delayed and frequently postponed visit. It was a gala occasion during which he was entertained in great style on board the flag-ship *Duc de Bourgogne*. In the evening the line-of-battle ships and the frigates in the harbor were dressed with lanterns and the entire city was illuminated, the town council having again voted candles, as they did on Rochambeau's arrival, to all those who could not afford to pay for them. Of course there were reviews and balls, at which the French officers were lionized and at which also the Des Touches expedition, the chances of its success and the fear of its failure, were fully discussed. After being cooped up in Rhode Island for nearly nine months, the French army was at last getting down to the business of war.

This was all very well, and Washington was no doubt pleased with the excellent *esprit de corps* he found in the French army, but he would have been still more pleased if Des Touches had acted with more sense of urgency. Tilly had returned to Newport on February 24 and, in anticipation of his report, orders for the embarkation of the grenadiers and *chasseurs* were issued the same day. On the following day, for reasons unknown, these orders were countermanded. Washington reached Newport on March

6, and by that time Closen reports that the companies of grenadiers from Bourbonnais and Soissonnais and of the *chasseurs* from Saintonge and Royal Deux-Ponts had already gone on board the transports. The wind was favorable on the seventh, and Washington did not understand why Des Touches did not give the order to hoist sail. On the morning of the eighth one of the ships ran aground, and it was not until sunset that the squadron finally sailed out of the harbor.

Arbuthnot in the meantime was busy refitting his ships after the gale. The damage had not been as serious as the French believed, and on the ninth of March he was ready for sea again. The news reached him on the tenth, and he "at once proceeded to sea in the hope of being able to fight the enemy before their entry to the Chesapeake, or if practicable to attack them there."[7] Although the French fleet had two days' start, the superior sailing of the British ships gave them the advantage. Arbuthnot passed his quarry in the night of the sixteenth and reached Chesapeake Bay a few hours ahead of the French. In the battle that followed the French had the advantage. Des Touches maneuvered his squadron with great skill, and though his force was inferior in gunpower he had the best of the exchanges. Two of the British ships were so seriously damaged that they had to pull out of the line, while only one of the French ships was disabled. In view of the damage he had inflicted on the British squadron, there was nothing to prevent Des Touches from sailing into the Chesapeake, landing his troops and going ahead with the plan to annihilate Arnold's force. Apparently neither Des Touches nor Arbuthnot wanted to press the action to a conclusion. Having disabled his opponent Des Touches seems to have thought that he had done enough. Possibly he underestimated the damage to the British ships, or he may have thought that the British squadron, in spite of being crippled, could still get into the Chesapeake before him and thus prevent him from landing his detachment. Whatever the reason, he returned to Newport without having completed his mission.

The failure of the expedition was a great blow to Washington because it meant that Arnold, who was running short of provisions, could now be supplied and reinforced by sea. Rochambeau, in his report of the engagement to Washington, attributed lack of success to the unfavorable winds. In his customarily polite reply, Washington appeared satisfied that his allies had left no stone unturned: "While I regret the disappointment of our plan, I cannot but admire the good conduct and valour displayed by Mr. des Touches. . . . It may, I think be fairly said that Great Britain owes the safety of her detachment under the command of Arnold to the influence of the Winds and not to the superiority of her Navy in the late affair."[8] He even wrote to the President of Congress that "the good conduct and bravery exhibited by our Allies on that occasion entitle them to the warmest thanks of the public," and Congress accordingly drafted and sent to Rochambeau an appropriate resolution of congratulation.[9]

So far Washington could not have shown more consideration for Rochambeau's feelings. He realized too how frustrated Vioménil must have felt at not being able to come to grips with the enemy. But whatever he might say to the French or to Congress, the failure of the operation still rankled, and he attributed it to what seemed to him unnecessary delays. If Des Touches had committed the whole squadron at once, while the British were still refitting after the storm, instead of sending out three small ships under Captain Tilly, nothing could have saved Arnold's force from destruction. Washington's irritation never finds its way into his official correspondence, but it did sometimes leak out in his private letters. One of these letters, addressed to his cousin Lund Washington, in which he expressed himself very clearly about the French not undertaking the enterprise "when I first proposed it to them," fell into British hands.[10]

Security arrangements were notoriously lax on both sides, so that Washington and Clinton were continually being informed of each other's movements through the capture of posts. This particular letter was captured by Loyalist partisans within a few miles of West Point. Clinton, seizing upon it as a means of making trouble between the two allies, promptly published it in Rivington's *Gazette,* the best-known Tory paper in New York. At the same time he made sure that a copy of this *Gazette* should reach Rochambeau.

Rochambeau was deeply hurt, as Clinton hoped he would be, by Washington's reflections on the French bungling of the operation, as reported in the intercepted letter. Up to that moment he had prided himself on his excellent understanding with the commander-in-chief. Was it, he ventured to ask Washington, a genuine letter that had appeared in the *Gazette*? He himself was not conscious of having failed in any way to carry out Washington's wishes. Tilly's small squadron had been sent out at the express wish of Congress and the state of Virginia, who had neither of them said anything about a detachment of troops. Washington's letter demanding a full-scale operation had not reached him until after Tilly had sailed. As for the subsequent delay, it was due to the difficulties Des Touches had had in getting the necessary supplies. The army had given Des Touches carte blanche so far as its own supplies were concerned. If Washington would consult the correspondence that had passed between them he could verify these facts for himself. In conclusion he reiterated that the King had put him under Washington's orders, and that for reasons of duty as well as inclination he would obey those orders as faithfully as any of Washington's own officers.

No man likes to eat humble pie, least of all when the dish is offered to him by a friend and an ally upon whom he is utterly dependent. There was nothing for it but to admit his mistake. No man ever grasped his nettle more manfully:

I assure your Excellency that I feel extreme pain at the occasion of that part of your letter of the 26th instant, which relates to an intercepted letter of mine published by the enemy. I am unhappy that an accident should have put it in their power to give to the world anything from me, which may contain an implication the least disagreeable to you, or to the Chevalier Destouches. . . . The enemy have fabricated whole letters for me, and even a series of letters; and it is not improbable that they may have given a different turn to some of my expressions in the present instance. It would however be disingenuous of me not to acknowledge that I feel the general import to be true. . . . Whatever construction it may bear, I beg your Excellency will consider the letter to a private friend, a gentleman who has the direction of my concerns at home, totally unconnected with public affairs, and on whose discretion I could absolutely rely. No idea of the same kind has ever gone to any public body. . . . My letter however was written in haste and might have been inaccurately expressed. I have lately learnt (though not officially) that the cause of the delay I have alluded to was a want of supplies for the fleet. Impressed with a real esteem for the Chevalier Destouches, I heard this circumstance with satisfaction. With this explanation, I leave the matter to his candor and to yours, and flatter myself it will make no impression inconsistent with an entire persuasion of my sincere esteem and attachment.

This honest explanation was all that was needed to heal what might have developed into a running sore. Rochambeau was too big a personality to nurse a grievance. Unless Des Touches should mention the article in the *Gazette,* in which case he would show him Washington's letter, the incident, so far as the French were concerned, was closed. In Greek mythology the goddesses had eagerly seized on the apple of discord, but luckily mortal men do not always behave as gods. When Clinton tossed his apple into the allied camp, Washington and Rochambeau threw it away. For one thing, they had other and more important business on hand. Rochambeau's son had just arrived back from Paris bringing with him, it was hoped, a favorable reply to the Hartford demands. The question whether Washington would be able to keep an army in the field, let alone win the war, all hinged on the letter in young Rochambeau's pocket.

N*otes*

1. Washington, *Writings,* XX, 173.
2. *Ibid.,* XX, 97.
3. Doniol, IV, 397.
4. Closen, p. 39.
5. Rochambeau, *Mémoires,* I, 256.
6. Washington, *Writings,* XXI, 61.
7. James, *The British Navy in Adversity,* p. 270.
8. Washington, *Writings,* XXI, 397.
9. *Ibid.,* XXI, 399.
10. *Ibid.,* XXI, 386.

N*ine*

THE FRIGATE *Amazone,* with the Vicomte de Rochambeau on board, had slipped out of Newport Harbor on October 28, run through the British patrol and landed at Lorient on the coast of Brittany on the fifteenth of November. It was a quick passage, and if the King and his ministers gave him a prompt audience, as he must have assumed they would in view of the importance of his dispatches, there was no reason why he should not report back to his father by the end of the year. The fact that it took over six months, instead of two, for Rochambeau to get a reply to his dispatches was not due just to the slowness of sailing ships—it would be another sixty years before steamships bettered the time of the *Amazone*—but to the deliberate methods of the French Ministry of War and the Ministry of Foreign Affairs. In the eighteenth century, before democracy had transformed it from the gentlemanly occupation of the few into a ghastly burden upon all mankind, war was still regarded as one of the various tools of diplomacy, and diplomats, as the young Vicomte soon learned, were not to be hurried.

The war in America was merely one of many pieces that had to be fitted into the international puzzle. Vergennes, a conscientious Minister of Foreign Affairs who surveyed the European scene from a strictly national point of view, had welcomed the revolt of the American colonies as a means of redressing the balance of power in Europe. With the exception of Benjamin Franklin, one of the supreme artists in diplomacy of all time, the American representatives in Paris were always inclined to bite the hand that fed them.

They marched into the Ministry of Foreign Affairs and virtually threatened Vergennes with blackmail. If France did not grant them immense subsidies at once, they might be driven to make their own terms with England and so leave France to carry on the war alone. Most conspicuous among the blusterers was John Adams. He hated to be under obligation to anybody and would never admit that America owed anything to France. On the contrary, France owed everything to America, thanks to whose tireless efforts, Europe was now for the first time allied against her ancient enemy.[1] Such talk might have proved disastrous to the alliance if Franklin had not been on hand to soothe Vergennes' feelings. It was not by such methods that America was likely to get the help Washington and Rochambeau so desperately needed. As Franklin wrote to the President of Congress, "an expression of gratitude is not only our duty, but our interest."[2]

While Vergennes was being subjected to Adams' arrogance, his own countrymen were pouring a very different story into his ears. To a great many Frenchmen, particularly French merchants, the war in America was a regrettable, though perhaps necessary, extension of the unending struggle for the West Indies. Their prosperity, and to a considerable extent the prosperity of France, depended on the sugar trade. What happened on the mainland was of importance only insofar as it affected the security of Guadeloupe and Martinique. The British were just as aware as the French of the revenue that poured into France from her West Indian possessions. At the end of the Seven Years' War a good many thoughtful Englishmen regretted the decision to keep Canada instead of Guadeloupe. They balanced the trade in sugar, rum, cotton, and coffee against the fur trade and thought that England had got decidedly the worst of the bargain.[3] In an age when imperialism was nakedly and unashamedly economic, Vergennes did not have to be convinced of the supreme importance of the sugar islands. Whatever France did or did not do for the American colonists, she must never weaken her hold on the West Indies. There was another complication. French policy in the West Indies was dependent on Spanish cooperation, and Spain was indifferent, if not actually hostile, to the attempt of any colony to establish independence. She was allied with France, not with America, and her only interest in the war with England was to obtain possession of Gibraltar.

The ramifications of the war in America were indeed endless. Rochambeau's politely insistent letters from his headquarters on Rhode Island reminded the King's ministers that the American Army was at the end of its rope, and that the French army in America was desperately short of funds. La Fayette's confidence was as unquenchable as ever, but the news that trickled across the Atlantic from other sources was not so optimistic. Benedict Arnold's treason, followed up by the tales of mutiny, were danger signals no responsible minister could ignore. Everything that Vergennes heard from Rochambeau was confirmed by the gloomy despatches of La Luzerne, the French representative with Congress, and again by Washington's own spokesman Colonel John Laurens. Washington's army was short of everything an army needed, food, ammunition, supplies, equipment, but most of all it was short of money. An army that is not paid cannot be fed, and an army that is not fed is bound to disintegrate.

No one questioned the accuracy or the urgency of these reports, but neither could anyone question the accuracy or the urgency of the reports of Jacques Necker, the Genevan banker who had been appointed director-general of finances. Necker had been chosen for this position as being an excellent man of business who, by dexterous financial juggling, could be counted on to bring some order into French finances without imposing any unpleasant taxes. Always ready to oblige, Necker piled up foreign loan on foreign loan so that temporarily at least the country should not feel the burden of war, but at the same time he warned the government that pouring France's wealth across the Atlantic must soon end in disaster. Nor was Necker the only minister pleading for economy. Of all people Montbarey, the Minister of War, was grumbling about the tremendous expenditures necessary for the successful prosecution of Vergennes' policies.

These were some of the problems confronting Vergennes when, on December 26, 1780, the Vicomte de Rochambeau arrived at Versailles and delivered into his hands the resolution drafted by Washington and Rochambeau at the Hartford conference. For one brief moment the Vicomte thought he would get everything he was asking for—a substantial sum of money, ten thousand men, and "many ships" (*beaucoup de vaisseaux*), but the sudden death of the Empress Maria Theresa put an end to his dream. Nothing could be done about sending reinforcements to America until it was seen what effect her death might have on the peace of Europe. Maria Theresa had just concluded the Treaty of Teschen, which averted war between Austria and Prussia. In her later years the Empress had been a strong influence for peace, but now that she was dead it was more than possible that a European war might break out again. England had just declared war against Holland, and the Court of France had decided to support the Dutch by sending a squadron out to the East Indies. These events had interfered with the Court's giving the detailed attention to Rochambeau's requests that they deserved. America would have to wait.

Vergennes was probably more easily reconciled to waiting than Rochambeau, but at the same time he was a tenacious man who never allowed himself to be sidetracked indefinitely. Though he was not insensitive to the complaints about the expense of the war, he had made up his mind that the British were just as war-weary as the French or Americans, and that if the Americans could be persuaded to play their part, one more vigorous campaign might well bring about the peace on which he had been gambling. Even before young Rochambeau had sailed, he had begun reorganizing the Cabinet with this end in view. The Comte de Maurepas was nominally the head of the government, but though he was not

lacking in intelligence, he was eighty years old and only too glad
therefore to surrender the initiative to the more energetic Minister
of Foreign Affairs. Obviously Montbarey, the Minister of War who
was known to be out of sympathy with Vergennes' policies, had to
be relieved; also M. de Sartine, the Minister of Marine, a former
police commissioner who had been promoted to cabinet rank
with disastrous results for everybody concerned. In their place
Vergennes appointed the Marshal de Ségur and the Marquis de
Castries. Rochambeau was delighted by these changes. Ségur was
an old friend, who like Rochambeau himself had been wounded at
Laufeldt and at Clostercamp. He possessed all the qualities
Montbarey lacked, a capacity for hard work, devotion to his profession, and the ability to say *no* to courtiers. If he was inclined to
be inflexible, that was a quality Rochambeau understood too.

The Marquis de Castries, the new Minister of Marine, was another competent officer in whom Rochambeau had the greatest
confidence. He had a son who was second colonel in the Saintonge
Regiment, and for that reason he took a particular interest in
American affairs. Rochambeau told Washington that Castries
could be relied upon to send over whatever was needed in the way
of supplies and reinforcements. Washington hoped it might be so,
but he had been hearing about reinforcements for so long he may
well have had his doubts.

In France the reaction to the changes in the Cabinet was no less
favorable than it was in Rochambeau's headquarters. At last the
war would be run efficiently. Instead of the confusion, the extrava-
gance, and the private quarrels which had paralyzed the last Cabinet, the new team could be counted on to work together in complete harmony.

The first news to reach Rochambeau from Versailles did not
refute these optimistic reports. La Pérouse returned in February
1781, bringing with him a million and a half francs in hard cash,
enough to keep the French army solvent for another few months.
The Vicomte de Rochambeau was to remain in France until the

Cabinet had finished debating the questions raised by the Hartford conference. He and the Chevalier de Barras, who was to take the place of Des Touches as commander of the squadron, sailed on March 24, bringing with them another substantial sum of money with a promise of more to come, six million francs in all, to be placed at Washington's disposal for the needs of the American Army. This six million francs was not a loan from the French government but a gift, and as such it was doubly welcome. Indeed it is hard to see how, without this last-minute assistance, even such a small army as Washington then commanded could have been kept in the field for another year. In other respects the reply to the resolutions was far from satisfactory. The Vicomte reports that he returned "tired and dissatisfied" with the results of his mission.[4]

The Vicomte's father must have been even more dissatisfied. Not only was Rochambeau's request for an additional ten thousand men refused, but the second division of the expeditionary corps which the King had promised him when he accepted the command, and for which he had been scanning the horizon ever since he sailed into Newport Harbor, was also countermanded. Vergennes and Ségur, who drafted the reply jointly, explained that even if it had been possible to send over these reinforcements, which it was not, they would have hesitated to do so. The Americans, like all young people jealous of their liberty, would not want to be under such obligations to their allies. The original intention had been that the French troops should serve as auxiliaries, not that they should constitute the main army. Ségur argued that should they send over the ten thousand men Rochambeau had demanded, the British would certainly do no less, and America would then become the main theater of war. There was therefore no likelihood that the tremendous expense involved in Rochambeau's recommendations would bring the war to an end any sooner. In support of the decision not to send over more troops the Council of Ministers pointed out that the Americans themselves had not asked for manpower. Through his representative John

Laurens, who was also the representative of Congress, Washington
had asked for money, which the French had repeatedly advanced,
though not to the fantastic amount Laurens had demanded, and
for sufficient naval power to enable the French and American
forces to plan their campaign with the knowledge that temporarily
at least they had achieved that superiority at sea without which
there could be no hope of victory. This request for naval superiority, which Rochambeau and Washington both agreed was essential, the Council of Ministers had done their best to meet.

Rochambeau would not have been human if he had not been
profoundly disappointed at not getting his reinforcements. He immediately wrote a stiffly polite reply to Ségur stating that, though
his request had been refused, he would do his best to carry out his
mission with the very limited means His Majesty had allowed him.
A wry comment in the letter about his son coming back to him
very much alone was as far as his ironbound sense of discipline
would allow him to go.[5] On second thought he may have decided
that the instructions from Paris were not quite so discouraging as
they seemed. By the same frigate he received a private letter from
the Marquis de Castries telling him that Admiral de Grasse had
just set sail from Brest with a squadron powerful enough to give
France and her American allies command of the sea.

Ségur had spoken in a general way about De Grasse having been
ordered to the West Indies to cooperate with the Spaniards in any
offensive operations against the British, either in the islands or on
the mainland. Castries was more specific. De Grasse was in command of a squadron of twenty vessels; he would find ten more in
the West Indies and eight in Rhode Island. With these forces,
which he could either unite or disperse, at his disposal, he would
be master of the North Atlantic coastline for some time at least,
and in a position "to act with you," added Castries, "in any enterprise you may wish to undertake."[6] In other words, De Grasse, if
he were so inclined, could venture north independently of his Spanish allies. While the West Indies was still the main theater of war,

De Grasse might be induced to embark on a sideshow in support of the Americans. In this one short letter, intended almost as a postscript to the instructions of Ségur and Vergennes, Castries foreshadowed the joint operations that led to Yorktown.

There were various other details in the instructions that did not appeal to Rochambeau at all. Among other things he was asked to facilitate as much as possible an expedition La Pérouse had in mind to Hudson Bay. It seems that La Pérouse had not wanted to return to America and that he had extracted a promise from influential friends at Court, as a condition for his going back, that he should be assigned a ship and 250 men with which to make an attack on various British trading posts in Hudson Bay. Rochambeau, who was short of men anyway, particularly disliked assigning men for a marauding expedition over which he had no control and which, even if it were successful, would have no effect on the outcome of the war. At the same time that La Pérouse was planning a sideshow in Canada, Des Touches was hoping to escape the tedium of war by embarking on another project of the same kind in Penobscot Bay. Rochambeau strongly disapproved of this plan also, but as he had no control over the Navy he referred the whole matter to Washington, in the hope that Washington would agree with him that their policy must be founded on concentration of force instead of dispersion. Fortunately Washington did agree. He was no more in favor of these forays than Rochambeau, and the subject was accordingly dropped, much to the disappointment of La Pérouse, Des Touches, and also of the state of Massachusetts which, looking ahead to the end of the war, was inclined to smile on all such expeditions as a means of guaranteeing its fishing rights in Canadian waters.

With the arrival of Barras and the potent letters from the new ministers Ségur and Castries, Rochambeau was eager for another summit conference. Washington proposed that they meet on the twenty-first of May at Wethersfield, a few miles south of Hartford, where the Connecticut legislature was at that moment in session.

He would bring with him General Knox and General Duportail, a French officer on his staff who could take La Fayette's place as interpreter. Again Rochambeau and Chastellux set out from Newport, this time on horseback instead of by coach, to confer with Washington at what was destined to be the most important conference of the war. At the last moment Barras, whom Washington was most anxious to meet, was detained in Rhode Island by the sudden appearance off shore of several British men-of-war.

The Webb house in Wethersfield, where the meeting took place, is not only still standing but, thanks to the Colonial Dames of Connecticut, in an excellent state of preservation. The charming rooms of the old house are just as they were when Washington and Rochambeau occupied them nearly two centuries ago. The visitor of today, if he has any historic imagination, can summon the two generals from the past, sit them down at the table, and watch them poring over their maps. The taverns where they took their meals have disappeared, but the Silas Deane house which the generals could see from their windows is still there, another outstanding example of the knowledge, taste, and generosity of the Colonial Dames. As for Wethersfield itself, no one will quarrel with the comment of one of Rochambeau's aides, the Baron Cromot du Bourg, who had only just arrived at his headquarters at the time of the conference. Wethersfield is "a charming spot," says the Baron. "It would be impossible to find prettier houses and a more beautiful view. I went up into the steeple of the church and saw the richest country I had yet seen in America. From this spot you can see for fifty miles around."[7]

In these ideal surroundings Washington and Rochambeau hammered out their plans for the next campaign. The laconic entries in Washington's diary give no impression of the proposals and counterproposals discussed and rejected.

In the earlier conference at Hartford, Washington had been at a disadvantage. He had no idea how many men he could muster for the next campaign or how they could be equipped. Rochambeau, on the contrary, knew exactly where he stood and he was also far more confident of his reinforcements. At Wethersfield the positions were not exactly reversed, but they were more nearly even. Washington still did not know whether he would be in command of an army of ten thousand or five thousand, but at least he was no worse off than before, and, thanks to the French, better off for clothing and equipment. Rochambeau arrived at Wethersfield feeling that his government had let him down. There was to be no buildup of his forces. Even the second division, which he had always counted on, was withheld from him. All that he could report at the conference was a possible reinforcement of six hundred recruits, which De Grasse was supposed to send him as soon as he had reached the Azores. He had now reached the point, which Washington had reached long before, where he did not believe in any reinforcmeents until they had actually landed in Rhode Island. Under these circumstances he was not in any position to impose a plan of campaign. He could only assure Washington, as he had assured him many times before, that his four regiments were at Washington's disposal, to be used in any way he saw fit.

Bearing in mind the failure of the recent operations against Benedict Arnold in Chesapeake Bay, Washington had now come back to his long-cherished scheme of an attack against General Clinton in New York. The two factors that contributed to this decision seemed to him unanswerable. In the first place, Barras was not prepared to transport the French army to Chesapeake Bay. Rochambeau had asked his colleague whether this was feasible and whether he could also assist the infantry in attacking the British positions in Virginia. Barras, who was perhaps still dreaming of operating by himself in Penobscot Bay, did not want to commit himself, and accordingly talked at length about the reinforcements to the British fleet. Obviously he shied away from any such large-scale operation as Rochambeau had in mind. But Washington had another and much stronger reason for harking back to his original plan of an attack on New York.

At the Wethersfield conference he was able to produce dispatches of Lord George Germain to Sir Henry Clinton, dated March 7, which had been intercepted by an American privateer. In these dispatches the British Minister directed Sir Henry to turn his immediate attention to the conquest of the southern states. Being thus advised of the enemy's plans, Washington was more than ever in favor of striking a decisive blow at New York, since the British forces there would necessarily be weakened. Rochambeau was not entirely convinced of the soundness of this reasoning. If Cornwallis and Clinton together, after subduing the southern states, were to go on and occupy Maryland and Pennsylvania as well by making another landing at the head of Chesapeake Bay, which was apparently the British intention, would not the spirit of resistance in the other states inevitably crumble and collapse? Washington did not think so. The moral effect of the capture of New York, in British hands since the beginning of the war and the mainspring of all their operations, would more than compensate for the temporary loss of the southern states.

Rochambeau was still not convinced. For the capture of New York naval cooperation was essential, and the heavy French ships of the line were unable to get over Sandy Hook bar. He based this opinion on the experience of Admiral d'Estaing, who had had the humiliating experience of bringing his fleet to New York and then being told by the pilot that it was absolutely impossible to take the ships inside the Hook. As to why the British ships were able to get in and not the French, it appeared that a French "sixty-four" drew twenty-seven feet, whereas a similarly gunned British ship drew only twenty-two feet.[8]

In spite of these arguments Washington stood his ground. Either the French and Americans had to proceed overland to Virginia or else they must conduct operations of some sort against the enemy in New York. He decided on New York. Having made as strong a case as he could for his own point of view, Rochambeau bowed to Washington's decision. This was no grudging surrender. Rochambeau was the ideal lieutenant. He had spoken his mind, and now he would carry out the commander-in-chief's plans to the best of his ability. Washington's summary of the conference is contained in his letter to the Chevalier de la Luzerne, written just before leaving Wethersfield:

The letter which I have the honor to inclose from the Count de Rochambeau will, I imagine, inform your Excellency of the intended march of the French army towards the North River. . . . I should be wanting in respect and confidence were I not to add, that our object is New York. The Season, the difficulty and experience of Land transportation, and the continual waste of men in every attempt to reinforce the Southern states, are almost insuperable objections to marching another detachment from the Army on the North River; nor do I see how it is possible to give effectual support to those States, and avert the evils which threaten them, while we are inferior in naval force in these seas. . . .[9]

Washington went on to say that Rochambeau and Chastellux agreed with him that, unless there should be some unexpected change in the situation, "the West India Fleet should run immediately to Sandy Hook . . . where, most likely, it will shut in, or cut off, Admiral Arbuthnot; and may be joined by the Count de Barras." This was not quite accurate. Chastellux agreed, but not Rochambeau, who thought that it must be left to De Grasse to decide for himself whether he could operate to better advantage in the Chesapeake or against New York. On May 28, five days after the end of the conference, he dispatched a frigate to De Grasse in Santo Domingo and painted a gloomy picture of the war, particularly of the war in Virginia. At the same time he pointed out that victory was still within their reach. It depended entirely on De Grasse. Nothing could be done without him, but with the naval superiority he could provide, and with the additional troops he might bring with him—this was essential too as the joint Franco-American forces were "very weak"—the picture might change almost overnight.

Washington had heard about French reinforcements so often and had been so often disappointed that he did not count on De Grasse with any certainty until a letter from Rochambeau, written on June 10, confirmed the arrival of the French admiral in the West Indies and assured Washington of his willingness to participate in an attack on New York or on the British forces in Chesapeake Bay. Not for many months had such encouraging news reached Washington's headquarters. It was encouraging for two reasons. It meant that the bogey of British naval superiority would at last be dispelled, and it meant also that if De Grasse could bring five thousand men with him, which Rochambeau seemed to think possible, the disheartening failure of the states to supply their quota of recruits would not necessarily prove fatal. Washington was so delighted by this news, which for the first time opened up smiling vistas of victory, that he began to let his imagination play with other schemes than the attack on New York. The next letter to Rochambeau shows that he is beginning to waver: "Your Excellency will be pleased to recollect that New York was looked upon by us as the only practicable object under present circumstances; but should we be able to secure naval superiority, we may perhaps find others more practicable and equally advisable."[10]

While Washington almost subconsciously was being won around to the possibility of making his main attack on Virginia, Sir Henry Clinton had come into possession of two letters which convinced him that the French and the Americans were irrevocably committed to an attack upon his position in New York. One of these letters, from Washington to General Sullivan, at that time a member of Congress, contained a full report on the Wethersfield conference.

The other letter, from Chastellux to La Luzerne the French minister, was even more explicit. Chastellux, who no doubt thought himself more a man of the world than Rochambeau—after all, Rochambeau was only a soldier whereas he was a philosopher and an Academician—reported on the deliberations at the conference and made it appear that it was he who had persuaded Rochambeau, much against his will, to accept Washington's plan of besieging New York. We can imagine how Sir Henry must have chuckled over his good fortune. Thanks to the alertness of his spies the enemy plan of campaign had been revealed to him. Instead of keeping the Chastellux letter to himself he could not resist sending it to Rochambeau with a covering letter warning him to be on guard against his associates. Rochambeau, always impeccable on matters of military procedure, replied requesting General Clinton "not to send any more flags of truce from now on, because they would be no longer received, since General Washington was the commander-in-chief of the combined armies."[11]

The extraordinary casualness with which both sides treated secret and confidential documents is one of the more curious aspects of the war. In the military training of the day no one seems to have paid any attention to security. Rochambeau was one of the few exceptions to the general carelessness. The courier who was caught with the Chastellux letter on him had another letter in his pouch to La Luzerne, a letter from Rochambeau, in which Rochambeau mentioned the possibility of a Chesapeake campaign, but fortunately this letter was in cipher and could not be decoded. Clinton therefore remained convinced that the attack was planned against New York. It is ironic that his interception of these letters turned out to be such a stroke of luck for Washington. As Mathieu Dumas puts it in his memoirs, "chance served better than the ablest spies could have done." So fortuitous was it that it has been suggested that Washington's letter was written not to enlighten Sullivan but to mislead Clinton, and that the interception of the letter was carefully planned. This notion, ingenious as it is, does not hold water. The captured letters stated the decision which had been actually reached, and it was not until De Grasse was heard from that Washington decided to bypass New York in favor of a combined attack on Cornwallis in Virginia.

Rochambeau found no difficulty in dealing with the Chastellux letter. He summoned the author, handed him the letter, and demanded an explanation. Since Chastellux had spoken of his chief's "incredible ignorance," it was not an easy letter to explain. There was nothing to say except that he had written it in a fit of bad temper, and that he was sorry. Rochambeau listened to his excuses, took the letter from him and told him he would put it where it belonged. Thereupon he threw it in the fire. The incident was closed.[12] Never one to harbor a grievance, Rochambeau remained on excellent terms with the Chevalier for the rest of the campaign. Before returning to France he wrote to Ségur, the Minister of War, recommending that Chastellux should be appointed in his place as a most capable officer and as one who could be counted on to maintain happy relations with the Americans.

In a matter of this kind Rochambeau could be generous, but he was not always an easy man to get on with. The Duc de Lauzun did not like him and complained that nobody else did, but Lauzun was something of a prima donna and his criticism cannot be taken too seriously. Rochambeau's own staff liked him, particularly Berthier, who thought he was like the father of a family, and Dumas, who speaks of his noble character. Closen and Cromot du Bourg were also devoted to him. At the same time Rochambeau could be crusty and irritable. He suffered occasionally from his old wounds, but he probably suffered still more from a sense of frustration. Owing to the unwillingness or the inability of his government to reinforce him he was condemned to play an idle role for ten months, during which time he was fully conscious of the restlessness of his officers and the bewilderment of his allies. At first the Americans had been impressed by the soldierly appearance and the strict discipline of the French regiments, but before long they began to wonder why these excellently equipped troops were not being put to use. Washington was one of the few who understood Rochambeau's predicament. Until the British blockade was raised, or until the British fleet sailed away of its own accord, his army had to be kept on guard in Rhode Island. Boston and Newport were the only two ports left capable of sheltering the French fleet, and the loss of either of them would have been disastrous.

Count Fersen, who really admired Rochambeau, reveals in his journal the low state of morale in the French army after the long months of inactivity: ". . . I am beginning to grow weary of M. de Rochambeau. He treats me with distinction, it is true, and I am very grateful for it; but he is distrustful in a way that is disagreeable and indeed insulting; he places more confidence in me than in my comrades, but what he grants me is meager enough; he has no more in his general officers, who are quite dissatisfied, as are the higher officers of the army." Eighteen months later, when Rochambeau was going home after leading the army to victory, Fersen sounds a very different note: "We saw the departure of M. de Rochambeau with regret; everyone was satisfied to be under his command. This is far from the case with the Baron de Vioménil. The Baron is very quick and high-tempered; he has not the precious *sang-froid* of M. de Rochambeau. He was the only man capable to command us here. . . . The wise, prudent, and simple conduct of M. de Rochambeau has done more to conciliate Amercia to us than the gain of four battles would have done."[13]

In other words, when all was said and done, old Papa Rochambeau, as his officers called him, was a good man to serve under. Testy he may have been, but he knew how to handle troops, and in every crisis on the field of battle or in the staff conference, his judgment was unerring.

One of the most talented as well as unquestionably the most difficult of his subordinates was the Duc de Lauzun. No officer in Rochambeau's army was more socially inclined or more determined to enjoy himself. At the same time he was a conscientious officer and the men in his Legion, most of them foreigners he had welded together into a fighting unit, were utterly devoted to him. Lauzun inculcated into his gay Hussars, Poles, Germans, and Irish, something of the swagger and the *esprit de corps* traditionally associated with the Foreign Legion. Owing to the lack of

forage in Rhode Island and the difficulty of finding adequate winter quarters Rochambeau decided, much to Lauzun's regret, to
move the Legion out of Newport. With this in mind he consulted
Colonel Jeremiah Wadsworth, the agent appointed by Washington,
from whom he had been buying horses for the Legion, and on his
advice settled on Lebanon, a small village near Willimantic. After
a few days in Providence, where the Duke gave a ball for his
officers, the Legion broke camp and marched on to its winter
destination. Lebanon was a long way from Newport and therefore
not at all to Lauzun's liking. He could only compare it to Siberia,
"a few huts dispersed in the immense forests."[14]

Chastellux gives us a charming account of dining at this outpost
of civilization with Lauzun and his officers. Governor Trumbull
happened to be there on this occasion, and he delivered a long
grace before dinner of which the Hussars understood not a word.
No one smiled but the stentorian "Amen" from twenty mus-
tachioed lips made him realize how glad they were it was over.[15]

Wherever he went Lauzun always made himself agreeable, and
he soon became as well-liked by the farmers of Lebanon as he had
been by the ladies of Newport, particularly Mrs. Hunter and her
three daughters. Rochambeau tells a story of one of the Duke's
friends in Lebanon asking him what line of work his father was in.
"My father is not in business," replied Lauzun, "but I have an
uncle who is a *maréchal*." He was speaking of the Duc de Biron, a
well-known field marshal of the day. "Indeed," replied the villager,
for whose benefit the word *maréchal* was translated as *blacksmith,*
"there are worse trades than that."[16]

Unfortunately Lauzun did not, like Chastellux, write a book
about America, but we glean something about his experiences here
from his memoirs and from the comments of his brother officers.
These memoirs titillated society, since the author appeared to be
on terms of extreme intimacy with everybody of any social importance, but they have not worn as well as many other memoirs of
the eighteenth century. They were not published until 1822, nearly

thirty years after his death. At the request of one of the ladies mentioned in what seemed to her an uncomplimentary manner, Talleyrand wrote a letter to the press denying their authenticity. There is no question, however, that the memoirs are genuine, though they were written hastily and the section dealing with America needs to be checked against other sources. In spite of his comments on Rochambeau, whom he did not like, Lauzun's account of his adventures in America is the most interesting section of the book.

Lauzun's quarrel with Rochambeau dated back to Rochambeau's refusal to give him command of the land forces in the Des Touches expedition. Whether it is true, as Lauzun claims, that Washington wanted him to have this command as being one of the few French officers willing to serve under La Fayette, Rochambeau not unnaturally picked his senior officer, the Baron de Vioménil, for this responsible assignment instead of Lauzun. The Duke was primarily a cavalry leader, and this was not a cavalry operation. In his memoirs Lauzun likes to make it out that Washington got on with him far better than with Rochambeau, and that he himself was often put in the awkward position of go-between. The basis for this claim was a certain change of plans in the disposition of the fleet at Newport, a change which irritated Washington but with which Rochambeau had nothing to do. It had been decided at Wethersfield that after Rochambeau left Rhode Island with his four regiments of infantry to join Washington on the Hudson for the attack on New York, Barras should move the fleet to Boston. Washington had thought that after the French army had been withdrawn from Newport, the fleet would be safer in the harbor of Boston, and he may well have been surprised that Barras had decided to stay on at Newport. The decision affected him in that the French now wanted a thousand militia for the protection of the Newport anchorage and the stores. After badgering the governors of Massachusetts and Rhode Island for recruits, he now had to come back to them again with a request for troops to serve under the French at Newport.

According to Lauzun, the change of plans threw Washington into such a rage that for three days he could not bring himself to answer Rochambeau's letter, but there is no indication of any such rage in Washington's own letters. He wrote in his usual courteous style to both Barras and Rochambeau, stating that he still held to his opinion but that he would not set up his single judgment "against that of so many Gentlemen of experience, more especially as the matter partly depends upon a knowledge of Marine Affairs of which I candidly express my ignorance."[17] At the same time, in deferring to the decision of Barras to remain in Newport, Washington renewed his appeal to Rochambeau for the earliest possible concentration of their armies in the vicinity of New York. There was no measure, Washington thought, "so likely to afford relief to the southern States as a serious menace against New York."

The decisions of the Wethersfield conference left both Washington and Rochambeau with a mountain of paperwork on their hands. Washington set himself to his letter-writing at once, preparing dispatches to the four New England governors calling upon them "in the most earnest manner to devise means to send into the field without delay the number of men which have already been voted for the completion of the Battalions of your State." As always, he was short of manpower and many of the recruits sent in he had had to discharge "on account of inability."[18] In talking about the American Revolution with La Fayette, Napoleon was always puzzled by the small numbers involved. The most important issues in the world were settled by encounters between patrols.[19] Washington would have been the first to agree with him. The fact was that his army was made up of farmers, men who had to be on their farms at seedtime and harvest. Few of them could be induced to enlist for the duration of the war, or even for a reasonably long term of service. They were fighting as citizens of Connecticut, or New Jersey or Pennsylvania, and when the danger to their particular state was averted, it seemed to them natural enough to go back to the farm. Rochambeau did not have to face that particular problem, and he was free also from the necessity of having to take orders from a Congress which was itself at the mercy of the several state governments, but for money, provisions, and transportation he was as hard put to it as Washington.

To move his four regiments from Newport to a point near Dobbs Ferry, where he joined Washington, taxed his quarter-master-general and his commissary to the utmost. Blanchard went ahead to make the necessary arrangements. Luckily he was a resourceful man, for he had plenty of difficulties to contend with, not only with the Americans but with his own general. The Americans were slow to make up their minds, and being desperately short of money, they demanded hard cash for everything they provided. Rochambeau was a perfectionist, and if supplies were not forthcoming at the very moment he had ordered them, Blanchard heard about it in no uncertain terms. On one occasion when Blanchard was blamed, unjustly he thought, for a shortage of bread, he complains that Rochambeau always assumed his officers were either rascals or idiots. Later on in his journal he admits that the general had his good qualities too. He knew his business, he had an excellent *coup d'oeil* on the field of battle. Perhaps he was not an ideal administrator but he knew how to get on with Washington, and by his own conduct, and the conduct of his troops, he left in America a favorable impression of the French nation.

On the ninth of June everything was ready, and on the morning of the tenth the first division, composed of the Bourbonnais and the Royal Deux-Ponts regiments, moved out of Newport under the command of the Baron de Vioménil. They reached Providence in the evening and made camp on the heights overlooking the city, where on the next day they were joined by the Soissonnais and the Saintonge. The spotless white uniforms of the French troops bore little resemblance to the garb of the ragged regimentals of the American Army. The French regiments were distinguished from each other by the color of their lapels, coat collars, and buttons. The Bourbonnais wore crimson lapels, pink collars, and white buttons; the Royal Deux-Ponts blue collars and lemon-colored lapels; the Soissonnais rose-colored lapels, sky-blue collars, and yellow buttons; and the Saintonge green lapels and yellow buttons. Altogether it was as brave a show as Newport and Providence had ever seen. The nearest approach to it was their own Rhode Island regiment, three quarters of which, according to Closen, "consists of Negroes, and that regiment is the most neatly dressed, the best under arms, and the most precise in its maneuvers."[20]

It was a proud moment for Rochambeau as he watched his regiments tramping out of Newport on their way to join General Washington. The long period of inaction had been more trying for him than for anybody else. He had been standing in the wings for nearly a year. Now at last he was to step onto the stage, and the world would see that his spick-and-span regiments in their cocked hats and white plumes were good for something more than parade-ground brilliance. Two of the regiments were especially dear to him as he had fought side by side with them in the Seven Years' War, with the Soissonnais in Minorca and with the Bourbonnais, *les petits vieux* as they were known in the French Army, at Clostercamp. They were the flower of the French infantry, and to Lieutenant-General Jean-Baptiste-Donatien de Vimeur, Comte de Rochambeau, commanding His Most Christian Majesty's forces in America, the French infantry was the most beautiful instrument in the world.

Notes

1. Doniol, IV, 416.
2. August 9, 1780; Francis Wharton, *Revolutionary Diplomatic Correspondence of the U.S.* 6 vols. 1889.
3. *English Historical Documents,* X, 775.
4. Weelen, 215.
5. Doniol, V, 470.

6. Doniol, V, 469.
7. *Magazine of American History*, IV, 295.
8. Freeman, *George Washington*, V, 48.
9. Washington, *Writings*, XXII, 103.
10. *Ibid.*, XXII, 108.
11. Closen, p. 110.
12. Rochambeau, *Mémoires*, I, 274.
13. *Magazine of American History*, III, 375; IV, 446.
14. Lauzun, *Mémoires*, p. 273.
15. Chastellux, I, 386.
16. Rochambeau, *Mémoires*, I, 259.
17. Washington, *Writings*, XXII, 157.
18. *Ibid.*, 110.
19. C. Blanchard, p. vii.
20. Closen, p. 92.

Ten

THE MARCH of the French army from Providence to Philipsburg in Westchester County, where the Americans were already encamped, took eighteen days. Rochambeau was chafing to get away but he had to spend eight days in Providence waiting for the artillery horses and oxen Colonel Wadsworth was having difficulty delivering. Commissary Blanchard also had his difficulties with the distribution of forage, bread, meat, and wood, but the army as a whole was in high spirits. At last it was on the move. The long stalemate was over. To the delight of everyone, from the commander-in-chief down to the youngest recruit, the curse of inactivity, which had been hanging over the French army for so long, had finally been lifted.

The general mood of excitement and anticipation is reflected in the journals of Rochambeau's aides. "At the beginning of a campaign," writes Baron von Closen, "everyone tries to provide for himself as best he can. I am starting out with two servants and four horses. . . . We marched on the 21st to Windham, a charming market town, where, incidentally there were many pretty women at whose homes we passed the afternoon most agreeably."[1] In a slightly different vein Baron Cromot du Bourg expatiates on the glories of the New England countryside: "The roads are almost all bordered with acacia trees which were at this time in flower and spread a charming perfume, so that it was easier for me to imagine myself walking in a garden than as leading a life of adventure two thousand leagues away from all to whom I am attached."[2] Obviously for these young aristocrats there was nothing very horrible about war. They looked forward to it as they might have looked forward to the grand tour. Closen was convinced that the campaign would be "extremely interesting" and that it would bring many other pleasures in its train, such as seeing other provinces and making new acquaintances. All of them were avid for experience. Mathieu Dumas tells us that he wanted to be able to say, like the pigeon in La Fontaine's fable, "I was there. This is what I went through."[3] The young men of today no longer look upon war as providing golden opportunities for enlarging their knowledge of the world, but however alien to the twentieth century, these were the sentiments, combined with a still more old-fashioned passion for military glory, that animated the men in Rochambeau's army.

Thanks to the inertia of General Clinton, who seemed to be hypnotized by the methodical activity of the men he was supposed to be fighting, the French regiments marched across New England and made the junction with Washington without having to strike a blow. Rochambeau was elated. His regiments had done 220 miles in eleven days of marching. There were not four provinces in France, he wrote the Marquis de Ségur, where they could have done this in a more orderly fashion. It had been expensive, he admitted, but the troops had not lacked for anything. Wherever they went, the people received them with blessings. Blanchard, who had to deal more directly with the civilian population, had a different story to tell, but Rochambeau in his letters to Ségur and to Washington glossed over all the difficulties. In all his dealings with the Americans he made a point of never complaining about anything.

The route of Rochambeau's army can be followed in the splendid set of plans drawn up by Alexandre Berthier. As one would expect of the man Napoleon later picked to be his chief of staff, these plans are the work of a perfectionist, an artist as well as a topographer. The contour work is beautifully executed, and the colors are as fresh and clear as when the maps were handed to Rochambeau a hundred eighty-five years ago. Rochambeau took

them back to France with him, and they have only recently returned to America.[4]

The encampments in chronological order of occupation are:
Providence, June 10–17; Waterman's Tavern, June 18; Plainfield,
June 19; Windham, June 20; Bolton, June 21; East Hartford, June
22; Farmington, June 25; Baron's Tavern, June 26; Breakneck,
June 27; Newtown, June 28; Ridgefield, July 1; North Castle, July
3; Philipsburg, July 5. On July 2, when they crossed the Connecticut border, the infantry regiments were joined by Lauzun's
Hussars who, starting from Lebanon, had made a covering march
by a more southerly route to protect the main forces from surprise
attack.

For the first three days the marches were fifteen miles each. The
roads were bad, particularly between Farmington and Newtown
—Breakneck,[5] says Closen, was well named—and the troops were
exhausted by having to manhandle the guns. After the fifth day of
marching several men deserted. The problem of desertion never
affected the French army as much as it did the Americans and the
British, but Closen notes that in the first week the Royal Deux-
Ponts lost three men and the Soissonnais nine. He is concerned
about this, "since all Germans find it attractive in the interior of
the country to become farmers or field-servants." The fact that the
Royal Deux-Ponts was a German regiment, just as German as the
Hessians and Anspachers they were fighting, is sometimes forgotten. The difference between them, an important one, is that the
Deux-Ponts, though they may not have spoken French, were fanatically loyal to France, all of which proves that in the eighteenth
century the conceptions of loyalty and nationality did not necessarily
coincide.

The Deux-Ponts also differed from the other French regiments
in that some of the men had wives. Rochambeau's host at Bolton,
a Presbyterian minister, suggested to the wife of one of the men in
the regiment that she leave him one of her daughters, whom he
would adopt as his own child. He even offered to pay thirty louis

for her, but the grenadier and his wife refused to give her up, even for this enormous sum. This is the only reference in any of the journals kept by officers to the wife of a French soldier, but when the four regiments returned to France in 1783 they carried twenty women and six children with them, including, let us hope, the wife and daughter of the Royal Deux-Ponts grenadier.[6]

In spite of the bad roads and the unexpected heat spell—four hundred men dropped from fatigue in one day's march—the traditional gaiety of the French soldiers won all hearts. Rochambeau's chaplain, the Abbé Robin, who liked his comforts and who grumbled in a good-natured way about the lack of them, was proud of the way his countrymen bore up under the hardships of the march. "Without books," says the good Abbé, "to take my mind off my fatigue, and without ink, I often sit down to write with the sap of a plant, happy if I may only be left to myself for a while. But no, from two o'clock in the morning the roll of the drums orders me to tear myself away from my hard bed, roll up this movable home of mine, mount my horse and follow at a snail's pace the poor infantryman trudging along under the weight of his knapsack. Even when we arrive at the new campsite we have to wait during the hottest part of the day for the baggage wagons. Sometimes it is almost sunset before our weakened stomachs get any food in them. Stretched out on the dusty ground, panting with thirst, I have often wished—like the Rich Man in the parable—that another Lazarus would dip the tip of his finger in the water to quench my thirst. Our young officers brought up to a life of luxury stand the strain with a spirit that makes me blush for my weakness." Two of the officers, the Vicomte de Noailles and the Comte de Custine, went the whole way from Providence to Yorktown on foot at the head of their troops.

"What astonished me," continues the Abbé, "is the lighthearted gaiety of the French on all these grueling marches. Americans whom curiosity leads by thousands into our camp are immediately made to feel welcome. Our bands play for them, which they enjoy enormously. Officers, soldiers, and Americans, men and women, all dance together. It is the feast of equality, the firstfruits of an alliance which must surely prevail between our two nations."[7]

Though the Abbé does not say so in so many words, credit for the morale of the French army and the favorable opinion it had won for itself, even before it had been in action, must go to Rochambeau. The journals of Berthier and Dumas are more explicit. To Berthier, Rochambeau was the father of the family, ever watchful over their conduct as over their professional competence. Dumas mentions the discipline he maintained in his army, his "undeviating sense of justice and his noble and perfect subordination to General Washington."[8] Other men had paid tribute to these qualities, but Dumas, a more astute observer, puts his finger on another aspect of his chief that the others had not noticed. If Rochambeau and Washington made such a happy combination it was due in no small part to Rochambeau's understanding of the difficulties against which Washington had to struggle. It is remarkable that a man brought up as Rochambeau had been, trained in an army where class distinctions were still of paramount importance, should have accommodated himself so quickly to the very different structure of society in America. Nor did the delays inherent in democratic administration irk him as much as we might have expected. He was interested in the American experiment, and ten years later when France was trying to set up a constitutional government he was always harking back to the way the Americans did things.

In his lonely eminence Washington must have welcomed Rochambeau's tacit sympathy. He was never as intimate with him as he was with La Fayette, whom he came to regard almost as his own son, but as an ally no one could have taken Rochambeau's place. The bone of contention between them, whether the main attack should be made against Clinton in New York or against Cornwallis in Virginia, never jeopardized their relations. Rochambeau's son, the young Vicomte, tried to make out that Washington wanted to attack New York because he would be in command of that operation himself, whereas if they marched south he was afraid Rochambeau and De Grasse might well be able to defeat Cornwallis without any help from the Americans.[9] There is of course no evidence to support this theory in any of Rochambeau's own writings, and it is entirely foreign to Washington's character. Washington was never jealous of anyone, least of all of anyone who was contributing to the great cause of independence.

Certainly he would have liked to capture New York, and the juncture of the two armies within ten miles of the enemy outposts offered him an opportunity of feeling out the enemy's defenses. He might capture one of the forts at the northern end of the island, and even if the attack failed it would probably confuse General Clinton and prevent him from sending further reinforcements to Cornwallis in Virginia. The attempt was made and it did fail. In his memoirs the Duc de Lauzun relates at some length the part that he took in this operation. According to his account an American detachment under the command of General Lincoln was to descend the Hudson, then cross over from the Jersey shore for an attack on the outer forts near Spuyten Duyvil. His own Hussars supported by American dragoons were to make a forced march arriving at the appointed rendezvous in time to prevent any reinforcement of Fort Knyphausen, which the main body would by that time be attacking. "I reached the place as ordered," wrote the Duke, "though the bad roads and the terrible heat made the march very difficult."[10] From then on everything went wrong. In crossing the river the troops ran into a British foraging party who spread the alarm. Almost before a blow could be struck, the advantage of surprise was lost. Fersen says that the corps which the Duc de Lauzun hoped to surprise had been forewarned of his arrival by a deserter and that the moment the legion appeared several small columns hidden behind trees had debouched at once, thus forcing him to retire.

From Lauzun's own narrative, which is not confirmed by Wash-

ington's report, it would appear that General Lincoln made the
mistake of attacking before Lauzun's cavalry were in position and
that he arrived barely in time to save the Americans from complete
defeat. As it was, Lincoln had two or three hundred men killed or
taken prisoner. This is almost certainly an exaggeration. In his
report on the operation to the President of Congress, Washington
says "General Lincoln had about 5 or 6 men killed and about 30
wounded in this skirmish."[11] Whatever the facts about this very
confused operation (and the American, French, and British accounts are impossible to reconcile with each other), nothing was
gained from it beyond the opportunity of making a close reconnaissance of the British defenses in the northern part of Manhat-
tan.

Washington may have been disappointed by the meager results
achieved, but if so he kept his disappointment to himself. In the
same report to the President of Congress he was careful to speak
highly of the cooperation he had received from the French: "I
cannot too warmly express the obligations I am under to the Count
[Rochambeau] for the readiness with which he detached the Duke
de Lauzun, and for the rapidity with which he pushed the march of
his main body that he might have been within supporting distance
had any favorable stroke upon the enemy below given us an opportunity of pursuing any advantage which might have been gained."

All through the month of July Washington was hoping that
he might have ten thousand troops available for the operations
against New York, which is what he had assured Rochambeau at
Wethersfield he would have, or rather what he hoped he would
have. Washington was wise enough to make no hard-and-fast
promises about the number of men under his command at any
given time. As it turned out, his requests to the various governors
for recruits met with a very disappointing response. Governor John
Hancock of Massachusetts did not even acknowledge his letters.
"This puts me in rather an awkward situation," writes Washington
with extraordinary restraint, considering that he had already writ-

ten Hancock six times, "as I cannot give His Excellency Count Rochambeau, who has formed a junction with me, that official assurance of support which I had promised upon the faith of the States, when I had an interview with him at Wethersfield."[12] On July 15, instead of the ten thousand men on whom he had been counting, the muster rolls give the rank-and-file strength of the continental army as 5835.[13] Under these circumstances, and until he heard more definite information as to what De Grasse was able to do, Washington could not hope to attack New York. Even with Rochambeau's help the best he could do was to probe the defenses in the hope that Clinton would withdraw men from Cornwallis' command and so relieve the pressure on Virginia.

Discouraged though he must have been by the apathy of Congress as well as of the governors, and by his own consequent inability to plan the next campaign, Washington spent the month of July profitably enough cementing the good relations that had already been established between the two armies. He and Rochambeau continued their reconnaissances, as if preparing for action, and on July 22–23 they made a demonstration in front of Kings Bridge and near Morrisiania in the course of which Rochambeau, according to one of his aides, spent twenty-four hours on horseback. He himself tells us in the memoirs of another reconnaissance when he and Washington slept under a hedge on an island in Long Island Sound and were very nearly caught by the tide. They finally returned to the mainland in an open boat with their horses swimming behind them.

If these operations were barren of any military results, they went a long way toward refuting the wishful thinking of Lord George Germain, who predicted that the junction of the French troops with the Americans would produce such friction that "Mr. Washington will find it necessary to separate them very speedily, either by detaching the Americans to the southwards or suffering the French to return to Rhode Island. . . ."[14] The junction of the two armies, as it turned out, produced just the opposite result. The

Strategical Preliminaries to YORKTOWN

RHODE ISLAND

NEW YORK
CONNECTICUT
HUDSON R.
Newport
West Point
White Plains
New York
LONG ISLAND
BARRAS
PENNSYLVANIA
DELAWARE R.
SUSQUEHANNA R.
Philadelphia
NEW JERSEY
ELK R.
GRAVES AND HOOD
Baltimore
Annapolis
MARYLAND
Mount Vernon
POTOMAC R.
VIRGINIA
CHESAPEAKE BAY
ATLANTIC OCEAN
Richmond
Gloucester
Williamsburg
Yorktown
CAPE HENRY
NORTH CAROLINA
DE GRASSE

① WASHINGTON AND ROCHAMBEAU
② LAFAYETTE
③ ST·SIMON

SCALE IN MILES
0   25   50   75

French officers were as impressed by what they now saw of the American Army as they had already been by Washington. Closen, who was constantly at Rochambeau's side, probably echoes the general's own feelings in expressing his delight at getting a closer look at the American soldier: "It was really painful to see these brave men, almost naked, with only some trousers and little linen jackets, most of them without stockings, but, would you believe it? very cheerful and healthy in appearance. A quarter of them were Negroes, merry, confident and sturdy."[15] According to Closen, who was not always accurate though he was an intelligent observer, Negroes constituted a very important element in the American forces during the Revolution. We know that Congress first forbade the use of Negroes as soldiers, but the order was rescinded on January 16, 1776, because of the need for manpower. It is estimated that during the six years of fighting five thousand Negroes at one time or another served as regular soldiers.[16]

The reconnaissances and the occasional brush with the enemy, in which both armies took part, gave Frenchmen and Americans the opportunity of taking the measure of each other. In the long march to Yorktown, and still more in the Yorktown trenches, the experience gained in the supposedly idle month in front of New York was to prove invaluable. For the officers on Rochambeau's staff the skirmishing, the foraging expeditions, the reviews, and the ceremonial visits of Washington were a welcome change after the inactivity of Newport. Count Dumas' vignette of his "bivouac" between the Bronx and the Saw Mill rivers, in an area now engulfed by the great parkways, shows how readily the French adapted themselves to their new surroundings: "My friend Charles de Lameth, the two brothers Berthier, who had lately arrived from France and joined our staff, and myself, established our bivouac near the headquarters of General M. de Béville [the Quartermaster-General of the army] in a very pleasant situation, between rocks and under the shade of magnificent tulip trees. We amused ourselves in ornamenting this little spot, and in a short time and at a very trifling expense we had a very pretty garden. General Washington, who was taking a survey of his line, desired to see us. We had been apprised of his visit, and he found on our camp-tables, the plans of the battle of Trenton and several other actions of the war."[17]

Berthier describes this Arcadian retreat in even more detail. Their *cabinet de travail* was a grassy clearing in the woods where, shaded by tulip trees, they entertained Washington with a little light refreshment after what we may be sure was an excellent lunch with General Béville. Washington drank several glasses of Madeira and punch, after which they mounted and escorted him back to his headquarters. Berthier adds that the General, in spite of his modesty, was obviously pleased by the maps and plans they had assembled for this occasion, illustrating his victories.

The diaries of these officers are full of references to such exchanges of courtesy. James Thacher, an American doctor, tells of a dinner given by the officers of the Bourbonnais to the officers of the Virginia regiment to which he was attached. They were received in an elegant marquee, the menu consisting of excellent soup, roast beef, and so on, served in the French style. The doctor regretted, as so many other Americans have regretted under similar conditions, that he did not speak French. Blanchard, the querulous French commissary, was not so well pleased with the dinner he attended at Washington's headquarters. "The table," he says "was served in the American style, and pretty abundantly; vegetables, roast beef, lamb, chickens, salad dressed with nothing but vinegar, green peas, pudding and some pie, a kind of tart generally in use in England and among the Americans; all this being put upon the table at the same time. They gave us on the same plate beef, green peas, lamb, etc."[18] Blanchard was also not pleased with the weak coffee and the absence of bread. Obviously certain national characteristics were already clearly established. A French officer dining in an American mess in the last war would have had the same experience as Blanchard except that he would not have been called upon to drink twelve or fifteen healths in Madeira.

During these six weeks when the French and American armies

were shaking down together, General Clinton watched, waited, and did nothing. He might have attacked Rochambeau on his march from Providence to White Plains, or he might have seized the opportunity to reoccupy Newport, which Rochambeau had had to leave practically undefended. He might have recalled Cornwallis from Virginia, or have gone to his support. Above all, he might have launched a determined attack on the French and American armies when they were withdrawing from their positions near New York to King's Ferry, near Peekskill, where they crossed the Hudson. The French officers were amazed that the English did not come out from New York, at least to harass their retiring columns. The Duc de Lauzun remarks that the march was badly organized, that the route chosen lay across marshy ground, and that the artillery and the wagons were stuck in the mud for thirty-six hours, with only his Hussars and a battalion of *chasseurs* to cover the retreat. Once again the British had let a golden opportunity slip through their fingers. For Washington and Rochambeau, Clinton's failure to strike at this moment was as unaccountable as it was welcome. No one could understand it, friend or foe. William Franklin, the Governor of New Jersey who, unlike his famous father, refused to have anything to do with the patriot cause, was completely mystified: "Every measure of Sir Henry Clinton since he came to the command has been so far beyond the view of vulgar capacity that this in particular strikes with less force and is in some degree buried against a multiplicity of more unaccountable actions. And we have only one lament that we have not penetration to fathom the policy of his deep laid schemes. For deep laid they must be because unintelligible."[19]

The simplest explanation of Clinton's conduct of affairs throughout this critical period would seem to be either that he had lost the will to win or that he was another Braddock, stubborn as well as incompetent. But such a facile interpretation of Sir Henry's character does not fit the facts. He had already proved that he was devoted to the King's interests, or at least what the King thought to be his interests. He had fought under the Duke of Brunswick in the

Seven Years' War, in which, like Rochambeau, he had been severely wounded. Evidently the Duke of Brunswick, one of the
ablest soldiers of the day, admired him, for he was recommended
for promotion at the end of the war "as a reward for proved
merit." Early in 1775 Clinton was ordered to America. He took
part in the Battle of Bunker Hill where he again distinguished
himself by intervening at the critical moment. That he was capable
of winning victories is proved by the Battle of Long Island, in
which he planned the envelopment of the American army, drove
Washington out of New York, and failed of complete success only
because General Howe, the commander-in-chief at the time, refused to exploit the victory. In the spring of 1780, by which time
he had succeeded Howe as commander-in-chief, he gained the one
solid British triumph of the war by capturing Charleston and its
garrison of five thousand at a cost of only 268 killed and wounded.

A recent study of Clinton's generalship concludes that, far from
lacking ability, "he had quite as much as his more famous colleagues and, with the possible exception of Greene, quite as much
as his opponents."[20] How then are we to account for his supine
behavior in New York during the months of July and August 1781
when, as one of his own officers puts it, "the enemy have been
suffered to come within sight of our posts, to retire from thence
again, to pass the Hudson, and to advance a good way into Jersey,
without molestation or obstruction; while the army in Virginia was
nearly deprived of one-half of its strength, and is now entirely
unprepared for being attacked by a fleet and an army."[21]

The principal clue to Clinton's unaccountable shilly-shallying is
to be found in Downing Street. Lord North himself was never
convinced of the wisdom of the war he was conducting, and his
two principal lieutenants, Lord George Germain, Secretary of State
for the American Colonies, and Lord Sandwich, First Lord of the
Admiralty, were probably as thoroughly incapable as any two ministers he could have chosen. For his conduct at the Battle of
Minden in the Seven Years' War, Lord George was tried by court-
martial and adjudged "unfit to serve His Majesty in any military

capacity whatsoever." This was the man chosen to direct the war for the suppression of the revolt in the American Colonies. Lord Sandwich was, if anything, even less suitable for the office he held. For corruption and incapacity Sandwich's administration is unique in the history of the British Navy. Between 1771 and 1778 he received six million pounds for the Navy, and at the end of it all there was nothing to show. No one knew where the money had gone, but His Majesty's ships were still as unseaworthy and undermanned as they had been before the money was appropriated.

With such men at the helm it is not surprising that the campaign in America made little headway. Clinton in New York, Cornwallis in Virginia, and Germain in London were all attempting to control operations at the same time. No wonder they came to grief. A strong commander-in-chief, a Wellington or a Marlborough, might have won the war in spite of the Cabinet, but those men were sure of themselves, and Clinton was not. He was so tentative in dealing with his colleagues that they never knew what he expected of them. His reaction to the threat presented by Rochambeau and Ternay was thoroughly typical of his mentality. Instead of drawing up a plan of operations and putting it into immediate effect he sketched out three schemes of action and sent them off to Admiral Arbuthnot for his opinion as to which, if any, were feasible. Arbuthnot, who was always eager to put Clinton in the wrong, sidestepped the decision and then blamed Clinton for not making it himself. As we have already seen, by the time Admiral Graves had arrived and Clinton was ready to act, it was too late. Rochambeau had entrenched himself on Rhode Island, and the Americans were there to support him.

Clinton was one of those very deliberate generals who are always postponing action in the hope that within another twenty-four hours the situation will have become clearer. When everything was exactly to his liking, as at Charleston, he could act with decision. But the set piece the overcautious general insists upon does not occur often. For Clinton it occurred only once. He understood the role of sea power and the fact that his armies could not venture far from the sea without risking disaster, far better than Cornwallis, but unlike Cornwallis he was always haunted by the fear of failure. Unable to impose himself on his colleagues because he was never willing to take the blame if his plans went wrong, always hoping to be relieved and yet never quite ready to resign, Clinton's only solution was to wait and do nothing. In his private quarters he enjoyed drawing up plans for future operations, and his plans were usually sound, but the time was never ripe for putting them into effect.

In explaining why he did nothing while Washington and Rochambeau were camping on his doorstep, Clinton trots out the old excuse used by the equally cautious McClellan in discussing his plans with Lincoln. McClellan was proud of the Army of the Potomac, but he could never use it because he believed himself outnumbered. So it was with Clinton. If the reinforcements he had demanded had arrived on time, things would have been very different. On August 11, when he was finally joined by twenty-four hundred German recruits he would "probably have tried a brush" with Washington, had "a favorable opportunity offered anywhere near my lines." Needless to say the favorable opportunity did not occur. Clinton remains the classic example of the man who wrapped his talent in a napkin and did nothing with it. His nemesis was himself. By risking nothing he ended by losing everything.[22]

Notes

1. Closen, pp. 83, 85.
2. *Magazine of American History,* IV, 213.
3. Dumas, I, 10.
4. Among the Rochambeau Papers recently acquired by the Paul Mellon

Library is the following list of marches and camp sites between Providence and Williamsburg:

1   Camp à Providence le 10 & 11 Juin . . . Cette marche s'est faite par eau.
2   Camp à Watermans Tavern le 18 Juin.
3   Camp à Plainfield le 19 Juin.
4   Camp à Windham le 20 Juin.
5   Camp à Bolton. Le 21 Juin.
6   Camp à East Hartford le 22 Juin.
7   Camp à Farmington, le 26 Juin.
8   Camp à Barn's Tavern, le 26 Juin.
9   Camp à Break-Neck, le 27 Juin.
10   Camp à New-town, le 28 Juin.
11   Camp à Ridgebury, le Ier Juillet.

12   Camp à Bedford, le 2 Juillet.   } Sur la même
13   Camp à North-Castle, le 3 Juillet.   } feuille.

14   Camp à Phillips'burg, le 5 Juillet.

15   Camp à North Castle, le 19 Aoust.   } Sur la même
16   Camp à Huntz-Tavern, le 21 Aoust   } feuille.

17   Camp à King's Ferry, ou Verplank, le 22 Aoust.
18   Camp à Hawen-Staw, le 24 Aoust.
19   Camp à Suffrantz, le 25 Aoust.
20   Camp à Pompton-Meeting-House, le 26 Aoust.
21   Camp à Wippany, le 27 Aoust.
22   Camp à Bullion's Tavern, le 29 Aoust.
23   Camp à Sommerset-Courte-House, le 30 Aoust.
24   Camp à Prince-Town, le 31 Aoust.
25   Camp à Trenton, le Ier Septembre.
26   Camp à Read-Lion's Tavern, le 2 Septembre.
27   Camp à Philadelphie, le 3 Septembre.
28   Camp à Chester, le 5 Septembre.
29   Camp à Wilmington, le 6 Septembre.
30   Camp à Head-of-Elk, le 7 Septembre.
31   Camp à Lowev-Ferry, le 9 Septembre.
32   Camp à Bush-Town ou Hertford, le 10 Septembre.
33   Camp à White Marsh, le 11 Septembre.
34   Camp à Baltimore, le 12 Septembre.

35   Camp à Spurier's, le 16 Septembre.
36   Camp à Scott's House, le 17 Septembre. } Ces quatre camps
37   Camp à Annapolis, le 18 Septembre.   } se trouvent sur
38   Camp à Arche's-Hupe, le 25 Septembre   } la même feuille.

39   Camp à William's Burg, le 26 Septembre . . . Fin.

A similar list with minor alterations will be found at the end of the Abbé Robin's *Nouveau Voyage dans l'Amérique Septentrionale.*

5. *Breakneck*, which does not appear on the maps of today, is the name of a hill near the north end of Quassapaug Lake, near Middlebury, Connecticut.

6. Closen, p. 85.

7. Robin, p. 36.

8. Dumas, I, 68.

9. Weelen, p. 219.

10. Lauzun, *Mémoires*, p. 281.

11. Washington, *Writings*, XXII, 331.

12. *Ibid.*, XXII, 340.

13. *Ibid.*, XXII, 388.

14. Jusserand, *The School for Ambassadors*, p. 68.

15. Closen, p. 89.

16. Herbert Apthequer, *The Negro in the American Revolution* (New York, 1940).

17. Dumas, I, 43.

18. Blanchard, p. 80.

19. Fleming, *Beat the Last Drum*, p. 95.

20. Willcox, *Portrait of a General*, p. ix.

21. Frederick Mackenzie, *Diary*, 2 vols. (Harvard University Press, 1930) II, 606.

22. Willcox, *Portrait of a General*, p. 524.

Eleven

━━━━━━•❦•━━━━━━

WHILE WASHINGTON was reluctantly coming to the conclusion that as a result of the failure of the states to comply with his requests he would have to give up the long-cherished attack on New York, and while Clinton was congratulating himself that he had not been attacked, the destinies of America were being decided by Admiral de Grasse in the West Indies. After the Wethersfield conference letters had been despatched to De Grasse virtually begging him to come to the rescue but leaving it to him as to whether he should sail for Sandy Hook or for the Chesapeake. As we already know, Washington inclined to New York while Rochambeau, who was much concerned over La Fayette's predicament in Virginia, favored a concentration of force in the Chesapeake. De Grasse read the numerous dispatches carefully—he had heard from Washington and La Luzerne as well as from Barras and Rochambeau—and then made his momentous decision. Obviously such an appeal coming from men for whom he had the greatest respect could not be ignored. The point he chose as his destination was the mouth of Chesapeake Bay. There was no time to be lost. He began preparing for the expedition at once.

The contrast in the relations between Washington and Rochambeau and Rochambeau and De Grasse on the one hand, and between Clinton and Graves, Clinton and Arbuthnot, or Clinton and Cornwallis on the other is sufficient in itself to account for the outcome of the war. Clinton was certainly badly served by his admirals. Germain may have been criminally wrong-headed in not relieving Clinton and yet treating Cornwallis as if he held an entirely separate command, but in spite of the utter confusion in the British plan of operations, the war might still have been lost if Rochambeau and Washington had not understood each other so well, and if De Grasse, *"comme bon Français,"* as he wrote to Rochambeau, had not been so willing and eager to contribute to the success of their over-all strategy.

De Grasse, who had only recently been promoted to the rank of lieutenant-general (rear admiral), was exercising his first independent command. The orders he had received from Paris had merely suggested, not required, that he should take his fleet to New York or to Chesapeake Bay. His first duty was to safeguard French interests in the West Indies. If he had failed in that, he would have been given short shrift in Paris. Fortunately he did not fail. He protected French interests in the islands and at the same time deprived the British of the command of the middle Atlantic during the critical months of September and October 1781. By so doing he sealed the fate of Cornwallis and virtually ended the war.

Seven months later his flagship, the *Ville de Paris,* was a riddled hulk and he himself a prisoner of Admiral Rodney. That is another story, a Shakespearian tragedy representing a dramatic reversal of fortune, but it had no effect on the future of the thirteen colonies.

The inability of the British generals and admirals to sink their differences and cooperate with each other for the good of their cause is well known. Washington profited by it, just as a generation later the Duke of Wellington profited by the bickering of Napoleon's marshals in Spain. Rochambeau's difficulty in paving the way for a concerted plan of action is not so well known. Once victory has been achieved it is apt to look as if it had been inevitable, but there were moments in 1781 when it seemed anything but inevitable to Washington and Rochambeau. Washington's problem can be summed up in the one word *manpower.* As late as August 5 he was writing to Governor Clinton of New York that he might have to adopt a defensive plan, that if "the States will not or cannot fill their Continental Battalions . . . we must end our Operations in Languor and disgrace, and perhaps protract the War to the Hazzard of our final Ruin."[1] He was always chary of exact figures, but his letter to De Grasse, written from Dobbs Ferry on July 21, leaves no doubt of his predicament: "The French force consists of 4400 men. The American is at this time but small, but expected to be considerably augmented. In this however we may be disappointed. And as the time of your arrival and the succour you may bring are altogether uncertain no definitive plan of operations has been or can be fixed."[2] Rochambeau speaks of Washington's handful of men *("une poignée de monde"),* not more than four thousand, and though in a month's time it may grow to six or seven thousand, which Rochambeau doubts, that will be the *"ne plus ultra."*[3]

Rochambeau's own problems had been no less galling. No sooner had he landed than La Fayette began badgering him to take the offensive. He had had to explain to La Fayette that he intended to deal directly with Washington himself, not through an intermediary. He had been bitterly disappointed by the failure of the French government to send him the second division he had been promised. Having assured Washington of this second division of another five thousand men that would be arriving within a matter of weeks, he had to tell him at their next conference that his government had changed its mind about sending him reinforcements. Possibly he might get another six hundred men, if De Grasse found it possible to send them, but that would be all. Among his own officers he had been conscious of an undercurrent of restlessness due to the inactivity to which they were condemned. The Des Touches expedition to Chesapeake Bay, which was to have cooperated with La Fayette in cornering Benedict Arnold, ended in an inconclusive action in which Des Touches inflicted some damage on the British ships, but he was unable to get his troops ashore. He therefore returned to Newport without having accomplished his mission. Through letters intercepted by the British and forwarded to his headquarters, Rochambeau learned that Washington had been critical of the way this operation had been handled. Rochambeau had no control over the Navy, and the naval officers were a constant thorn in his flesh. Most of them had no conception of over-all strategy. La Pérouse, with the full approval of the Minister of Marine in Paris, wanted to mount an operation of his own in Hudson Bay, while Barras, who was senior to De Grasse and therefore not subject to his orders, wanted to make a name for himself by attacking British shipping off Newfoundland.

Instead of wringing his hands and complaining that everybody was against him, as Clinton did, Rochambeau listened patiently to all their proposals and asked them to consider whether their plans would contribute to the final result they all had at heart. In his letters to Ségur and to Necker he betrays his anxiety about funds. The army must pay its way, and it can only do that with hard money. While to them he excoriates the American jobbers and speculators who are making money out of their French allies, he never breathes a word of these complaints to Washington. Like Washington, Rochambeau was imperturbable. Only to his own countrymen, and to De Grasse in particular, did he confide his hopes and fears. America was at bay, at the end of her resources; the paper money was worthless. Washington's army, even with the addition of his own corps, was not strong enough to fight a decisive campaign, either in New York or in Virginia. Everything depended on De Grasse. He must come, and he must come at once, with all the ships, the money, and the men he could lay his hands on. The winning cards were in his hands. He must play them.

So much has been said about the difficulty of raising funds for the American Army that we are apt to forget that Rochambeau too was always worrying about money. As recently as June 3 his paymaster had warned him that the funds remaining in the military chest would be sufficient to support the army only up to August 20, assuming that the contractors would be able to continue their purchases with those drafts. The funds that ought to arrive with the convoy would extend the time to October 20. Unfortunately the rate of exchange on French bills was from twenty-eight to thirty per cent at discount, and there was no reason to suppose it would become less ruinous. Finally, it would not be possible to find, at whatever price, enough hard money in the United States to meet the needs of the army. M. Tarlé, the paymaster—or *Commissionnaire Coordonnateur,* to give him his exact title—stated that the rate of exchange on French drafts was far more favorable in the French islands, and it would therefore be of the greatest advantage to the King if Rochambeau would call for the help of the Navy in the Antilles up to the amount of 1.2 million livres.[4] Rochambeau listened to the gloomy report of his paymaster and relayed the essential facts to De Grasse.

The answer to his appeal could not have been more heartwarming. It reached Rochambeau's headquarters on August 15 and was immediately transmitted to Washington. By that time De Grasse would already be at sea. He had planned to weigh anchor August 13 and head straight for Chesapeake Bay. He would bring with him from the West Indies detachments from the Gâtinais, Agenois, and Touraine regiments, together with siege mortars and field artillery, some three thousand men in all, under the command of the Marquis de Saint-Simon.[5] Also, in accordance with Rochambeau's request, he would somehow have raised and would have on board with him the 1.2 million francs demanded. De Grasse asked only that he be employed promptly and effectively. He expected to be in Chesapeake Bay by the end of August, and he would have to be on his way back to the West Indies by the middle of October. He was bound to be back by a fixed date, as Saint-Simon and the troops he brought with him had been promised to the Spaniards with whom France also had an alliance, for an expedition against Florida.

The generous response of De Grasse, all the more welcome to

Washington as well as to Rochambeau because he stated so precisely when and where he was arriving and what forces he would bring with him, was all that was needed to galvanize Washington into action. Until then, through no fault of his own, he had been unable to shape the plan of campaign. Now at last he knew exactly what forces he would have at his disposal at a given time. The various pieces in the puzzle were at last beginning to fall into place. No doubt he gave up the New York enterprise with some regret, but he accepted the Yorktown alternative with a good grace. Possibly he might induce De Grasse to extend his stay in American waters so that they could make a joint attack on Charleston and Savannah and so end the war in a blaze of victory. Washington was dreaming, but his dreams were not fantastic or incredible. Surely this time he was not mistaken. After plodding through the darkness for so many years, suddenly there was a gleam of light at the end of the tunnel.

If the long arm of De Grasse could reach out as far as Elkton, at the head of Chesapeake Bay, and supply him with vessels for transporting the troops down the Bay, the five-hundred-mile march in midsummer, which had always been Washington's chief objection to a large-scale offensive in Virginia, would be shortened by half. Rochambeau, delighted that Cornwallis apparently persisted in his resolution not to leave Virginia, was already looking forward to the day when the allied forces converging on Yorktown would make him repent of his resolution.

Thanks to De Grasse, the plan which he had always favored and which he had been tactful enough not to press for too vigorously, was now at last coming into its own. There were difficulties still to be ironed out. Barras, who wanted to play a lone hand, did not take kindly to the notion of operating under the orders of De Grasse. Unlike Washington and Rochambeau, he never appreciated the value of a full concentration on the vital spot. "I regret that my proposed expedition meets with such strong opposition from you," he wrote to Rochambeau. "I thought it, and still think it, to be more advantageous to the common cause than a junction with De Grasse. . . . However, as the opinion of yourself and Washington is opposed to mine, I have decided to sail to Chesapeake with my fleet, bringing along your artillery and some transports."[6] This was just the letter Rochambeau had been hoping to get. More than ever his eyes were now fixed on Yorktown. Cornwallis, believing that his supply line was safeguarded by the Navy, was quite unaware of his danger. Only Rochambeau knew that slowly, inexorably, the trap was closing.

The series of misunderstandings between Cornwallis and Clinton which culminated in the disaster of Yorktown were inherent in the characters of the two men. One was an aggressive, fighting general, ready to take desperate chances in the hope of destroying the enemy, the other a constitutional worrier who could never bring himself to move until he was satisfied every element of risk had been eliminated. Only the most definite instructions from London could have induced them to sink their differences and act together in the common cause, but instead of sending such instructions, Lord George Germain seemed to take a willful pleasure in playing the two men off against each other. At one time Germain toyed with the idea of appointing Cornwallis commander-in-chief in place of Clinton. There was much to be said in favor of the change, as Clinton and Cornwallis were known to be at odds with each other, but he ended by making the worst possible decision. He did not relieve Clinton or promote Cornwallis, but communicated separately with both men, thereby encouraging them to fight separate wars in which neither supported the other or knew of the other's progress.

Clinton, as we have seen, reached the high point of his career in the capture of Charleston on May 12, 1780, the week after Rochambeau set sail from Brest. Indeed, the fall of Charleston had been the first news to greet Rochambeau on his arrival in American waters. Flushed with this victory Clinton hurried back to New York, taking part of the army with him, having received intelligence that a French fleet escorting troop transports was on its way to the American coast. Cornwallis was left in command in the South with a force of twenty-five hundred men, around which it was hoped the Loyalists would rally. Thus the victory at Charleston led to a dangerous division of the British forces. Before leaving, Clinton issued a proclamation calling on the country people to return to their allegiance, an appeal which would have met with more success if the country people had been convinced that the British Army was ubiquitous enough to protect them from the fury of the patriots.

At first everything went well. Cornwallis struck out boldly from Charleston and seemed to be carrying everything before him. At Camden he met and defeated Horatio Gates, the conqueror of Burgoyne, and was so elated by his victory that he marched on into North Carolina intent on seeking out and destroying whatever troops might be sent against him. Clinton was aghast at such tactics. Cornwallis had not yet pacified the back country around Charleston, and here he was plunging northward on the assumption that the war in South Carolina had already been won. Worse than that, he had chosen a route inland instead of advancing along the coast where he would have been sure of cooperation from the fleet. By striking into the interior he cut himself off from his supplies and at the same time subjected himself to attacks from guerrilla bands which never allowed him a moment's peace. Although Lieutenant-Colonel Tarleton, commanding his cavalry, displayed great energy in countering the operations of these partisans, he finally wore himself out pursuing shadows. The popular uprising inspired by such men as Francis Marion the "Swamp Fox," and Thomas Sumter, the "Gamecock of the Revolution," proved an essential factor in the climax at Yorktown.

The replacement of the inefficient Gates, after his defeat at Camden, by General Nathaniel Greene was another blow to Cornwallis' hopes of a triumphant progress through the Southern states. Greene was probably the ablest general in the Revolution produced by either side. His strategy was to draw Cornwallis farther and farther into the back country and at the same time avoid any general engagement. Cornwallis managed to win a Pyrrhic victory at Guilford Court House on March 15, 1781, but the "victory" deceived nobody, least of all Cornwallis himself. As Charles James Fox said in the House of Commons, "Another such victory would destroy the British Army." Greene withdrew from his position, and the militia, which made up a large part of his force, dispersed to their homes. But Cornwallis, owing to heavy casualties and the impossibility of feeding his army, was compelled to forgo any further operations and retreated down the Cape Fear River to Wilmington.

Clinton, in the meantime, was quite in the dark as to what had happened, and when the news of Cornwallis' costly victory reached him, he assumed that the long march north had been successful in spite of his forebodings, and that both North and South Carolina had been completely pacified. Having heard of Cornwallis' arrival at Wilmington he embarked a force of seventeen hundred men as reinforcements, never dreaming that the Loyalists in the Carolinas, encouraged to come out and declare themselves, had been left to their fate. He was fully alive to what such abandonment meant, but presumably Cornwallis knew what he was doing. In any case he was not man enough to order his subordinate to return to Charleston. Cornwallis, still intent on the offensive and confident that he had the support of Lord George Germain in London, was now ready to stake his military reputation on the conquest of Virginia. General Phillips, one of the most capable of the British commanders, and General Benedict Arnold, who was proving as aggressive a fighter on the British side as he had been on the American, were already actively engaged in Virginia ravaging the country around Richmond. Cornwallis was eager to join them. Whatever advantage Greene had gained at Guilford Court House would be cancelled if he had to face the larger combined force Cornwallis now envisaged.

The sequel to Cornwallis' march north into Virginia is well known. General Phillips died a few days before Cornwallis joined forces with Arnold. He was an irreparable loss to Cornwallis personally, as well as to the British Army. Arnold was recalled to New York to create a diversion which would keep the French and Americans from sending troops south. The diversion, an attack on New London, succeeded only in still further blackening Arnold's reputation among his old friends. Fort Griswold was captured and New London burned, but Washington and Rochambeau marched on to Yorktown.

Once again Cornwallis found himself unable to come to grips with his enemy. Greene carried the war into South Carolina and cleared the British out of every position they had occupied except Charleston. Unable to go to their support, Cornwallis undertook to catch La Fayette, whom Washington had sent down to Virginia to put a stop to Benedict Arnold's marauding expeditions. With the help of the French squadron under Des Touches, Washington hoped that La Fayette would succeed in cornering Arnold's small force, that he would compel him to surrender, and that he would then have the exquisite pleasure of hanging him as a traitor. As we have seen, the plan failed. La Fayette was no more able to corner Arnold than Cornwallis was able to corner La Fayette. The armies marched and countermarched. The Marquis would hit and run, but he never risked a general engagement. There were many narrow shaves and on one occasion General Anthony Wayne, who was a fighter like Cornwallis himself, almost precipitated a disaster, but the agile La Fayette always just managed to extricate himself.

While he was wondering how long the game of hide and seek would last, Cornwallis finally received a definite order from Clinton to take up a defensive position at Portsmouth and send away every man he could spare to New York. Clinton had gathered from an intercepted letter that Washington was going to attack New York in full force, and he decided therefore to call in all the troops he could lay his hands on. A few days later another letter from Clinton reached Cornwallis countermanding the order and informing him he could keep the whole force at present under his command. On the strength of these conflicting orders which he could not understand, Cornwallis gave up his pursuit of La Fayette and allowed himself to be shepherded down the peninsula between the York and the James rivers, to fortify himself at Yorktown and to remain there until he knew what was expected of him. It was a bad position and he would need more troops if it were to be made a permanent base, but at least he would be in touch with the Navy.

The explanation of Clinton's *volte-face* was that he himself had just received peremptory orders from London that the British forces were to push their conquests from the south to the north. As usual Lord George was acting on information that was already out of date. On hearing the report of Cornwallis' victory at Camden, he had jumped to the conclusion that South and North Carolina had now been won back to their allegiance to the King. Disgusted with Clinton's inactivity, he decided to back Cornwallis to the limit. Clinton realized that he was being bypassed, but instead of insisting that his resignation be accepted he clung half-reluctantly to the position of commander-in-chief, at the same time washing his hands of responsibility for whatever might befall the King's forces in the South.

The tangle of mistakes in which Clinton and Cornwallis involved themselves is not easy to unravel, and the controversy between them continued to rage long after the war was over.[7] Clinton's weaknesses have already been analyzed. Cornwallis' were of a different variety. Under another commander-in-chief, capable of giving clear-cut orders and willing to assume responsibility for failure as well as success and ready to back him to the limit, Cornwallis might have succeeded. Certainly he would have avoided the disaster at Yorktown. In many ways he was the ideal divisional commander. He was a born leader of men, a good tactician who knew how to handle troops on the battlefield, but he was not a strategist. He never understood, for instance, that he could not win the war in the South without Loyalist support. Nor could he hope to rally the Loyalists, and far less the fence-sitters, who made up the bulk of the population, by merely marching through the countryside. Without occupying the country he could not organize his supporters, and he could not occupy any spot for more than a few days so long as he was out of touch with the fleet. His supplies reached him by the tall ships of the Royal Navy, and by depriving himself of those supplies he condemned himself to a war of movement. The army could not stay long in one area, or it would starve. It is ironic to think that, far from rallying the Loyalists to his side, Cornwallis probably raised more troops for the American Army than Washington. While Washington was pleading with the States to send him recruits, the Carolina farmers, as soon as the war came close to their own homes, joined Marion and Sumter of their own accord. They would never have been willing to fight for New York or New Jersey, and if Cornwallis had shown any signs of repeating his victory at Camden they would probably not have come out at all. As it was, the Loyalists stayed at home and the fence-sitters rallied to the winning side.

All this time, while Clinton and Cornwallis were at loggerheads, while Lord George Germain believed that everything was going according to plan, and while Washington was wondering whether New York might possibly fall into his grasp, Rochambeau was praying that Admiral de Grasse would be able to elude the British Navy and lead his ships into Chesapeake Bay. Luck had been against Rochambeau for the past year, but this time the gods were on his side. Not only was De Grasse willing and eager to cooperate, but also by great good fortune on his way to the Chesapeake he captured all the enemy vessels that were sighted. The British therefore had no knowledge of his movements. The British commanders were not even aware that their sea line of communications was threatened by a superior force. Rodney knew that De Grasse had sailed, but he assumed the Frenchman would convoy the homeward-bound trade with a strong squadron and only detach twelve or fourteen ships to the American coast. He himself was in bad health at the time and could not decide whether he would take the fleet north to New York or return home on a long-delayed sick leave. This irritated Hood, his second in command: "It is quite impossible," complained Hood, "from the unsteadiness of the Commander-in-Chief to know what he means three days together; one hour he says his complaints are of such a nature that he cannot possibly remain in the country and is determined to leave the command to me; the next he says he has not thought of going home."[8]

Finally Rodney settled for home and sailed on August 1 after handing over the command to Hood. At the same time he sent letters to Admiral Graves in New York recommending him to make a speedy junction with Hood so that the enemy might meet a "proper reception on their arrival." If Graves had not been at sea at the time these dispatches reached New York, De Grasse might never have reached Chesapeake Bay, in which case Cornwallis would have escaped from the trap, but from now on until Rodney returned to the West Indies the British Navy was dogged by misfortune. Graves being at sea, the senior naval officer opened the letter, took a copy, and then hurried the sloop off to find the Admiral. But the letter never reached Graves, as the Captain of the sloop, apparently not aware of the importance of his mission, went in chase of a privateer and brought her into action. He captured her but was himself taken immediately afterward by three other privateers. Another sloop, sent by Hood to Graves with a letter announcing his early arrival in New York, met with the same luck. She was captured and taken into Philadelphia.

Graves was thus cruising on the lookout for a French convoy in complete ignorance of the real state of affairs. Failing to sight the convoy he returned to Sandy Hook, anchoring there on the sixteenth of August. He then read the duplicate of Rodney's letter, but still did not know that Hood was on his way north. By this

time Clinton had again decided that something should be done
about the French fleet in Rhode Island. Plans had been discussed
before, and Graves had agreed to cooperate, but now he withdrew
the offer on the plea that one of his ships had to be refitted and one
remasted. Once again Clinton and Graves might have complained
of bad luck. Maybe the ships did need refitting, but history has
always insisted that "men at some time are masters of their fate."
Graves was one of those commanders, like Clinton, who allow
themselves to be mastered by circumstances. They both lived
through those critical days when the future of the thirteen Colonies
was hanging in the balance without ever realizing that the fault was
not in the stars but in themselves.

One of the principal causes of their "bad luck" which is often
overlooked was noted at the time in the diary of Lieutenant
Mackenzie, a British officer in the New York garrison. After commenting on the escape of the French fleet from Newport, which
took place on August 25 after Barras had finally been persuaded
to join forces with De Grasse, the observant lieutenant puts his
finger on a fatal weakness in the British Navy:

I cannot help remarking how frequently we suffer by sending small
vessels with the most consequential dispatches. Three or four instances
have occurred this month, viz *The Swallow*, 14 guns, and *The Active*
about the same force, taken or destroyed coming from the West Indies
with dispatches from Sir George Rodney, the *Dispatch*, an armed brig
of 12 guns, taken going from hence with dispatches to Admiral Graves;
and the *Swallow* dispatch boat, taken coming from the Chesapeake. . . .
It may be observed that the French hardly ever act in this manner;
whenever they have anything of importance to communicate, it is done
by means of a Frigate, so that a misfortune of this nature hardly ever
happens to them. I fear our Admirals wish to keep the Frigates cruizing
for prizes, which is thought better than employing them in carrying
letters, however important.[9]

Certainly it is true that the French frigate *Concorde* plied between Rochambeau in Newport and De Grasse in the West Indies

without mishap, whereas the brigs and sloops carrying no less important letters between the British admirals were always coming to grief. It might be supposed in view of the chapter of accidents that befell the British that all the bad luck was on one side, and that the concentration of Barras and De Grasse, Washington and Rochambeau around Yorktown proceeded smoothly according to plan. Actually they had plenty of misfortunes of their own to contend with, any one of which might well have proved disastrous if they had not been buoyed up by confidence in each other, as well as by the feeling that they were at last riding the tide to victory.

De Grasse in particular had to contend with accidents that would certainly have shattered the confidence of a less determined man. Having postponed the sailing of the Europe-bound convoy so that he could take his entire fleet to the Chesapeake, he was in the midst of his preparations when one of his big ships, the *Intrépide,* a seventy-four, caught fire as a result of the carelessness of a ship's clerk who had gone down into the cockpit to draw some brandy. Through some carelessness in the handling of his lantern a fire was started which quickly spread through the hold. Fortunately there was time enough to tow the ship out of the roadstead, but the small vessels that towed her out were hardly two cable lengths away when the stern sprang into the air and the great ship exploded. Two days later he learned that one of his frigates had also been destroyed by fire with a loss of some two hundred men. In spite of these blows De Grasse pushed ahead with his plans so rapidly that the fleet was ready to sail from Cap Français, Santo Domingo, even earlier than he expected.

Not the least of his many difficulties was the raising of the 1.2 million livres which Rochambeau considered almost as essential to the success of the cause as the ships and the men he and Washington were both counting upon. De Grasse offered to pledge his own plantations in Santo Domingo in security, as well as his estate in France, but the offer was not accepted. He then enlisted the help of the Spanish director-general of the customs, then residing in Cap

Français, but the money was actually raised in Havana by Francisco Miranda, the South American patriot who at this time was still a lieutenant-colonel in the Spanish Army. Miranda had recently distinguished himself by his share in the Spanish campaigns against the English in Florida, notably in the capture of Pensacola. According to legend he was so popular with the ladies of Havana on account of these exploits, not to mention others in which the ladies were more directly concerned, that he persuaded them to offer their diamonds to De Grasse, to help defeat the hated English who had stormed and captured the city in the last war.

The story may well be apocryphal. What we know for certain is that Miranda procured the money in Havana, and that when De Grasse took his fleet through the narrow channel between the Bahamas and Florida the frigate *Aigrette* with the precious cargo of 1.2 million livres (or their equivalent in gold piastres) came out from Havana to join him. We know also that, thanks to the extraordinary resourcefulness of De Grasse and Miranda, a financial crisis which would have affected both the French and American armies was successfully averted. Washington had written to Robert Morris, the financier of the Revolution, to try to secure "a month's pay in specie" for his men, as they had again been showing signs of discontent, and the Northern regiments were balking at the prospect of the long march to Virginia. "A little hard money," Washington said, "would put them in a proper temper." Morris just managed it. He raised thirty thousand dollars in cash, of which twenty thousand was borrowed from Rochambeau! The ministers of Louis XVI had already learned that it was an expensive proposition to launch thirteen colonies on a career of independence, but the actual day-by-day difficulties of providing funds to meet every emergency were known only to Rochambeau.

The old Bahama Channel, through which De Grasse chose to bring his ships instead of taking the shorter route outside the Bahamas, had the reputation of being tedious and difficult, but the fact that it was unfrequented made it less likely that the British would learn of his destination. In making their way through the channel between Cuba and the Bahamas one ship was nearly lost when the helmsman gave the wheel a wrong turn and ran her into the breakers, but the De Grasse luck still held. A strong favorable wind carried the fleet through the Channel, and after a most successful voyage up the American coast during which they captured several small English ships, De Grasse anchored his ships in Lynnhaven Bay at the entrance to the Chesapeake on the thirtieth of August.

A pleasant surprise awaited him when a boat came out from the shore carrying a man identified only as "one of the principal citizens of Virginia," who asked which was Lord Rodney's flagship. One of the crew who spoke English told him to come aboard, and it was not until he was in the Admiral's cabin that he discovered his mistake. The boat was taken, and found to contain excellent melons and other refreshments which were promptly eaten in honor of Lord Rodney. This incident, which is recorded with obvious relish by one of De Grasse's officers,[10] though trivial in itself, is significant as indicating how completely successful De Grasse, Rochambeau, and Washington had been in concealing their plans from the enemy. Not one of the frigates that shuttled between Barras, Rochambeau, and De Grasse had been captured, so that while the French and Americans knew that Rodney had returned to England and that De Grasse was on his way to Yorktown, Clinton and Cornwallis knew nothing at all about De Grasse and confidently expected that Rodney would be appearing at the head of an all-powerful fleet at any moment either off Sandy Hook or in Chesapeake Bay.

The arrival of De Grasse on schedule at the point agreed upon was the first and most important feature in Rochambeau's general scheme of concentration. No one was more elated by the news than Washington. He had accepted the Yorktown plan not because he liked it but because he knew he was dependent on De Grasse for everything, for men and for money as well as for ships, and the time limit De Grasse imposed on his stay in American waters left him no other choice. Washington's entry in his diary for August 14 makes this perfectly clear:

Matters having now come to a crisis and a decisive plan to be determined on, I was obliged, from the shortness of Count de Grasse's promised stay on this Coast, the apparent disinclination of their Naval Officers to force the harbour of New York and the feeble compliance of the States to my requisitions for Men, hitherto, and little prospect of greater exertion in the future, to give up all idea of attacking New York; and instead thereof to remove the French troops and a detachment from the American army to the Head of Elk [i.e., the head of Chesapeake Bay, Maryland] to be transported to Virginia for the purpose of co-operating with the force from the West Indies against the Troops in that State.[11]

Even so, Washington could hardly believe that Cornwallis would be obliging enough to let himself be trapped in Yorktown. Surely he would send his troops to New York as soon as he scented the trap, or else fight his way back to South Carolina. Washington had been disappointed so often that he did not allow himself to be optimistic. He knew that Rochambeau was a man of his word, but could Rochambeau answer for De Grasse? Might not De Grasse sail back to France at the last moment as other French admirals had done, D'Estaing and Guichen, or might not his fleet turn out to be something like that phantom second division at Brest that was always on the point of sailing and had never arrived?

Some such thoughts must have been racing through his head as the Continental Army followed by the French troops marched through Philadelphia on their way to Yorktown. In Philadelphia he received a number of friends at the City Tavern and then went on down Market Street to the house of Robert Morris, which had been put at his disposal for his headquarters. At eight o'clock on the morning of September first, a dispatch from New York brought news that the British fleet, consisting of the squadron of Admiral

Graves and the thirteen ships brought from the West Indies by Admiral Hood, had just sailed. Hood's copper-bottomed ships had reached Chesapeake Bay before De Grasse and, not finding him there, had concluded that he was headed for New York. If Hood had taken his time he might have intercepted De Grasse, and with his superior maneuverability might well have defeated him. As it turned out, the tortoise profited by not winning the race. While Hood was crowding on sail to reach New York, De Grasse had landed his troops and sent them up the river to join La Fayette. The fleet had anchored in the James River, and Cornwallis' route of escape had been effectually blocked off.

Of all this Washington knew nothing. In a letter to La Fayette, written on the second of September, he confesses that he is "distressed beyond expression to know what is become of the Count de Grasse, and for fear the English fleet, by occupying the Chesapeake (towards which my last accounts say they were steering) should frustrate all our flattering prospects in that quarter. I am also not a little solicitous for the Count de Barras." It was not until, pushing ahead from Philadelphia, he had reached Chester that a lonely horseman met him with the glorious news that that punctual man, De Grasse, was already in Chesapeake Bay with twenty-eight ships of the line and three thousand troops. Rochambeau, weary after the long march to Philadephia, had preferred to go by water. Sailing down the Delaware, says Baron von Closen, was "the prettiest trip imaginable."[12] No doubt it was, but they had no opportunity to tell Washington about it. As they came up to the dock, there he was, waving his hat in one hand and a white handkerchief in the other. Never had they seen the commander-in-chief so excited. As they landed, he clasped Rochambeau in his arms. Yes, it had all come true. De Grasse was there, in Chesapeake Bay. The troops were already ashore. Cornwallis was trapped!

Notes

1. Washington, *Writings,* XXII, 468.

2. *Ibid.,* 401.

3. Doniol, IV, 637; V, 495.

4. *Ibid.,* V, 477.

5. Claude Anne de Rouvroy, Marquis de Saint-Simon, who commanded the regiments transported by De Grasse, belonged to a younger branch of the family of the famous duke, the author of the memoirs. His cousin, Count Claude Henri de Saint-Simon, the future founder of the Saint-Simonian sect, also served in the expedition.

6. Doniol, V, 524.

7. The series of misunderstandings between Cornwallis and Clinton, and the pamphlet war conducted by their partisans after Yorktown, is examined in great detail by Benjamin F. Stevens in *The Clinton–Cornwallis Controversy* (London, 1888).

8. James, *The British Navy in Adversity,* p. 264.

9. Mackenzie, II, 604.

10. Karl Gustav Tornquist, a Swedish officer who served with De Grasse. His account of his experiences, *The Naval Campaigns of Count de Grasse during the American Revolution, 1781–1783,* was translated from the Swedish by Amandus Johnson (Philadelphia, 1942).

11. George Washington, *The Diaries of George Washington, 1748–1799* (edited by John C. Fitzpatrick; 4 vols., New York, 1925), II, 254.

12. Closen, p. 121.

Twelve

THE VILLAGE OF YORK, now called Yorktown, which Cornwallis chose to fortify and defend, with or without the approval of the commander-in-chief (the question is still being debated) was not in any sense a natural fortress. The terrain had none of the features that would have appealed to a military engineer. "Nothing but the hope of relief," said Cornwallis afterward, "would have induced me to attempt its defense." It stood on the banks of a river, about thirty feet above the water line. From the river it could be defended with some chance of success, but on the land side it lay wide open to attack.

Founded in 1691 on land owned by an ancestor of George Washington, Nicholas Martiau, a French Walloon, Yorktown had been until about 1750 the busiest port on the Chesapeake. Most of the tobacco crop raised on the Tidewater plantations, amounting to about fifty thousand hogsheads a year, was shipped from Yorktown. With the gradual development of the upper valley of the James as a tobacco-growing area of importance, Yorktown declined but up to the Revolution it still had a considerable shipping business. On the bluff above the masts and yards of the ships in the river were perched the church, a few stores, the courthouse, and the homes of the merchants. Some of these houses, in particular the fine house of Thomas Nelson where Cornwallis established his headquarters, were excellent specimens of the best building of the period. Nelson, a man in his seventies, shared the house with Cornwallis and they were the best of friends. As a secretary of the Virginia legislature in Loyalist days, he did not take sides in the Revolution, unlike his cousin (another Thomas Nelson) and his two sons, who were ardent patriots.

All through the dog days of August, while the thoroughly disgruntled Cornwallis was fortifying Yorktown and the smaller village of Gloucester, half a mile away across the York River, in accordance with what he believed to be Clinton's orders, Washington and La Fayette, Rochambeau and De Grasse were praying that no suspicion of what was in store for him would induce him to change his mind. As long as he sat tight in Yorktown they were perfectly content to have him fortify himself as much as he chose. Their heavy artillery would easily level whatever earthworks he found time to raise. But there was still much that might go wrong. Though Washington's iron reserve had given way to an outbreak of optimism when he heard that De Grasse was anchored in the York River and that the three regiments he had brought over with him were already ashore, a moment's second thought must have reminded him that the battle was not yet won. De Grasse and La Fayette were poised for the kill, but where was Barras? Not a word had been heard from him since he had been persuaded against his better judgment to give up his Newfoundland venture and join forces with De Grasse in Chesapeake Bay. Until he arrived safely with the French siege artillery and the Americans' reserve of "salted provisions," the beautifully intricate structure designed by Rochambeau, which was beginning to show such promise, might suddenly collapse like a house of cards.

On the very day that the good news about De Grasse reached Washington in Chester, a French lookout frigate posted off Cape Henry reported sails on the horizon. De Grasse hoped that it might be Barras' squadron that had been sighted, but it turned out to be the British fleet from New York under the command of Admiral Graves. No one was more surprised than Graves to discover an immense fleet flying the *fleur de lis* confronting him. After all Clinton's blunders and the misunderstanding between the British admirals in the West Indies and in New York, it seemed as if fate had relented and given to Admiral Graves one last chance to win the war. As one British historian puts it, "Graves was in a position almost beyond the wildest dreams of a sea commander. His whole fleet was running down before the wind, and his enemy was before him, working slowly out of the harbor. He had only to fall on their van with full force and the day was his."[1]

From De Grasse's point of view the enemy could not have appeared at a worse moment. His smaller craft were still engaged in landing troops and many of his crews were still ashore, but he had to go out and fight. The desultory action that extended over the next five days has been rightly described as "one of the least inspired and most decisive naval battles of the century."[2] Graves had two golden opportunities to bring a superior force to bear on the enemy—at the outset, when the French fleet was working out of harbor in disorder, and later on when their van was out of supporting distance from their center and rear. For some inexplicable reason he failed to take advantage of either. He had also failed to intercept and destroy Barras' squadron before it sailed from Rhode Island. In the engagement that followed three of his ships were badly mauled, one of which had to be abandoned and blown up. Of De Grasse's fleet two ships were injured seriously. The casualties on both sides were about even. An apologist for Graves might say that he suffered a tactical defeat in what was after all only a naval skirmish, but the indirect outcome of this naval skirmish was nothing less than the birth of the United States of America.

At a Council of War held on board Admiral Graves' flagship on September 13, it was decided that, owing to the position of the enemy, the condition of the British ships, and the season of the year, it was impracticable to give "effectual succour" to Cornwallis. It was also decided that the fleet should return to New York at once for repairs. In the meantime Barras had slipped into Chesapeake Bay and joined De Grasse without firing a shot. If the British fleet in this engagement had been commanded by Admiral

Hood instead of Admiral Graves, the result might have been very different, but Graves, as senior to Hood, had taken over the command of the combined squadrons. Though not a man or a ship in Hood's squadron had been touched, he was not permitted to engage the enemy. By the time Graves was ready to listen to the opinion of a younger man it was too late. Barras had already arrived, and with the addition of his squadron the odds were overwhelmingly on the French side.

Once again it was Lieutenant Mackenzie, an obscure lieutenant of the Royal Welsh Fusiliers stationed in New York, who realized far more clearly than the commanding officer on the spot how much was at stake. On September 15 Mackenzie noted in his diary: "Should our fleet be defeated the loss of the whole army under Lord Cornwallis is much to be dreaded, the consequence of which would be that we could no longer attempt to prosecute the war against the Rebels, and must necessarily admit their claim of Independence: on the contrary, should our fleet be successful & gain a decisive victory over that of France, we have a prospect of defeating the united forces opposed to Lord Cornwallis, and thereby putting an end to the Rebellion, for in that case I am convinced the Rebels could never assemble another Army."[3]

Mackenzie's estimate of the situation was faultless. If Rochambeau could have read it, he would have chuckled with approval. Yes, that was the way he had planned it. He was lucky to find in De Grasse a man equal to the emergency, but it was he who had insisted on the concentration of every ship and every man at the vital point. The arrival of De Grasse and Barras on schedule was entirely a result of his quiet persuasiveness. The transportation and quartermaster arrangements for the French, as well as the American, army on the long march from the Hudson to the York River were all made by Washington. This too required the nicest sense of timing. Washington was all too familiar with the problem of moving troops without adequate means of transport, but at least he did not feel, as he had so often been made to feel before, that he was living on "false hopes and temporary devices." Some of the devices might still be temporary, but the hopes were not false. De Grasse had arrived, Barras was expected, and Cornwallis had not stirred. Best of all, on reaching Williamstown on September 15 Washington had learned that De Grasse, of whom nothing had been heard for several days, was back again in Chesapeake Bay with two captured frigates after a favorable if incomplete engagement with the British fleet. The British admiral had admitted defeat by sailing back to New York without making any further attempt to break the blockade. French vessels would now be available for transporting the troops on the shores of the upper Chesapeake down to Yorktown. No wonder Washington was hopeful, more hopeful than he had been at any time since the war began. For the first time his army, the French Army, and the French Navy were in position to deal a vital blow. The great concentration had begun in earnest.

It was just a month since Washington had come to the hard decision to give up his long-cherished plan of attacking New York. Rochambeau did not agree with him about New York, though he would have supported him loyally if Washington had insisted, but De Grasse had left no choice. Since De Grasse could not, or would not, bring his ships over the bar at Sandy Hook, Washington was forced to go south. On the morning of Friday, the twenty-fourth of August, he directed that the army be supplied with three days' rations, and on the following morning the long march from King's Ferry on the Hudson to Yorktown, Virginia, was under way. General Lincoln, with the light infantry and the First New York Regiment, headed the column. The French broke camp the same day, the Lauzun Legion leading the van, followed by the first division of the French army, composed of the regiments of Bourbonnais and Deux-Ponts. The Baron de Vioménil commanded this corps. They took the route through Hackensack to Suffern, where they encamped. The second division, consisting of the regiments of Soissonnais and Saintonge, was commanded by the Vicomte de Vioménil. They brought up the rear with all the baggage and stores.

Not until August 29 did it become generally known in the army that the objective was no longer New York. Up to the last possible moment Washington had wanted to make Clinton believe that the armies were crossing the Hudson and marching south for an attack on Staten Island and Sandy Hook. With this object in view Rochambeau ordered his commissary to build a bakery at Chatham, New Jersey, opposite Staten Island. "I let him into the secret," says Rochambeau, "and told him that my real intention was to feed the army from this bakery on the march as far as Philadelphia, but that it was necessary to make the enemy think by all this that the object was to attack the Hook and Staten Island. He kept his secret and accomplished his task well."[4]

While Clinton was bracing himself to withstand a siege, the two armies were marching unhampered through the Jersey countryside, a much pleasanter province, according to the Abbé Robin, than Connecticut. In New Jersey the inhabitants were mostly Dutch or Alsatian by extraction, and they were more friendly as well as more prosperous than the New Englanders. The Abbé was delighted with the array of fruits and vegetables which greeted them wherever they made camp. What puzzled him was that the farmers' wives were different from any farmers' wives he had seen in France. They were well dressed, some of them even wore jewelry, and their farm wagons, which they drove themselves, were drawn by two, and sometimes three, spirited horses. Without knowing it the Abbé was bowled over by the now-familiar "American standard of living," something that was first noticed by his compatriot, St. Jean de Crèvecoeur, and that has continued to astound foreigners ever since.

For the French officers the hundred thirty miles from King's Ferry to Philadelphia was something of a holiday outing. They visited Passaic Falls, which made Closen long to see Niagara, toured the battlefield of Trenton, where they heard from the lips of Washington himself how he had outwitted the Hessians, and stopped in Princeton to take a quick look at the College. The Abbé Robin was impressed by the brick buildings, several stories high, with twenty-five windows across the front; also by the curious orrery built by David Rittenhouse, but nothing they had seen or done since they marched out of Providence excited them as much as their entry into Philadelphia. Like all good tourists they were delighted to find the shops full of merchandise of every description, some of them not inferior even to the Petit Dunkerque, a famous shop in Paris near the Pont Neuf, a *"magasin de frivolités,"* much patronized by the young bloods of the day.[5]

The American Army marched through Philadelphia in a cloud of dust, but on the next day, September 3, when the French arrived, the conditions were perfect. Rochambeau, who never missed an opportunity of putting on a good show, made the most of the occasion. The troops halted about a mile outside, brushed off their uniforms, put on their decorations, and then marched into the city, down Front Street and up Vine Street, with the flags flying and the bands playing, just as well turned out as they would have been on the day of a royal review in Paris.

Rochambeau, who had arrived the day before, rode out to meet them with his staff, and placed himself at their head. The effect on the ladies, particularly of the Soissonnais regiment with rose-colored lapels on white uniforms, is said to have been devastating.

The next day this regiment gave an exhibition exercise of the manual of arms. At least twenty thousand persons, many of them in carriages, notes the Abbé Robin, watched this exhibition. The Abbé, who was not entirely unaware of worldly distinctions, was distressed by the long black coat worn by the President of Congress, the Honourable Thomas McKean, at this ceremony. "The worthy Pennsylvanians," he concludes, "are as far below us in knowledge of etiquette, as we are below them in the science of legislation." McKean was obviously not entirely at ease on this occasion. When the troops deployed before Congress, with the general officers at the head of their brigades, he asked Rochambeau whether he should salute or not. The General replied that in

France when the French troops marched past in review, the King did return the salute. Mr. McKean was still worried. If he took the salute, would he not be thought to be assuming the trappings of royalty? In the end he solved this nice problem of protocol by proposing that the thirteen members of Congress take off their thirteen hats at each salute of the flags, which they accordingly did. The President of Congress may well have been right. Those thirteen members represented thirteen sovereign states, and the day was still far off when they would come together as one nation.

At the close of this review, which still lives in legend among the old families of Philadelphia, the Chevalier de la Luzerne, who lived in a style worthy of his sovereign, gave a dinner for a hundred eighty guests. Unfortunately, Washington and Rochambeau, who had already gone on ahead to Chester, could not be there. At this dinner the Minister had the pleasure of announcing the tremendous news about De Grasse. While the officers were drinking toasts and climbing up on the tables to pronounce funeral orations on Cornwallis, Charles Thomson, Secretary of the Continental Congress, "the Sam Adams of Philadelphia" as John Adams called him, arrived to offer his congratulations. His thin wrinkled face, his deep-sunk eyes, his unfashionably short white hair, and his plain black clothes must have struck a strange note in that colorful, carefree company. To the dedicated Charles Thomson, who was translating the Septuagint and the New Testament when he was not sitting at his Secretary's desk listening to the debates, these young men were imbued with a passion for political liberty. Maybe they were, but liberty was not the only factor involved. To Fersen, Closen, the Berthiers, the Duc de Lauzun, and all the other gallants who had tumbled over each other to get a place in the expedition, the revolt of the English colonies in America offered the adventure of a lifetime, a welcome relief from the stultifying routine of garrison duty.

To Washington and Rochambeau the war was certainly not a lark, nor were they thinking of it at the moment as a sacred cause.

They saw it in a more prosaic light as a problem in logistics. How were they to get the troops to Virginia in time to support La Fayette and the Virginia militia, and prevent the escape of Cornwallis? Washington was as disappointed by the lack of shipping at Chester as he had been at Trenton and Philadelphia. In addition to Rochambeau's four thousand he had to move two thousand Continentals and a regiment of artillery. He had already been delayed by the difficulty of finding horses for the French, but the absence of shipping was even more serious. Would he never be free from the nagging problem of transport! The Delaware had failed him as a water highway. Perhaps he would do better on the Chesapeake. Surely ships would be waiting for him at Elkton, the "Head of the Elk" as he called it, at the head of the Bay. But again, his diary tells us, there was nothing but a pitifully inadequate flotilla awaiting him: "Finding upon my arrival at the Head of the Elk a great deficiency of Transports, I wrote many letters to Gentn. of Influence on the Eastern Shore, beseeching them to exert themselves in drawing forth every kind of Vessel which would answer for this purpose. . . ."⁶ Unfortunately, British gunboats had already combed the Bay and sunk or captured most of the craft available. Into the few boats that had been assembled Washington and Rochambeau agreed to embark about two thousand men, twelve hundred Frenchmen and eight hundred Americans. The French detachments included one battalion of grenadiers from the Soissonnais and from the Bourbonnais, and the infantry of Lauzun's Legion. The American troops consisted mostly of a regiment of artillery. At the last moment it looked as if the Americans would not embark unless they received at least part of their long-overdue back pay. Washington was at his wit's end, but Rochambeau stepped into the breach by lending him fifty thousand livres, one third of all the funds he had left. More than ever, they both thanked God that De Grasse had brought with him, as they had already heard at Chester, the generous supply of hard cash he had requested.

The remainder of the troops were to continue the march to Baltimore, where Washington hoped that the "Gentlemen of Influence" would have bestirred themselves and supplied him at last with the shipping he had been asking for so repeatedly. Having made all his dispositions to the best of his ability, Washington set out on the last lap of his journey. He was eager to be on the road again, eager to reach Yorktown, and perhaps even more eager to visit Mount Vernon en route. The matter-of-fact entries in the diary allow us to follow him step by step: "Judging it highly expedient to be with the Army in Virginia as soon as possible, to make the necessary arrangements for the siege, and to get the Materials prepared for it, I determined to set out for the Camp of Marqs. de La Fayette without loss of time and accordingly in Company with the Count of Rochambeau who requested to attend me, and the Chevr. de Chastellux set out on the 8th and reached Baltimore where I received and answered an address of the Citizens."[7] On the following day, September ninth, he reached "my own Seat at Mount Vernon," a hundred twenty miles from the Head of the Elk, where he stayed until the twelfth. Three days later he was at Williamsburg, within easy reach of Yorktown.

The casual reference to his covering the hundred twenty miles from the Head of Elk to Mount Vernon in two days gives us some idea of the stamina of the man. Rochambeau and Chastellux took it more easily. They may have wanted to spare their horses, or perhaps Rochambeau with his usual tact may have guessed that Washington might well enjoy a day alone at Mount Vernon before his guests arrived. It was over six years since Washington had set foot in his own home, and Rochambeau, a happily married man himself, knew what it would mean to the Washington family to have a day to themselves. Not that Washington could have had much time to enjoy the society of his wife or to get to know the four little step-grandchildren, who had all been born since his departure. There were orders to be written to the militia brigadiers about putting men to work on repairing roads and the landings at the fords to be used by the army wagons and the artillery must be made practicable. At the same time he had to spend some hours with the manager of his estates, and to get ready for Rochambeau and his staff who were only twenty-four hours behind him. There was no shortage of food at Mount Vernon, at least during the summer months, and we may safely assume that Rochambeau was delighted with the good cheer that was offered him, though he does not happen to speak about it in his memoirs.

Unfortunately the general was not much of a reporter, but Jonathan Trumbull, Jr., who was Washington's secretary at the time and who was getting his first insight into the life of a great Southern plantation, wrote admiringly in his diary: "A numerous family now present. All accommodated. An elegant seat and situation, great appearance of opulence and real exhibitions of hospitality and princely entertainment."[8]

Rochambeau's stay at Mount Vernon, one day and two nights, did not leave him many hours for relaxation, otherwise he might well have commented on Mrs. Washington's hospitality. He too had important instructions to send out about the route the army was to follow. After a last conference with Washington he writes to the Baron de Vioménil, his field commander, that he must use his own discretion as to whether to wait for shipping at Baltimore or continue the long march by land. Washington was still hopeful that the "Gentlemen of Influence" would come to the rescue, but Rochambeau had his doubts. Just as Washington had always suspected that the second division Rochambeau was so confident about might never materialize, so Rochambeau was now skeptical of Washington's plan to save time by transporting the army in small boats down Chesapeake Bay. At Trenton and again at Philadelphia Washington had hoped to ferry the troops down the Delaware to Wilmington, then march them the short distance over the head of Chesapeake Bay, where more shipping would be waiting. Each time something had gone wrong. For one reason or another the shipping was not available. What reason was there to suppose that they would meet with better luck at Baltimore?

On September 11, their one day of rest at Mount Vernon, the

two generals must have spent some time discussing logistics. The
main body of the army was still held up on the wrong side of the
Susquehanna. A few ferryboats had been collected, enough to put
the infantry across the river by slow stages, but quite inadequate
for the artillery and the wagons. Mathieu Dumas, who was in
charge of the crossing, was fortunately a resourceful man. Hearing
that there was a ford twenty miles from the mouth of the river he
investigated it, and reported to the generals that it was just feasible. The river bottom consisted of boulders and the water was
from three to four feet deep, but everything was rafted across with
few accidents and by September 13 the army was in Baltimore.
The men were short of rations, result of the delay in getting the
wagons across the Susquehanna, but they scented victory ahead
and were in good spirits.

Rochambeau guessed right about Baltimore. General Vioménil
found a few boats there, all of them so small and so badly
equipped that he refused to put his troops on board. They would
do better swinging down the roads on their own legs than sitting
for several days in the miserably cramped quarters which were all
the little boats furnished. The Comte des Deux-Ponts was afraid
they would be too late, that by the time they got to Yorktown it
would be all over, but General Vioménil assured him that he had a
positive statement from the Comte de Rochambeau himself that
siege operations would not be begun until the French army arrived.

However disappointed the French may have been by the inability of their allies to provide them with transportation, their spirits
were soon raised by the glorious news from De Grasse. He had
gone out to meet Admiral Graves' squadron on September 5, and
for the next five days nobody knew what had happened to him.
Tangible, and most welcome, proof of the victory reached Vioménil when he marched into Annapolis. There, waiting for him, was a
captured British frigate with a letter announcing the victory. Even
more important from the point of view of the foot-weary army was

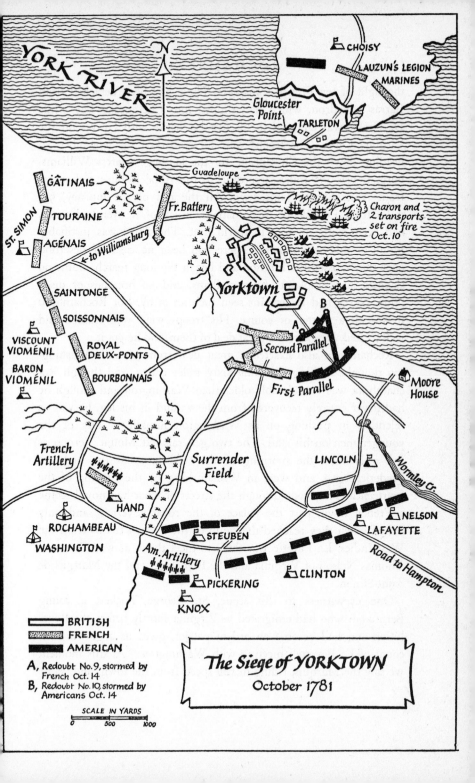

The Siege of YORKTOWN
October 1781

YORK RIVER

CHOISY
LAUZUN'S LEGION
MARINES
Gloucester Point
TARLETON

GÂTINAIS
TOURAINE
St. SIMON
AGÉNAIS
Guadeloupe
Fr. Battery
Charon and 2 transports set on fire Oct. 10
←to Williamsburg
Yorktown
SAINTONGE
SOISSONNAIS
VISCOUNT VIOMÉNIL
ROYAL DEUX-PONTS
BARON VIOMÉNIL
BOURBONNAIS
A
B
Second Parallel
First Parallel
Moore House

French Artillery
Surrender Field
LINCOLN
Wormley Cr.
HAND
NELSON
ROCHAMBEAU
LAFAYETTE
WASHINGTON
Am. Artillery
STEUBEN
CLINTON
Road to Hampton
PICKERING
KNOX

◻ BRITISH
▒ FRENCH
■ AMERICAN

A, Redoubt No. 9, stormed by French Oct. 14
B, Redoubt No. 10, stormed by Americans Oct. 14

SCALE IN YARDS
0   500   1000

the sight of ten French transports. These had been detached from
Barras' squadron, which had slipped into Chesapeake Bay while
De Grasse was engaged in his five-day battle with Graves off the
Virginia Capes. The troops were all embarked by September 21,
heading down the Chesapeake for the landings nearest Williamsburg. It was 178 miles, according to the Abbé Robin's reckoning,
from Annapolis to Jamestown. All the rest of the journey, 532
miles from Providence to Annapolis, much of it over bad roads,
had been made on foot in torrid heat. The Abbé was justifiably
proud of this achievement. There had been no cases of desertion
once they crossed the Hudson and began the long march south; no
sickness, no complaints from civilians, and no breaches of discipline. Never had Americans seen such an army. For Rochambeau
it was all a matter of course. His troops were well trained and
well treated. He exacted a great deal of them, and he got it.

Rochambeau also exacted a great deal from himself. Washington thought nothing of riding sixty miles a day, and though Rochambeau was considerably older than Washington and though he
had never entirely recovered from the wound in his leg, he was as
relentless in pushing on as Washington himself or any of the
younger men on his staff. The two generals left Mount Vernon at
five o'clock on the morning of the twelfth, spent the night at
Fredericksburg, and were in Williamsburg by the evening of the
fourteenth. They rode through the streets of what had now become
a French town, past the palace of the royal governor, and only
halted when they reached the camp of the French troops from the
West Indies. La Fayette was there to meet them, as was Governor
Thomas Nelson of Virginia and the French general the Marquis de
Saint-Simon.

One eyewitness to this scene, St. George Tucker, a young
Bermudan who had emigrated to Virginia shortly before the Revolution and had become an ardent patriot, gives us a glowing account of La Fayette's meeting with Washington: "At this moment
we saw the Marquis, riding in full speed from the town, and, as he

approached General Washington, threw his bridle on his horse's neck, opened both his arms as wide as he could reach, and caught the General around the body, hugged him as close as it was possible, and absolutely kissed him from ear to ear once or twice as well as I can recollect with as much ardour as ever an absent lover kissed his mistress on his return. I was not more than six feet from this memorable scene."[9] This letter may possibly be suspect as it was written in Tucker's old age, though he mentions the incident in a more matter-of-fact letter to his wife written on the day of the occurrence. Certainly it was a moving occasion for everybody concerned, for Washington most of all, whose plans had so often been frustrated and who now had the taste of victory in his mouth, but hardly less so for Rochambeau, who had been the first to conceive the great concentration and was now seeing it enacted before his eyes.

There was only one nagging question which no one could answer. What had happened to the fleet? Where was De Grasse? He had arrived, as he had said he would, by the end of August, and the troops he had brought with him were all ashore. Then on September fifth he had disappeared over the horizon to measure himself with Admiral Graves, and nothing had been heard from him since. If he had been defeated it was still possible, and even probable, that Cornwallis would be relieved. But no, De Grasse had not been defeated. On the night of Washington's arrival in Williamsburg news reached him that must have swept away any lingering doubts he may have had that Cornwallis might still escape him. In his diary Washington speaks of a "partial engagement" between the two squadrons. Strictly speaking he was right, but as a result of that partial engagement Admiral Graves had been driven back to Sandy Hook and De Grasse was left in complete possession of Chesapeake Bay. Equally satisfactory was the news that Barras' squadron from Newport, conveying the siege guns and the salted provisions, had eluded the British and joined him without mishap. Washington was even more delighted about the provisions than the siege guns, as the army had been on short rations for some time. Little or no flour was reaching the troops between the James and the York because the drought had shut down the mills. He had already written Governor Lee of Maryland, begging him to send down all the flour within reach. "An Army cannot be kept together without Supplies;" Washington reminded the Governor, "if these fail us, our Operations must Cease, and all our high Hopes will Vanish into Disappointment and Disgrace."[10]

The arrival of Barras put an end to these anxieties, but Washington was not yet entirely carefree. As soon as one difficulty was resolved another cropped up to take its place. Thank God the British fleet had been repulsed, and De Grasse was back at his old anchorage, but how long was he prepared to stay? In that same letter to Governor Lee Washington had written "our Prospects of success are most promising, if the Fleet will remain with us. . . ." He and Rochambeau must have an interview with De Grasse at once to make sure that he did remain at least until Cornwallis and his garrison had been bagged. An ominous note in De Grasse's letter announcing his success against the British had disturbed both of them. De Grasse urged there be no delay in their operations, for "the season is fast approaching, when, against my will, I shall be obliged to forsake the allies for whom I have done my very best and more than could be expected."

On the eighteenth of September, Washington and his party—including Rochambeau, La Fayette, General Knox, and Lieutenant-Colonel Alexander Hamilton—boarded the *Queen Charlotte,* a British prize recently captured by the French, and sailed to De Grasse's great 110-gun flagship, the *Ville de Paris.* As Washington climbed up on the quarterdeck, "the Admiral flew to embrace him, imprinting the French salute upon each cheek. Hugging him in his arms, he exclaimed, 'My dear little general.'" According to Washington's stepson, John Custis, who tells the story, the American officers were convulsed, and General Knox laughed until his fat sides shook.[11] Physically De Grasse was an imposing man. He was six feet two, and his sailors liked to say he was "six feet six on battle days." Washington makes no mention of any such incident in his diary or in his correspondence.

The results of the conference may not have been entirely satisfactory, but on the whole Washington got what he wanted. No doubt he and Rochambeau demanded a great deal of the Navy, and De Grasse was perhaps slightly testy before the interview was over. As he wrote Rochambeau afterward, he was a *"Provençal"* and a sailor, and they must therefore bear with him if he was quick-tempered. Washington wanted him to force the passage of the York River, to supply a number of men from the fleet for service on land, in addition to the three thousand men he had already put ashore, to lend "some heavy Cannon and other Artillery," and after the reduction of York to stay on long enough to block the British troops in Wilmington, and "to possess the Harbour of Charlestown." De Grasse hemmed and hawed over some of these requests, but he satisfied Washington on the most important point. He agreed to stay "upon these Coasts" until the end of October. That gave Washington about forty days in which to compel Cornwallis to raise the white flag. More time would have been desirable, but Washington had made the best bargain he could. As it turned out, he had eleven days to spare.

The conference ended in a formal dinner and a tour of the flagship, which everybody agreed was the finest ship afloat. It was late that night before Washington and his party went down the side to the waiting barge. A laconic note in Washington's diary for September seventeenth reveals one of the difficulties of the campaign of which we today are hardly aware: "I embarked on board the *Queen Charlotte* (the vessel I went down in) but by hard blowing and contrary winds did not reach Williamsburg again until the 22nd." In other words, while it took only a few hours for the party to get out to the admiral's flagship, it took them four and a half days to get back to the mainland. Under such conditions of wind

and weather it is hard to see how combined land-and-sea operations can ever have been successful. No one will deny that in this
last campaign of the war luck played an important part. It was
lucky for the cause of independence that Admiral Graves was
senior to Admiral Hood and that Rodney had to go back to England to recuperate just when he did. But there was no luck about
the way De Grasse chimed in with Rochambeau's plan, or in the
way he handled his ships.

In a book which had only just been published, *The Decline and
Fall of the Roman Empire,* a copy of which should have been in
Admiral Graves' cabin, Gibbon had remarked that the winds and
the waves were always on the side of the ablest navigators. At this
critical juncture the ablest navigator on these coasts was Admiral
de Grasse.

While Washington and Rochambeau were rolling about in
Chesapeake Bay, Cornwallis was unable to capitalize on the few
days' grace the weather had given him. All he could do was dig
more trenches and throw up more earthworks, which would soon
be blown to pieces by the French and American artillery. Only the
arrival of the British fleet could save him, but the British fleet
was nowhere to be seen. Cornwallis scanned the horizon in vain.
For the first time in the war the all-important naval supremacy had
passed into French hands; not for long, but long enough for Washington's purposes. Graves had gone back to New York to lick his
wounds and to talk things over with General Clinton. By the time
he was ready to try again, it was too late. The luck had changed.

Notes

1. James, *The British Navy in Adversity,* p. 290.
2. Willcox, *Portrait of a General,* 424.
3. Mackenzie, II, 623.

4. Rochambeau Mss. in Paul Mellon Library.

5. Jusserand, p. 78.

6. Washington, *Diaries,* II, 259.

7. *Ibid.,* 260.

8. Jonathan Trumbull's *Diary,* quoted by Freeman, V, 327.

9. Mary Haldane Coleman, *St. George Tucker, Citizen of No Mean City* (Richmond, 1938), p. 70.

10. Washington, *Writings,* XXIII, 116.

11.   George Washington Parke Custis, *Recollections and Private Memoirs of George Washington* (New York, 1860), p. 236.

Thirteen

Y ORKTOWN IS ONE of those decisive battles, like Gettysburg, which the protagonists would have preferred to fight elsewhere. Washington, as we know, had always had his eye on New York, and it had required some tact on Rochambeau's part to induce him to accept the Yorktown alternative. Cornwallis did not like the idea of Yorktown either, and claimed afterward that he was forced into fortifying it against his will. Fortunately for the cause of independence, Washington and Rochambeau had complete confidence in each other, and in De Grasse who, though occasionally temperamental and inclined to think that the Army expected him to do more than his share, always ended by cooperating with them. On the other hand it was common knowledge that Clinton and Cornwallis were forever at odds with each other. As the *Annual Register* put it in a masterpiece of understatement, "It does not seem that the Commander in Chief in New York and Lord Cornwallis entirely coincided in opinion with respect to the mode of conducting the war in Virginia."

Cornwallis had not foreseen a siege at Yorktown and did not begin to fortify himself there until the first days of August. Until he received Clinton's order to take a post and be prepared to defend it at all costs, he had looked upon Yorktown and Gloucester, on the two sides of the York River, as a temporary base for his army, conveniently accessible to the fleet, from which he could conduct operations in Virginia. If he had been given any choice in the matter, he would have picked Charleston rather than Yorktown to defend. All through the summer of 1781 he had been getting involved letters from Clinton which left him completely bewildered. He had had to give up his pursuit of La Fayette, after a successful brush with him at Green Spring Farm, and retire toward the coast to embark the troops Clinton suddenly demanded for the defense of New York. In accordance with these orders he abandoned the Williamsburg peninsula on which Yorktown stood, and crossed the James River to Portsmouth. Clinton had thus put an end to any further operations in Virginia, which Cornwallis had always wanted to make the principal theater of war.

The troops were already on the transports when the order was countermanded. Frightened by Germain's letters, Clinton now decided to use Cornwallis' post in Virginia as a springboard for a future offensive in the Chesapeake. Any such offensive would require a safe harbor for ships of the line, which Portsmouth did not provide. Cornwallis, who had been marching and countermarching between Williamsburg and Portsmouth, now was ordered to "secure either York or Old Point Comfort if either should be found to answer and could be put in a proper posture of defense within the time we had a chance of doing it in; but if not that he was to relinquish all views of a naval station for line of battle ships, and content himself with the one proposed in Elizabeth River."[1]

Clinton was incapable of giving a categorical order. He always hedged himself around with provisos so that he could disclaim responsibility for failure, but it was on the basis of these carefully phrased "orders" that Cornwallis made his decision. The report of his chief engineer on Old Point Comfort, at the tip of the Williamsburg peninsula, was unfavorable. The point would be difficult to fortify. It would not close the channel to the enemy and would therefore not afford protection to British ships. Since Old Point Comfort belied its name, at least as far as the Navy was concerned, Cornwallis felt himself condemned to Yorktown. Clinton believed it to be a healthy spot; Cornwallis did not find it so. He had no taste for the defensive role Clinton had designed for him, nor could he understand how it was, after six years of fighting, that the two British armies in America were being held immobile, one in New York and the other in Yorktown, by an enemy said to be at the end of his resources. With no great conviction he set about the construction of field works which, he wrote Clinton on August 27, "will be a work of great time and labour, and after all, I fear, [will] not be very strong."[2]

Three days later the French reached the mouth of Chesapeake Bay. A naval lieutenant rode down to the end of the peninsula and from Old Point Comfort counted thirty or forty ships within the Capes. While the French fleet moved into Chesapeake Bay for anchorage, the land forces under the Marquis de Saint-Simon went up the James River in longboats and landed at Jamestown. Cornwallis did not realize his danger even yet. He had made up his mind he was going to be relieved and that comfortable assumption blunted his initiative. He must have known he had more men under his command than Saint-Simon or La Fayette, but he did nothing to prevent their joining forces. It was as if something had gone out of him. The fighting instinct, the determination to come to grips with the enemy, had given way to a strange and most uncharacteristic listlessness. When left to himself he had acted with energy and self-reliance, if not always with good judgment, but at Yorktown he seems to have felt he was a pawn in somebody else's game. This was no longer his campaign. Clinton had ordered him to Yorktown, and Clinton would have to get him out.

Washington and Rochambeau must have been puzzled by Cornwallis' inactivity. They themselves were working on a definite schedule imposed on them by De Grasse. Victory was within sight, but it would not drop into their laps of its own accord. Cornwallis was a resourceful adversary, and there was still a loophole on the Gloucester side through which he might try to escape. Just before ordering the general advance from Williamsburg on September 28, Washington had to face another crisis, which was surmounted only by Rochambeau's help. After the interview with De Grasse on the *Ville de Paris* Washington and Rochambeau both felt that all the questions at issue with the Admiral had been successfully ironed out. De Grasse had agreed to remain in Chesapeake Bay until November 1, by which time Cornwallis would have been forced to capitulate. On arriving back at his headquarters at Williamsburg after the unexpected four days at sea, Washington found a report awaiting him that another British admiral, Rear Admiral Robert Digby, was off the coast of the United States with British transports and ships of the line variously estimated at from three to ten. The news did not seem particularly alarming to Washington, in view of the size of the French fleet, but after consulting with Rochambeau the news was duly passed on to De Grasse by Baron von Closen. The effect on De Grasse was very different from what Washington had expected. As Closen puts it in his diary, "The news of Digby's arrival and of the approaching departure of Hood's fleet from New York alarmed and disquieted these excitable gentlemen of the navy, who think only of cruises and battles and do not like to oblige or to cooperate with the land troops."[3]

De Grasse felt that the news about Digby called for a complete revision of plans. In his reply to Rochambeau he explained that he would have to leave his anchorage and go out to sea with the first favorable wind in order not to be caught in a mousetrap. He would leave Saint-Simon's troops ashore until such time as he could come back for them before returning to Martinique. In the event of his not being able to get back, on account of contrary winds or an unfortunate engagement with the enemy, Rochambeau could assume command of the troops himself. De Grasse then went on to speak of the possibility of his sailing north to New York, where perhaps he could do more for the common cause "than by remaining here, an idle spectator."

De Grasse's strange idea of sailing away in the hope of meeting the enemy somewhere outside New York, just when the presence of the French fleet in Chesapeake Bay was so essential to the success of their plans, must have struck Washington and Rocham-beau as utterly irresponsible. What was to prevent a British fleet from slipping into Chesapeake Bay to reinforce or even to relieve Cornwallis, just as Barras had slipped in while De Grasse was cruising out at sea? The two men replied to De Grasse immedi-ately, each in his own way. Rochambeau reminded him that at their last meeting he had expressed the greatest confidence of with-standing any naval forces the British might send against him. While Rochambeau would not venture an opinion on naval affairs, he could not understand why the appearance of Digby's squadron, the size of which nobody knew, should have occasioned such a complete change of plans. It was a friendly letter,[4] with repeated expressions of *mon cher Amiral* scattered through it, but it can have left no doubt in De Grasse's mind that Rochambeau was aghast at his decision.

Washington's reply was more formal. Couched in the scrupu-lously polite language he always used in addressing his allies, it began, "Sir: I cannot conceal from your Excellency the painful anxiety under which I have laboured since the receipt of the letter with which you honored me on the 23d instant."[5] Evidently these two letters served their purpose. De Grasse called a council of his ship captains to consider the situation, which resulted in a decision to stand by the original plan. Rochambeau and Washington breathed more easily. "You are the most amiable admiral I know," wrote Rochambeau on hearing the news. Washington expressed himself more sedately: "The Resolution that your Excellency has taken in our Circumstances proves that a great Mind knows how to make personal Sacrifices to secure a general Good. . . ."

With De Grasse once more in line, Washington could now con-centrate without fear of interruption on the business in hand. "The whole Army will March by the right in one Column at 5 o'clock tomorrow Morning precisely." So read the General Orders of Sep-tember 27, 1781.[6] The "whole army" amounted to just under sixteen thousand men, approximately eighty-three hundred Americans and seventy-five hundred Frenchmen. If we include the nineteen thousand seamen in the De Grasse fleet and the five thousand in the Barras squadron, the French forces at Yorktown, as compared to the Americans, were more than three to one. The nominal strength of Cornwallis' army was reported on September 15 as 8,885. Thanks to Rochambeau, the allies had concentrated their full force on the decisive point, and it was their overwhelming numbers that broke Cornwallis' resistance so soon.

The American Continentals were grouped in three divisions, commanded by La Fayette, Von Steuben, and Benjamin Lincoln. La Fayette, who was never hesitant to push himself forward, asked if Washington could not arrange to give him command of the three divisions, but Washington, though he hated to deny La Fayette anything, balked at that proposal. Lincoln was the senior officer and Washington saw no reason for putting La Fayette in his place. The militia, chiefly from Virginia, were under the command of General Thomas Nelson, Jr., a native of Yorktown, except for the troops on the Gloucester side under Brigadier General Weedon. The French wing of the allied army included Rochambeau's four regiments, the Lauzun Legion, and the three regiments from the West Indies.

Washington hoped that a generous spirit of emulation would actuate the allied armies, and in this he was not disappointed, least of all by Rochambeau. The one man who was slightly disappointed at the way things turned out was General Greene. "We have been beating the bush," he wrote to Knox, "and the General [Washington] has come to catch the bird."[7] Rochambeau had no such feelings. He never forgot that his troops were auxiliaries and that they must always yield the pride of place (*"céder le pas"* his orders read) to the Americans. This was to be Washington's victory. No man had done more to earn it, and Rochambeau would not have dreamed of claiming it for himself.

In the long march from the Hudson, Rochambeau had been separated from his staff, and now the family were all united again.

"I was really delighted to see him again," wrote Cromot du Bourg; "I had been separated from him for some time, and I can compare an aide-de-camp without his general to nothing but a body without a soul."[8] Rochambeau had one advantage over Washington in that he commanded a homogeneous corps, in which the officers all came from the same class, and in many cases had known each other for years. The Vioménil brothers, the Chevalier de Chastellux, the Duc de Lauzun, the Marquis de Saint-Simon, and the various colonels commanding the regiments, were all professional soldiers to whom war was the natural pursuit of a gentleman. In the American Army the officers had been drawn from every class. Among them were lawyers, merchants, innkeepers, and farmers. They had been hammered into shape by a long process of trial and error. That there was so little friction and so generous a spirit of rivalry between the two armies is one of the minor miracles of the Revolution.

The Baron de Vioménil, who commanded the grenadiers and the *chasseurs* in the advance guard of the French army, carried out his mission without a hitch. The army covered the twelve miles from Williamsburg and spread out to their designated campsites, forming a semicircle around Yorktown, as if they were on maneuvers. Closen complained of the heat and of the burning sand, but there were no casualties. As the combined columns appeared in sight, the British pickets fell back. Cornwallis, outnumbered two to one, was not risking his troops in the open. The investment of Yorktown, which began so auspiciously on the twenty-eighth, continued still more auspiciously during the next two days. To the great surprise of the French engineers who were studying the position, Cornwallis quietly abandoned his outer works on the night of the twenty-ninth without attempting to defend them. It was a move for which he was severely criticized afterward, and the only explanation for it seems to have been a letter from Clinton in New York confirming his belief that a relief expedition was on the way. Apparently his defenses were not completed because of the heat, the lack of tools, and the shortness of time. If he waited for the allies to advance he ran the risk of losing some of the forward redoubts and sustaining heavy casualties, while by retiring to the inner lines and husbanding his men, he would have at his disposal a compact striking force with which, he argued, he could withstand the superior forces of the enemy until Sir Henry arrived with his reinforcements.

Clinton certainly encouraged Cornwallis to think he was going to be relieved. He wrote an optimistic letter about embarking five thousand men and about the "joint exertions of the fleet and army to relieve you," but he did not actually promise anything. What he said was "There is every reason to hope we shall start from hence the 5th of October."[9] That was good enough for Cornwallis. Clinton's letter gave him the "greatest satisfaction," and he immediately replied: "I shall retire this night within the works, and have no doubt, if relief comes in time, York and Gloucester will be both in the possession of his Majesty's troops." As we all know, the relief did not come in time. Clinton and Graves went on dawdling until it was too late. The fleet did not sail from the Hook until October nineteenth, the day Cornwallis surrendered.

Washington and Rochambeau were as delighted to get possession of the outer works as Cornwallis was to abandon them. The siege of Yorktown had now begun. French *chasseurs* and grenadiers moved into two of the redoubts, while the American Light Infantry started the construction of a third. The ritual of siege operations was something about which Washington knew very little. The only officer in the American Army who had ever taken part in a siege was Baron von Steuben, the drillmaster of the Continental army, and Washington, who was always ready to learn from the foreign officers under his command, turned to him and to Rochambeau for advice. Both of them had had extensive experience of siege warfare in the Seven Years' War, in which they had served against each other.

The book of the rules for conducting a siege had been drawn up by the famous French engineer Marshal Vauban, whose great-grandnephew was at the moment serving as one of Rochambeau's aides. When the most advantageous ground had been chosen and marked, the besiegers began digging a line of entrenchments facing the besieged at a distance of eight hundred to a thousand yards, a convenient range for the artillery of the day. This line of entrenchments, in which batteries were erected, was known as the "first parallel." In planning the siege of Yorktown the allied engineers chose for the first parallel a line from the head of a deep ravine which half-encircled the town on the left to the York River on the right. Pending the arrival of heavy artillery, which Barras had brought with him but which had been delayed owing to the difficulty of finding ox teams to drag it from the landing, the infantry were kept busy collecting and constructing the siege material demanded by the foreign experts. Even the terminology of siegecraft had a strange sound in American ears. Who had ever heard of *gabions* (wickerwork baskets to be filled with earth to support embankments), or *fascines* (bundles of wood sticks for use in filling ditches), or of *fraises* (pointed sticks to be driven into embankments in an upright position) and *saucissons* (large fascines)? Except for a few bookish men who might have picked up a knowledge of these terms from their reading of *Tristram Shandy,* the farm boys who made up the bulk of Washington's army can hardly have made head or tail of the complicated *Regulations for the Service of the Siege,* fifty-two articles translated from the French, they were supposed to read in their spare time.

The whole problem of a siege centered around the artillery. After the artillery of the enemy had been subdued, if not silenced, trenches must be pushed out toward the front so that guns might be conveyed to the breaching positions and dug in there in redoubts. While this was being done the working parties and the batteries had to be protected against sorties. For this purpose Vauban devised the system of parallels to provide successive positions from which the men working in the trenches could be reinforced.

The destruction caused by the superior French artillery was a

great surprise to Cornwallis, who had not foreseen the arrival of
Admiral Barras with the French siege guns from Newport. Assuming that the British fleet was patrolling the sea lanes off New York,
he could not believe that Washington would have any heavy artillery at his disposal. As it turned out, the British batteries were so
completely overpowered that Washington was able to open the
second parallel, which would bring his troops within storming distance of the enemy works, far sooner than he expected. One by
one, Cornwallis' cherished illusions were to be shattered. He had
been sure that Rodney was on the heels of De Grasse, whereas
Rodney was on the other side of the Atlantic. He had been sure
that the Americans had no artillery to speak of, and within the
next few days he was to see his ramparts, his redoubts, even his
own headquarters in the Nelson house, being steadily pounded to
pieces. There was only one illusion to which he still clung—the
"certainty" that Clinton was moving heaven and earth to come to
his relief.

While Washington was directing the methodical approach to the
British lines in Yorktown he was keeping an eye on the enemy post
at Gloucester. From this post foraging parties, guarded by Tarleton's dragoons, were ravaging the countryside. It also provided
Cornwallis with an avenue of escape. Since De Grasse had refused
to send his vessels up the York River, fearing they might be destroyed by fire rafts, Washington decided that the Virginia militia
on that side of the river must be reinforced. He was not entirely
happy about the situation on the Gloucester side. General Weedon,
a former innkeeper, was not an aggressive fighter, and it was well
known that the Duc de Lauzun had no great respect for him.
Lauzun was chafing to match his Hussars against Tarleton's dragoons, while Weedon was more than content to keep out of Tarleton's way. Unfortunately Weedon was a general and Lauzun only a
colonel, and though Washington offered to order Weedon not to
interfere with the duke, Lauzun, who was a stickler for etiquette in
these things, said that he had always made a point of obeying his

superior officer. Evidently the Duke was one of those men who do not surrender their grievances easily.

Rochambeau, who had had some experience of Lauzun's touchiness and was to have still more, solved the matter for Washington by sending over the Marquis de Choisy, who was a senior to Lauzun and Weedon, to take Weedon's place. Choisy, a recent arrival in America who had come over with Barras, had a great reputation in the French Army as the hero of the siege of Cracow. In his memoirs Lauzun describes him as "a good and brave man, ridiculously violent, constantly in a passion, making scenes with everybody, and always without reason," but at least Choisy was a fighter. Under his command the Virginia militia and the Lauzun Legion, reinforced with eight hundred Marines from the fleet (requested by Rochambeau and lent by De Grasse very grudgingly), moved down toward Gloucester Point to halt the foraging parties and force the enemy into their fixed positions. On their way they collided with Tarleton's troopers, loaded down with corn they had collected.

This was just the occasion Tarleton and Lauzun had both been looking forward to. Only that morning, October 3, Tarleton had stopped to chat with a girl at a farmhouse and had told her he was eager to shake hands with the French duke. A few minutes later, Lauzun stopped at the same farmhouse. Had anything been seen of Tarleton? The young lady's answer sent him off in a whirl of dust. In the skirmish that followed, the two famous cavalrymen very nearly met hand-to-hand. As Lauzun made for his antagonist, one of his Hussars drove his lance into the horse of a British trooper. The wounded beast reared and plunged, and Tarleton was bowled over in the *mêlée*. The French Hussars thought he was killed, but he managed to extricate himself and mount another horse. By this time the infantry on both sides had gone into action, and the Virginia militia gave such a good account of themselves that Tarleton broke off the engagement and fell back on the camp at Gloucester. The whole scene is vividly described in the memoirs of the

American cavalryman "Light-Horse Harry" Lee, who had come up from General Greene with dispatches and remained at Yorktown for the siege in the unaccustomed role of observer. Although it was not an affair of any great importance, this brisk encounter, in which Lauzun's Hussars and the Virginia militia carried off the honors, seemed to hint at the greater success to come.

Incidentally, there was a certain *romanesque* quality about the clash between the two famous swashbucklers. The Duc de Lauzun already had been, and Colonel Tarleton would be when he got back to England, one of the lovers of "Perdita" Robinson, the most beautiful English actress of the day.

Meanwhile, on the other side of the river, French and American troops were steadily digging their way nearer to the British lines. By the evening of October sixth, Yorktown was completely encircled. The American sector stretched from the headwaters of Wormley Creek on the right of the line to the York–Hampton road. The center and the left of the line, reaching to the York River west of the town, was built and manned by the French. Rochambeau was amazed at the skill of the Americans in adapting themselves to this new kind of warfare. During the next few days one unit followed another on fatigue duty with precision and dispatch. By the afternoon of October ninth, work on the redoubts had been completed, the last *saucisson* was in place, and the guns were ready to fire. According to legend the first shot from an American battery was fired by Washington himself.

The devastating effect of the bombardment was reported by Thomas Nelson, in whose house Cornwallis was quartered. Although he himself had not taken sides in the war, his two sons were serving in the trenches with the American militia. They were so appalled by the destruction that they persuaded Washington to send a messenger into town under a flag of truce asking that the old gentleman might be allowed to pass through the lines. The bombardment had done so much damage, said Nelson, that the British had been forced to take shelter under the cliff, where

Cornwallis had established his headquarters in a cave. Nelson also reported that a small boat had slipped into the river with assurance from New York that a fleet of thirty ships would arrive to relieve Cornwallis within seven days. Far from discouraging the allies, this last item of news was received with delight, as indicating that Cornwallis would be forced to capitulate if the relief did not arrive.

After two days of bombardment the enemy batteries were so completely overpowered that Washington was ready to open the second parallel, which would bring his troops within storming distance of the enemy lines. Digging began at dusk on the eleventh of November, and before morning on the twelfth the troops were covered. "Lord Cornwallis' conduct," Washington wrote that day, "has hitherto been passive beyond conception; he either has not the means of defence, or he intends to reserve his strength until we approach very near him. A few days must determine whether he will or will not give us much trouble."[10] Cornwallis was running short of ammunition, but he was not yet at the end of his rope.

Two strong redoubts in the British lines blocked the extension of the second parallel on the allied right. Before work could proceed, these redoubts, No. 10 near the river, a square position manned by about seventy men, and No. 9, a five-sided strong point held by approximately a hundred twenty-five near the road from Yorktown to the Moore House, would have to be reduced. As soon as they were captured the allied artillery would be in a position to enfilade the whole British camp. These two redoubts were the key to Yorktown. If Cornwallis lost possession of them, his position was untenable.

To keep alive "the generous spirit of emulation" on which Washington counted so much, redoubt No. 9 was assigned to the French, and No. 10 to the Americans. Baron Vioménil, Rochambeau's second in command, a quick-tempered man who liked to have things his own way, was ready to storm his redoubt before the second parallel was dug, but Rochambeau would not risk lives

unnecessarily. Dumas reports that he gave Vioménil "a noble lesson" by reconnoitering the redoubt for himself. Taking only his
son with him, he descended into a ravine on one side of the redoubt and climbed up under the defenses to a point from which he
could examine the damage that had been done to the enemy works.
Either he was not noticed or else the British were so impressed
by his coolness that they held their fire, but he returned to the
trenches unscathed. He was not satisfied with what he had seen.
The abattis and the palisades were still intact. The artillery fire
must be redoubled in order to level the parapet. Tomorrow he
would see if the pear was ripe.

For the rest of the day, while Vioménil was chafing, the artil-
lerymen pounded the abattis. Finally, at eight o'clock in the evening of October fourteenth, Rochambeau decided that a successful
assault was practicable. Both redoubts had to be stormed at the
same time. Four hundred Americans, drawn from La Fayette's
Light Infantry Division and commanded by Lieutenant-Colonel
Alexander Hamilton, advanced to the attack of No. 10. At the last
moment there was a slight dispute as to who was to have the honor
of leading the attack. La Fayette had entrusted the command of
the American column to his own aide, the Chevalier de Gimat.
Hamilton at once protested. He happened to be the field officer of
the day and he demanded the privilege as his right. When La
Fayette tried to keep his promise to Gimat, Hamilton went over
his head and appealed to Washington, who decided in his favor. It
was characteristic of Hamilton to insist on a right that might very
well lead to his death, and it was equally characteristic of Washington to forget that Hamilton had only recently resigned from his
position of secretary and aide in a fit of temper, and to grant his
request.

The French storming party consisted of four hundred grenadiers
and *chasseurs* of the Gâtinais and Royal Deux-Ponts. To command this detachment, Vioménil picked Lieutenant-Colonel Guillaume des Deux-Ponts. It was an assignment every other colonel

envied him. In his journal, the young Count recalls how he received the command: "Everybody wished me success and glory, and expressed regrets at not being able to go with me. That moment seemed to me very sweet and very inspiring. I shall never forget the tenderness showed me by my brother." Twelve years later, when he was dodging the guillotine, Colonel Guillaume des Deux-Ponts may well have looked back with some nostalgia to the carefree days at Yorktown when he stormed redoubt No. 9 and planted the *fleur de lis* on the highest point of the parapet. There were others taking part in the attack who may, too, have reflected afterward that this was the supreme moment of their lives. As the grenadiers of the Gâtinais Regiment were going up to the attack they heard a familiar voice calling to them. *"Auvergne, Auvergne sans tache!"* It was their old colonel, Papa Rochambeau, calling to them, reminding them of forgotten campaigns in the Seven Years' War when he had been a colonel of the regiment. Since then, the Auvergne and Gâtinais regiments had been amalgamated, and the name Auvergne had been suppressed. Give us back our old name, shouted the veterans, and we will fight to the last man. "They kept their word," says Rochambeau, "charged like lions, and lost a third of their effectives."[11] On his return to France, Rochambeau spoke of their gallantry to the King, who saw to it that the regiment got back its old name of Royal Auvergne.

Such was the *esprit de corps* in the two assaulting parties that both redoubts were quickly taken. According to Hamilton's report, his troops carried their objective within ten minutes, with a loss of nine killed and thirty-one wounded. The capture of redoubt No. 9, which was more strongly held, took longer. Part of the abattis was still undamaged, and the French suffered heavy casualties before the garrison was overwhelmed. Colonel Deux-Ponts himself was knocked out and temporarily blinded by flying stones and sand. The few minutes that elapsed before the French could announce the capture of their redoubt gave La Fayette the exquisite pleasure of offering assistance to Vioménil. The offer may have been made in a spirit of "generous emulation," but if so Vioménil did not care for it. Like most of the senior officers in Rochambeau's army, Vioménil did not take kindly to La Fayette's airs and graces, though he was full of admiration for the intelligence as well as the gallantry of the American storming party.

Rochambeau was equally pleased with the way Vioménil and Deux-Ponts and the troops under their command had carried out the assault. In the King's name he gave two days' extra pay to the four companies of grenadiers and *chasseurs* who took part in the operation. The capture of the two key redoubts marked the beginning of the end. The day after they were taken, Rochambeau wrote to De Grasse that he expected Cornwallis to surrender within a week. His guess was accurate. There was nothing to interfere now with the construction of the second parallel, and as soon as that was finished, and the batteries mounted in the captured redoubts, Cornwallis would have to choose between the annihilation of his entire force or surrender. In a last letter to Clinton, after the capture of the redoubts, Cornwallis warned the commander-in-chief of what he must expect. "The safety of the place is so precarious," wrote Cornwallis, "that I cannot recommend that the fleet and army should run great risk in endeavoring to save us."

Even though he saw the handwriting on the wall, tradition demanded that he make one desperate sortie. Accordingly, on the night after the redoubts were captured, he launched a counter-attack in the hope of crippling the batteries that had just been brought up into the second parallel. At about four o'clock in the morning, three hundred fifty picked troops slipped over the hastily erected parapet and into the main trench of the second parallel. After a sharp struggle they gained possession of an advanced French battery belonging to one of the West Indian regiments. They had only had time to spike the guns with the tips of their bayonets when Chastellux came up with the French supports and drove them out with heavy losses. It was a gallant effort but it accomplished little, for within a few hours the spikes had been removed and the guns were in action again. Washington dismissed the sortie as "small and ineffectual . . . of little Consequences to either party."[12]

Cornwallis was now more than ever aware of the desperateness of his situation, and at long last he determined on the step Tarleton had hoped, and Washington had feared, he might take at the beginning of the siege. On the night of the sixteenth he began to pass his troops across the river to Gloucester, in the hope of breaking through Lauzun's Legion and the Virginia militia, marching north into Maryland and perhaps eventually reaching New York. He can hardly have had much hope of success and, as it turned out, this last faint hope of escape was frustrated by the weather. Washington and Rochambeau do not mention the episode, but Cornwallis' most generous adversary, Light-Horse Harry Lee, a man who knew a good deal about forced marches, did not think the plan impracticable. "This bold conception," wrote Lee in his memoirs, "bespoke the hero, and was worthy of its author. Nor can it justly be deemed so desperate as was generally supposed." Cornwallis made his arrangements with the greatest care. He planned to abandon his baggage and to leave a detachment behind to care for the sick and wounded and to arrange for their surrender. The rest of his army he hoped to ferry across the river during the night in sixteen large boats which had been got ready for the purpose. After the first boatload had got across, a sudden squall blew up against which his clumsy flatboats could make no headway.

From that moment Cornwallis must have known it was all over. By the time the storm died down, it was daybreak and the enemy batteries were opening fire again. There was no hope of stealing away from Yorktown except under cover of darkness. His defenses had been demolished. Sickness as well as the enemy artillery had taken its toll.

The British had over two thousand men in the hospital when they surrendered, whereas the losses inflicted by enemy gunfire amounted to only 552. French and American casualties were even lower, 253 for the French and about 130 for the Americans, though that figure does not include the losses among the militia which were not recorded. In other words, in this battle which was to affect the history of the world so profoundly, fewer than a thousand men were killed or wounded. Truly, as Napoleon remarked to La Fayette, it was unbelievable that such momentous victories and consequences should have been achieved at so light a cost.

Cornwallis might have held out a day or two longer but, hopelessly outnumbered as he was, he knew that when the final assault came, it could have only one end. He had given up all hope of relief, and Washington, as he could see, was closing in for the kill. Under these circumstances he made his great decision. On the morning of the seventeenth of October—by a curious coincidence the anniversary of Burgoyne's surrender—a drummer in red mounted the British parapet on the left where some of it was still intact, and began to beat a "parley." As for being heard, "he might have beat away till doomsday," wrote Ensign Ebenezer Denny of the Pennsylvania Line,[13] but with him appeared an officer waving a white handkerchief. No one could have mistaken its meaning. An American ran forward to meet him, bandaged his eyes with the handkerchief he had been waving, and led him to Washington's headquarters. The General was writing to De Grasse at the moment. He looked up from his paper, broke the seal of the letter that was handed to him, and read:

Sir, I propose a cessation of hostilities for twenty-four hours, and that two officers may be appointed by each side to meet at Mr. Moore's house to settle terms for the surrender of the posts at York and Gloucester.

I have the honour to be, etc.

Cornwallis.

At about the same time that the drummer boy was beating his parley the British fleet under Admiral Graves was beginning to straggle out of New York, but it did not sail from the Hook until the nineteenth, the day of the surrender. Troubles in the dockyards may have delayed the fleet, yet it is hard to escape the impression that, with the exception of Admiral Hood, no one in the British higher command in New York had any sense of urgency about the rescue of the beleaguered army in Virginia. Finally, on October 24, the fleet appeared off Cape Charles. Small craft scouring the coast for news picked up a boat containing a white man and two Negroes. They had escaped from Yorktown on the eighteenth, the day after Cornwallis had asked for terms, and they had heard no firing since. Their story was soon confirmed by Loyalist refugees, who had no illusions about the fate that awaited them if they were caught and were therefore eager to reach New York. Whether or not Graves should have gone into the Bay to attack De Grasse is open to question. Clinton, who sailed with the expedition, thought that Graves could have forced an entry, but Clinton was always ready to recommend heroic measures as long as he was not responsible for the outcome. Evidently Graves decided that a fleet drawn up on the defensive was too hard a nut to crack. Perhaps he felt he was not the man to lead a forlorn hope, for on October 29 he swung about and headed for New York. By the time he got there, Cornwallis' letter announcing his "mortification" at having to give up the posts of York and Gloucester had already arrived. It was not pleasant reading, either for the commander-in-chief or for his naval colleague.

The terms of surrender were quickly arranged. Cornwallis tried to get the same easy terms as had been granted to Burgoyne at Saratoga, but Washington drove a harder bargain than Gates. He refused to accept the condition that the British troops be sent back to England upon a parole not to serve against France or America again. Incidentally, Congress had refused to honor the Saratoga "Convention" stipulating that the British troops be returned to

England, and Washington was in no mood to ask Congress for any such concession now. Instead, he promised to march the troops off as prisoners of war "to such parts of the country as can most conveniently provide for their subsistence." At two o'clock on the afternoon of October nineteenth, the British Army, spick and span in a new issue of uniforms, marched out of Yorktown along the York-Hampton road to the melancholy tune of "The World Turned Upside Down." They were led not by Cornwallis, but by his second in command, Brigadier General O'Hara. Cornwallis himself was sick, but he sent his sword by O'Hara to be given up to Washington. According to Dumas, who had been ordered to direct the British troops to the place of surrender, General O'Hara had been going to surrender his sword to Rochambeau. "Guessing his intention," says Dumas, "I galloped on to place myself between him and M. de Rochambeau, who at that moment made me a sign, pointing to General Washington, who was opposite to him, at the head of the American army: 'You are mistaken,' said I to General O'Hara, 'the commander-in-chief of our army is on the right.' I accompanied him, and the moment he presented his sword, General Washington anticipating him, said, 'Never from so good a hand.' "[14]

This episode may be apocryphal. It is never given in the American accounts, which represent O'Hara on foot, doffing his hat and murmuring an apology for his chief's illness. As he offered his sword, Washington motioned him to General Lincoln, his second in command, who took it and handed it back immediately. Rochambeau corroborates the fact that O'Hara offered his sword to him, and that he waved him on to Washington, but he makes no mention of the graceful reply overheard by Dumas.

The illness of Cornwallis, genuine or not, has left a bad taste in the mouth of American historians. It may very well have been genuine. Yorktown was a hotbed of disease, and both Rochambeau and La Fayette had been down with fever at various times during the siege, but somehow on such an occasion posterity has felt that Cornwallis should have forgotten about his fever and surrendered his sword himself, just as a greater man than Cornwallis was to do eighty years later at Appomattox. "Light-Horse Harry" Lee, the father of the man who surrendered at Appomattox, thought that Cornwallis had yielded to "sensations which his great character should have stifled. He had been unfortunate, not from any false step or deficiency of exertion on his part, but from the infatuated policy of his superior, and the united power of his enemy, brought to bear on him alone. There was nothing with which he could reproach his brave and faithful army: why not then appear at its head in the day of misfortune as he had always done on the day of triumph."[15]

On the basis of this "sickness" and on the strength of a derogatory remark attributed to him by La Fayette twenty years later— "the boy cannot escape me"—the very name Cornwallis has become almost a synonym for arrogant insolence. Actually Cornwallis was scrupulously polite in all his dealings with his enemies, and most explicit in acknowledging the courtesy with which he had been treated after the surrender. La Fayette never produced the letter in which Cornwallis is said to have referred to him as "the boy," and the fact that he kept the insult to himself for so long, and never mentioned it until he felt the need of a little flattering publicity, is highly significant.

The other French officers were far more generous. Closen, who visited Cornwallis immediately after the surrender, says that "his appearance gave the impression of nobility of soul, magnanimity, and strength of character." The British officers were now gentlemen in distress, and they were treated accordingly. Washington and Rochambeau, Vioménil and Steuben invited their distinguished prisoners to dinner, and extended every courtesy to them. Dr. James Thacher, whose journal shows that he had an instinct for the poignant detail, tells a story which in itself refutes the legend of Cornwallis' arrogance: "On one occasion, while in the presence of General Washington, Lord Cornwallis was standing with his head uncovered, his Excellency said to him politely, 'My Lord, you had better be covered from the cold'; his Lordship, applying his hand to his head, replied, 'It matters not, Sir, what becomes of this head now.' "

Whatever cruelties were practiced by the two armies during the war, and there certainly were cases of senseless butchery on both sides, the surrender of Yorktown took place in an atmosphere of old-fashioned chivalry. Washington was adamant on only one point. He refused to have any dealing with Loyalists who had been with the British at Yorktown. They were not to be exempt from punishment, and it was only with the greatest difficulty that Cornwallis managed to smuggle a few of them onto the *Bonetta,* the ship that carried his dispatches to Clinton. In other respects the victors treated their enemies with every consideration. A charming letter from the Vicomte de Noailles to Cornwallis, accompanying a book he was lending him, the second volume of a well-known treatise on tactics by the Comte de Guibert, which was at that time the talk of Europe, suggests the sort of relationship that existed between Cornwallis and his enemies. The Vicomte, evidently a booklover, asks Cornwallis not to lend the volume to anybody else, as it was in no condition to be passed around.

Other British officers besides Cornwallis were deeply touched by the attitude of the victors in their moment of triumph. "The Americans," says Captain Samuel Graham, "behaved with great delicacy and forebearance," but naturally enough the British felt more kinship with "that sweet enemy, France" with whom they had been fighting for hundreds of years, than with the "rebels" whom they looked upon as members of the family who had gone wrong. In the final report in which he gives his own account of the catastrophe, and which he published when he reached England, Cornwallis makes this distinction very clearly. He has no complaint to make against the Americans. Far from it: "The treatment, in general, that we have received from the enemy since our surrender has been perfectly good and proper, but the kindness and attention that has been shown to us by the French officers in particular—their deli-

cate sensibility of our situation—their generous and pressing offer
of money, both public and private, to any amount—has really
gone beyond what I can possibly describe, and will, I hope, make
an impression on the breast of every British officer, whenever the
fortune of war should put any of them into our power."[16]

As soon as he reached New York, Cornwallis repaid the loan
Rochambeau had made him, and at the same time took the opportunity of sending him a good supply of cheeses and English beer.
That ended their relationship until, five years later, their paths
crossed for the last time.

Shortly after returning to France, Rochambeau had been appointed Governor of Picardy and Artois, and Calais was his headquarters. In 1786, Cornwallis passed through Calais on his way
out to India, and Rochambeau gave a dinner in his honor. He
mentions the incident in one of his letters to Washington. Apparently it was an agreeable occasion. Cornwallis was very polite, but,
"as you may believe," adds Rochambeau in his funny English, "I
could not drink with him your health in toast."[17]

For Cornwallis, Yorktown was the end of the war, a war he was
only too ready to forget. As a loyal servant of the King, he had
done all that he could to subdue the rebellious colonists, no man
could have fought harder, but he had not believed in the war and
in the House of Commons he had persistently voted against the
measures which brought it about. A long career of useful service
still lay ahead of him. As Governor-General of India and Viceroy
of Ireland, a post in which he gained the good will of both Catho-
lics and Protestants, he more than redeemed, in his countrymen's
eyes, the surrender at Yorktown. For that defeat, the most cata-
strophic England had ever suffered, he was never held responsible.
There were plenty of other scapegoats to be found, in Westminster
as well as in New York.

For Rochambeau the battle of Yorktown marked only the successful termination of another campaign. He did not foresee, any
more than Washington did, that though peace negotiations dragged
on for a year and a half, there would be no more fighting. Within a

few weeks of the capitulation he was writing to Ségur, the Minister of War, demanding men and money for the next campaign. Again he reminds the Minister, as he had so often done before, that the Americans were at the end of their rope and that it would be difficult for them to keep an army in the field for another year under any conditions, and quite impossible unless France were prepared to support it.

Rochambeau was a modest man. He would have been less than human if he had not prided himself on the planning of the whole Yorktown operation, but he never claimed it as his victory. He had planned it, but Washington and De Grasse had accepted the plan and put it into effect. Luck, as he pointed out to the Minister, had also played an important part. If any of the timing had gone wrong, if a single one of his letters to De Grasse had been intercepted, the campaign would have ended very differently. In this campaign he had had to gamble, and he had won. His corps and Washington's army, Barras and De Grasse had all converged on Yorktown at the right moment, just as he had planned. All the same, the margin of victory had been uncomfortably narrow. Next year he hoped the government would not be so niggardly. He wanted more leeway.

Writing from his headquarters in Williamsburg, three thousand miles from Paris, Rochambeau could not know that when Cornwallis surrendered at Yorktown, France was just as much at the end of her rope as America. The American war had already cost France the equivalent of fifty million dollars. She could do no more. The French people might not be aware of it and the Court might choose to ignore it, but Necker, the Minister of Finance, knew and stated very clearly in his famous *Comte Rendu* (1781) that the moment had arrived, as it does in all wars, when exhaustion imposes peace on the victors as well as on the vanquished. The disastrous defeat of De Grasse in April 1782, following so soon after Yorktown, just when France was basking in the sunshine of victory, made peace all the more imperative. In England the question was no longer how can the colonies be subjugated, but rather how much of the empire in America could be salvaged. For once, Lord North was speaking for the nation when he exclaimed, on hearing the news of Yorktown, "Oh God, it is all over. It is all over."

Politicians and diplomats would now take over where the armies and navies had left off. Washington and Rochambeau were too close to the war to see it in its proper perspective. To them, Yorktown was merely the fortunate culmination of a well-planned campaign, but they did not see it as the grand finale of the American Revolution. London knew better. Yorktown was at once the end and the beginning, the end of an unnatural war and the beginning of an unpredictable experiment.

Notes

1. Clinton, *The American Rebellion*, p. 311.
2. Cornwallis, *Correspondence*, I, 118.
3. Closen, p. 133.
4. Doniol V, 544–48.
5. Washington, *Writings*, XXIII, 136.
6. *Ibid.*, 147.
7. Francis S. Drake, *Life and Correspondence of Henry Knox* (New York, 1873), p. 68.
8. *Magazine of American History*, IV, 444.
9. Cornwallis, *Correspondence*, I, 121.
10. Washington, *Writings*, XXIII, 231.
11. Rochambeau, *Mémoires*, I, 294.
12. Washington, *Writings*, XXIII, 231.
13. Freeman, *Washington*, V, 376.
14. Dumas, I, 52.
15. Henry Lee, *Memoirs of the War in the Southern Department of the United States* (New York, 1870), p. 513.
16. Cornwallis, *Correspondence*, I, 121.
17. Library of Congress. Letter from Rochambeau to Washington, dated January 1786.

Fourteen

ASHINGTON'S REPORT TO CONGRESS on the capitulation of Cornwallis' army was characteristically prosaic: "Sir, I have the honor to inform Congress that a Reduction of the British Army under the command of Lord Cornwallis is most happily effected."

The rest of the dispatch was taken up with tributes to "the unremitting Ardor which actuated every Officer and Soldier in the combined Army on this Occasion," and to "the very chearfull and able Assistance" of Rochambeau and De Grasse.[1] Colonel Tilghman, a man Washington later described as "having left as fair a reputation as ever belonged to a human character," and whom he selected to deliver the momentous news to the President of Congress, clattered into Philadelphia early in the morning of October 24, five days after the surrender. The newspapers of the day told how the German watchman who led Tilghman to President McKean's door, went on his way waking the townspeople with the cry: "Basht dree o'glock, and Gorn-val-lis isht da-ken."[2]

It is significant that Tilghman, who like most of the officers in the Continental Army had not been paid, arrived in Philadelphia without a penny in his pockets. Congress felt that it should furnish him with hard money for his expenses but, says one of the members, Elias Boudinot of New Jersey, "there was not a sufficiency in the Treasury to do it, and the Members of the Congress, of which I was one, each paid a dollar to accomplish it."[3]

In all the excitement over Yorktown the emptiness of the Treasury could not be ignored. Nor could it be ignored that though La

[233]

Fayette in the long run was right in calling the capture of Corn-wallis the fifth act of a tragedy, the British were still in possession of New York, Charleston, and Savannah. As it turned out, the fifth act dragged on interminably, so that peace, when it did come, was almost an anticlimax.

Washington's chief anxiety immediately after Yorktown was that France, the great ally who had already done so much for the cause of independence, might now lose interest and leave the Americans to fend for themselves. Already, in January 1782, he was writing to La Fayette, who had returned to France as soon as possible, there to enjoy what Jefferson called his "canine appetite for popularity" about the necessity of a further "aid of money, which would enable our financier to support the expenses of the war with ease and credit. . . ." Washington was also insistent on the importance of maintaining naval superiority. He could not help being disappointed, though he had been warned of it beforehand, that De Grasse should have sailed away so soon after the capitula-tion. He hoped that he might stay on for a few weeks longer than he had intended, to cooperate in an attack on Charleston, but it was not to be. Having more than kept his promises to the Ameri-cans, De Grasse now felt that he must keep his promises to the Spaniards in the West Indies. Maybe he had some inkling of what fate held in store for him, for in the moment of triumph he wrote Rochambeau a very depressed letter. De Grasse was a sick man during the siege of Yorktown and, like Cornwallis, he was unable to attend the capitulation ceremonies. "You would be sorry for me, my dear General," he writes in a postscript, "if you could see the state I am in. I can neither talk nor write. My condition gets worse every day, and I don't know what the end will be; the longer I live, the more convinced I am that a man of sixty is no longer fit for such a command as I am burdened with now."[4]

With the departure of De Grasse there was no hope of any further offensive. For the French government the American conti-nent was only a minor theater of war. The sugar islands of the

West Indies, which contributed so much to the national economy, were considered much more important than the poverty-stricken colonies of the mainland. Washington accordingly wended his way north, leaving Rochambeau in Virginia to form a link between General Greene in the Carolinas and his own army, which now again resumed its post on the Hudson. On the way north he stopped in Philadelphia to appear before Congress. There was no fanfare, salute, or parade. Congress congratulated him on the glorious success of the allied army in Virginia, hoped that he would press the war vigorously in the South, and at the same time reminded him that it was important to dismiss surplus officers and to reduce all expenses as far as possible. It was the old familiar story. The Army must continue to produce results. Congress would urge the states to contribute the necessary recruits and supplies, but of course it could promise nothing of itself.

Rochambeau made his headquarters in Williamsburg, where the townspeople entertained him and his staff to the best of their ability. "One could not be more hospitable," says Closen, "than are the inhabitants of Williamsburg to all the army officers; they receive them very cordially in their homes and do all in their power to provide entertainment for them (according to the custom of the country, however). In this city, the fair sex, although they are not the prettiest I have seen, form a very agreeable and, in general, very well-bred society. Perhaps the oppressively hot climate of Virginia has some influence upon the inhabitants; it is probably the reason for their being less gay and much less active than those in the north."[5] Closen goes on to illustrate the effect of climate by pointing out that the Southern ladies dance the Minuet infinitely better than "those up North," but they are not so good in the more lively Schottische.

The town of Williamsburg offered few resources other than its university, the College of William and Mary, to which King Louis XVI sent "two hundred volumes of the greatest and best French Works." Here Rochambeau, who was not yet proficient in English, doubtless had many opportunities of conversing in Latin, as he had done with Ezra Stiles in Providence. At the same time, for the benefit of those less classically inclined and to relieve the inevitable tedium of garrison life, he made a great point of entertaining the gentry of the neighborhood. It was part of his creed that wherever the French Army found itself it must not only seek out the King's enemies and defeat them, but it must also contribute to the amenities of life. The French Army was essentially a civilizing agency. So successful were these efforts that it may fairly be said that Rochambeau's officers created in America an image of the French as an agreeable people that has never been effaced.

Inevitably there was some friction between the military and the civilian population, though this was reduced to a minimum by the admirable discipline of the French troops. Americans have never taken kindly to the practice of billeting. As one householder complained, "there is a degree of harshness in a soldier's coming and taking a man's house that our people have never been used to, nor can they put up with it quietly," yet he admits that the French soldiers were "a set of very orderly men."[6] Certainly they were far more orderly than either the British or the Americans. Contemporary accounts agree that the billeting was an unpleasant practice, but that if you had to take soldiers into your home, you were better off with the French.

One of the difficulties—and this has an ominously modern ring —was over the question of Negroes. While patriots were proclaiming the sanctity of independence, runaway slaves were in the habit of attaching themselves to French and British officers. Many of Cornwallis' officers being sent back to New York found themselves taking along with them Negro servants they had never seen before. Washington issued very strict orders on this subject, and Rochambeau did his best to comply with them, but it was no easy task. The Governor of Maryland was particularly insistent that he should make himself responsible for the return of the runaways, but what could he do? The whole question of surrendering Negroes

who had attached themselves to the French army was further complicated by the fact that early in the war Lord Dunmore, Governor
of Virginia, proclaimed freedom for all rebels' slaves who would
join him, and soon several hundred Negroes, known as Lord
Dunmore's Ethiopian Regiment, with *Liberty to Slaves* inscribed
across their chests, were in service. By the end of 1779 Sir Henry
Clinton as commander-in-chief had extended Dunmore's offer
throughout the colonies.[7]

Quite apart from any action of the British, the colonists' right to
independence was difficult to square with the right to enslave others. Many of the French officers, especially Chastellux and Count
Fersen, were outspoken in their condemnation of slavery and strikingly accurate in predicting that it would not be long before Virginia broke away from the Northern states. It must have been
difficult to explain to them that the doctrine of independence did
not apply to Negroes. Rochambeau does not mention slavery in his
letters or in his memoirs, but since the Vernon house in Newport,
which he occupied for nearly a year, belonged to a man who made
a fortune in trading for rum, he may well have been aware of the
infinite ramifications of slavery. If he ever had the leisure or the
inclination to dig into the town records, he might have learned that
"in 1756, William Vernon and William Redwood, well-known and
respected Newport merchants, took a note for 353 gallons of rum,
payable in good men and women slaves, men at 110 galls each,
and women at 95 galls each."[8]

Rochambeau, however, was not one for delving into archives,
nor did he have time, like Chastellux, to speculate on the incon-
sistencies of mankind. While Chastellux went on an extended tour
of the United States, notebook in hand, Rochambeau stuck close
to his headquarters in Williamsburg. What with balls and fox hunting, and an occasional cockfight—"something to see once out of
curiosity, but the spectacle is a little too cruel for one to enjoy"
—the winter passed pleasantly enough. On the fifteenth of December Congress ordered public celebrations to be held throughout the

country for the capture of Yorktown. In accordance with the instructions of King Louis XVI a *Te Deum* was sung in Williamsburg, and at the same time in every church in France. Rochambeau gave a big dinner for the leading residents of Williamsburg, followed by a ball. "Everyone," says Closen, "was very much pleased with it."

By this time congratulations were trickling in by every vessel arriving from France, from Spain, and from the West Indies. In the victory dispatches carried to France by the Duc de Lauzun and the Comte des Deux-Ponts, on separate ships in case of capture, Rochambeau had recommended a number of his officers for promotion and decoration, and the reply to these recommendations was eagerly awaited. Not all of them were granted. Deux-Ponts, the man who had led the assault on the redoubt, was made a full colonel and given the coveted order of St. Louis. Vioménil received the governorship of a province worth twelve thousand francs a year. Chastellux was given another province, the Berthier brothers were appointed to the general staff of the Army, and the grumbling but devoted Blanchard, among many others, received a substantial pension. Conspicuous among those who were passed over was the Duc de Lauzun, a man Rochambeau did not like personally but recognized as a very efficient officer, and whom he had specially recommended for promotion. Lauzun complained that he was ignored in the honors list because he was not popular with the King, which was quite likely in view of his attentions to Marie Antoinette, and because the Minister of War and the Minister of the Navy were both enemies of long standing. Castries, the Minister of the Navy, was annoyed with Rochambeau for not having chosen his son, a colonel in the Saintonge Regiment, for the honor of bringing the great news to Paris.

Rochambeau had done his best for his officers. Perhaps he had asked too much of them. In any case the popular hero was not Lauzun or Deux-Ponts, or anybody else in Rochambeau's army, but La Fayette. That great artist in publicity was hailed as the real victor of Yorktown. Though the dispatches reached Paris some time before he did, it was La Fayette who first brought home to the French people that France had been doing great things in America, great things in which he himself, as the friend of Washington, had had the lion's share. Vergennes and Franklin were as eager to listen to his exploits as were the King and Queen. Poets and pamphleteers were busy with his name. In the theaters and the cafés ballads and songs that referred to ancient heroes were now applied to him and sung with a new zest. It was roses, roses all the way. In a few years the Paris crowds would be treating him very differently. Only once more, at the end of his life, when he returned to America on a carefully stage-managed triumphal tour, would he inhale again the intoxicating aroma of adulation so essential to his well-being.

The honors list, when it finally reached America, was as disappointing to Rochambeau as to some of his officers. He would have liked for himself the decoration of the *cordon bleu* to add to the order of St. Louis, and he had no hesitation in telling Ségur that was what he had expected. His son, too, should have been given a regiment at once, instead of a vague promise that the King would bear him in mind in the event of a vacancy. These things were pinpricks, and if Rochambeau had been a perfectly well man they would probably not have affected him. But he was not well, and he was not young. The summer climate of Virginia did not agree with him, and he suffered continually from ague and fevers. In the eighteenth century a man of fifty-six, particularly a man who had spent most of his life in the Army and had never entirely recovered from old wounds, was already looking forward to retirement. As he wrote Ségur, he could keep going in moments of crisis, while the campaign was still on, but his infirmities got the better of him when there was nothing to fight but the steamy climate and the mosquitoes. He would like to come home as soon as possible.

Ségur teased him about his ailments. He had wanted to be relieved even before Yorktown, and was he not happy now that the government had decided that he could not be spared? The Minister of War was a tactful man. He said just the right things to the crusty old general. He told him that France was proud of him, that he had more than fulfilled all the hopes of the government, and he saw to it that the King and Vergennes wrote him equally complimentary letters. That was all very well, but Rochambeau was not entirely satisfied. Along with the compliments he was aware of a certain undercurrent of criticism. Some of his officers had been writing home that he was too much of a martinet. It was perfectly true. Rochambeau rode his army on a tight rein, officers as well as men, and he was proud of it. Except for Chastellux the academician, whom he regarded more a literary man than a soldier and to whom he allowed indefinite leaves of absence, there was no relaxation of discipline. Thanks to this discipline and to his relentless insistence on training, the Army had won golden opinions for itself. Rochambeau hoped that Paris would pay no attention to the chatter of the discontented.

In these days of instant communication by radio, telephone, and teletype, it is hard to remember that when Rochambeau wrote a letter from his headquarters in Williamsburg to the Minister of War in Paris, it took a good three months to get an answer. Sometimes letters never reached their destination at all, as in the case of a dispatch he forwarded to De Grasse from Paris, which was captured by a British frigate fifty miles off Yorktown. Fortunately this dispatch contained nothing more momentous than the compliments of the government. Owing to the slowness of communications, misunderstandings and complaints were apt to fester before they could be rectified.

Rochambeau had one serious complaint with the government at home, and it was a very familiar one. The government could not make up its mind what it wanted him to do. A commander-in-chief of an expeditionary force is either bedeviled by instructions that are too explicit or he is left entirely in the dark. Rochambeau often felt that he lived in a strange limbo into which news from the outside world never penetrated. Time dragged on, and even by the middle of 1782, more than eight months after the surrender of Yorktown, nobody knew whether there would be another campaign or not. The British could not be ousted from New York or Charleston without the assistance of the French Navy, but after Rodney's victory over De Grasse in the West Indies the French Navy could no longer be counted upon as a factor in the American war. So long as the British flag flew over New York, the United States could hardly claim to be entirely free, nor could it expect unconditional acceptance of its independence at the peace table.

Meanwhile the indefatigable La Fayette in Paris had managed to pry another six million francs out of the French Treasury. Though he had talked theatrically about Yorktown being the fifth act of the tragedy, he was intelligent enough to know that the best way to get the British off the stage, and to ring down the curtain, was to prepare vigorously for the next campaign. The six million francs was a loan to be paid quarterly beginning in March 1782. The French made it thoroughly clear that this was as far as they were prepared to go. In spite of what La Fayette said, Vergennes was not satisfied with the attitude of Congress. The French alliance, instead of stimulating the Americans to greater effort, seemed to have operated as a sedative. They were not prepared, as the Dutch had been in their struggle for independence, to sacrifice everything for liberty. He did not question the gallantry of the American Army, but there was not enough of it. It is the big battalions,[9] insisted Vergennes, that decide victory. Where were they? Out of a population of three million, how many in America were devoting themselves to the cause for which France was contributing so much? It was an awkward question.

Congress could not produce the big battalions. The governors of the states, to whom Washington had so often pleaded in vain for recruits and for supplies, were now less than ever prepared to exert themselves. The British were said to be putting out peace feelers, and under those conditions it was hopeless to expect Americans to gird themselves for battle. In a letter to his father, written in August 1782, Fersen reports that the English "have forbidden their partisans, 'tories' and 'refugees' as they are called, to make incursions or expeditions into the country without a permit signed by the commandant of the place." He also states that General Carleton, who had taken Clinton's place, had addressed a "very polite" note to General Washington informing him that the King had granted independence to America and that he was sending a man to Paris to treat for peace. Such reports were taken up eagerly in the newspapers, but Washington remained completely skeptical and persisted in his warnings against "languor" and neglect of defense.

General Greene, in the South, was another of those preparing for the next campaign. He would have liked Rochambeau to march his army down through the Carolinas, and to join forces with him in an attack on Charleston. Greene had been so successful that by the end of 1781 the British had been forced to abandon every position in South Carolina except Charleston, and he was confident that that last stronghold could be captured without the help of the French Navy. Reports had now reached him that the British were sending reinforcements to Charleston, and he would welcome any help that Rochambeau could send him. However tempting the request may have been, for Rochambeau was always uneasy when his troops were idle and he was anxious to cooperate with Greene as far as possible, he decided against it. The King's orders still held good that the corps must not be divided, and it was obviously impossible to protect Virginia against a possible British attack and at the same time send troops down to South Carolina. He would send Lauzun's Hussars down to the Carolina border, but that was as far as he could go. Unless Greene were hard-pressed, which he was not, for the British reinforcements never materialized, he would keep his troops in and around Williamsburg, halfway between Washington and Greene, ready to support either as the occasion demanded.

That was the arrangement he had come to with Washington immediately following Yorktown, but after eight months of inactivity, what we should call today a phoney war, Rochambeau felt the need of another conference with the commander-in-chief. If there was to be a summer campaign, either in South Carolina or in the North against New York, they must start planning it at once. If, on the other hand, the rumors about peace were correct, he must begin thinking about getting his troops home. There was also the eternal question of money to be considered. Rochambeau was down to his last penny (*notre dernier sol*). After ordering that *Te Deums* be sung all over France, Versailles seemed to have forgotten it had an army in America.

Having heard from the West Indies that the Marquis de Vaudreuil with his squadron, the remnant of the De Grasse fleet, would reach Boston early in August, Rochambeau decided to march north. The army broke camp at Williamsburg on July 1. It traveled in four divisions, a day apart, at the rate of twelve to fourteen miles a day. Rochambeau ordered that they should start at 2 A.M. and make camp by daybreak, so as to avoid the excessive heat to which the troops were not accustomed and which Rochambeau thought "did not permit of any movement." Chastellux, just back from one of his sightseeing tours, marched at the head of the first division, composed of the Bourbonnais Regiment. The second, the Deux-Ponts, was commanded by the older brother of the man who had led the assault on the redoubt. The third, the Soissonnais, was led by the younger Vioménil, and the fourth, the Saintonge, by the Marquis de Custine, whom Rochambeau had had to discipline for drunkenness during the siege of Yorktown but who was now once again in favor. Custine's fondness for the bottle, coupled with a tendency to speak his mind too openly, was to prove fatal to him. He was guillotined while in command of one of the Revolutionary armies for incompetence, and for speaking disrespectfully of the republican government.

Washington, still on the Hudson, was more than ready for a

conference, and agreed to meet Rochambeau halfway, in Philadelphia. There was of course much to be discussed, and an entirely new situation to be faced since the French Navy had now lost command of the American waters. The dream of capturing New York with the help of the French Navy, which had always haunted Washington, faded again, but now, resourceful as he was, he turned to another scheme, one that he and La Fayette had often talked over—the invasion of Canada. Since an attack on New York was no longer feasible, and since Charleston was too far away, why should not the allied armies launch an offensive against Quebec? The attempt had been made earlier in the war under Montgomery and Benedict Arnold, while he was still a loyal American, and it had very nearly succeeded. With a much better equipped army and with the help of his French allies, Washington had high hopes of capturing Quebec, driving the British out of Canada and ending the war with another resounding victory.

Tentatively he broached the plan to Rochambeau, who pointed out in the friendliest way that his orders did not permit him to operate outside of the thirteen colonies. He would have to refer the plan to his government, which would involve a delay of at least three months, but in the meantime he would do what he could to occupy the British in New York while Washington made his attack on Canada. Being a tactful man he did not say that he had been warned by his government not to be drawn into any campaign for the conquest of new territory. Vergennes, the man who was chiefly responsible for the American alliance, was not prepared to have the new republic spread over the whole continent. In the eyes of that astute politician the peace of the world, which meant the balance of power, would be better served if Canada remained in British hands. By all means let the British keep Canada. It would involve them in continuous friction with their former colonies, and prevent them from interfering with French projects in other parts of the world.

Very wisely Washington dropped the Canadian offensive. He

was not strong enough to attempt it alone, and he probably sensed that the French government would have no part in it. Rochambeau could not have been more considerate, and the two men remained on excellent terms. Indeed, Washington was able to do Rochambeau a good turn by helping him dissuade Admiral Vaudreuil from going off on a private marauding expedition in Penobscot Bay. It is strange what an extraordinary fascination Penobscot held for the French Navy. Vaudreuil was only following in the footsteps of Des Touches, La Pérouse, and Barras. All of them had wanted to borrow troops from Rochambeau for attacks on outlying British posts. Even if the attacks had been successful, which was unlikely, they would have had no influence on the course of the war. Fortunately Washington agreed with Rochambeau that the expedition would serve no purpose and that Vaudreuil would be running the risk of being bottled up in Penobscot Bay, since a new British squadron known to be on its way to New York would soon be on his heels.

Between them, Rochambeau and Washington dampened Vaudreuil's ardor. His policy of striking at the enemy wherever found was a generous one and it did him credit, but in this particular case, from Rochambeau's point of view at any rate, there were other factors to be considered. More and more Rochambeau was becoming convinced that the struggle for American independence had been won, and that if there were to be any more fighting it would be in the West Indies. After the long inactive winter in Virginia he had been anxious to return home to confer with Ségur on the next campaign. He himself hoped to retire, but there were several others who could take his place. If the Baron de Vioménil, now in France, came back to America he would be the obvious choice. Otherwise Rochambeau would be more than satisfied to leave Chastellux in command. By the end of September the situation had changed. Young French noblemen eager for service overseas were still pouring over from France, but from now on they would not be fighting side by side with the Americans.

A letter brought over to Rochambeau by the Comte de Ségur, son of the Minister of War, ordered him to embark his regiments as soon as possible in Admiral Vaudreuil's ships, now refitting in Boston. They were to sail for the West Indies. There they would be under the command of the Baron de Vioménil, who would put himself at the disposition of M. de Galvez, the Spanish general in command, just as Rochambeau had put himself at the disposition of Washington. Versailles had taken note that the British had written off the war with America, with whom they now wanted to make an independent peace. The British were said to be willing to make peace with France too, but they were both hoping to consolidate their position in the West Indies before sitting down at the bargaining table. It was to offset the effect of Rodney's victory that Versailles transferred its attention to the Caribbean. Rochambeau was now at liberty to come home on the first vessel available.

He was very much at home in America by this time. He was gradually becoming more fluent in English and in writing he expressed himself clearly if not always idiomatically. Though he may not have made friends as easily as Chastellux, one of the few men who would joke with Washington, or as Lauzun, who became so devoted to the Hunter family, he was on pleasant terms with all kinds of Americans. Everybody liked him and respected him. Count Fersen thought that the friendly and unassuming behavior of the general had done more for the cause of independence than any number of successful battles, while the overworked commissary Blanchard admitted that though he was sometimes unjust to his subordinates, no one could have given Americans such a favorable impression of France as Rochambeau.

An incident that occurred at King's Ferry on the Hudson, where the French troops on their way to Boston were reunited for a few days with their Yorktown comrades, illustrates Rochambeau's ready understanding of the ways of democracy. In the midst of the festivities a certain captain of the militia, on whose property one of the French brigades had been camping, presented Rochambeau

with a bill for fifteen thousand francs for the firewood that had
been cut on his property. Rochambeau thought the bill excessive
but he referred the man to the commissary, whose duty it was to
attend to such matters. The next morning just as the army was
breaking camp, "a man approached me," says Rochambeau, "and
addressed me in the most respectful manner. He said he was perfectly aware of the services I had rendered his country, and that he
had the greatest respect for me, but that he was obliged to do his
duty. With that he produced a warrant, and placing his hand gently
on my shoulder he said, 'You are my prisoner.' 'Very well,' I
replied, 'take me away with you—if you can.'[10]

" 'No, Monsieur,' replied the sheriff, 'there is no question of
that, but now that I have done my duty I beg you to permit me to
withdraw quietly.' "

Rochambeau continued his march at the head of the column,
and the matter was referred again to the commissary. In the end
the aggrieved captain of militia was very glad to receive two thousand francs instead of the exorbitant fifteen thousand, which even
his friends thought outrageous. Any American who served in
France during either of the world wars will recognize the story as
following a familiar pattern. Allies are notoriously suspicious of
one another, but fortunately Rochambeau was an exception to the
rule. He did not, on the basis of one incident, draw up an indict-
ment against the whole American nation.

By the end of the war Rochambeau had won an enviable reputation for himself among friends and foes alike. During the long
period of inaction following his arrival in Newport, the Americans
had not known what to make of him or his army. La Fayette had
done him a disservice by giving it out that he was overcautious,
that he did not understand the need for immediate action, but the
Yorktown campaign had cleared away all such misconceptions.
After being an unknown quantity for nearly a year, the quiet, self-
effacing French general stood revealed as the architect of victory.
In conference and in the field, at Hartford and Wethersfield as well

as at Yorktown, Rochambeau had proved himself an invaluable ally, quick to understand Washington's difficulties and enormously competent in devising means of overcoming them.

After Yorktown, while he was in Williamsburg, complimentary addresses poured in on Rochambeau from Congress, from the legislatures of the various states, from governors, mayors, and universities, congratulating him on his services to their cause. He was particularly pleased by the address from the mayor and the inhabitants of Williamsburg, offering their thanks not only for the services rendered by the General in his military capacity, but "for your conduct in the more private walks of life, and the happiness we have derived from the social, polite, and very friendly intercourse we have been honored with by yourself and the officers of the French army in general, during the whole time of your residence among us."

The quality of the man was recognized by the British, for whose defeat he was also so largely responsible, as well as by his countless American friends. Remembering his consideration for them in their hour of humiliation, it seemed natural to turn to him to save the life of Captain Asgill of the Guards, a prisoner who had been sentenced to death in reprisal for the execution by the Loyalists of an American militia captain. The British claimed that Asgill, an officer in Cornwallis' army, was covered by the terms of surrender, while Congress insisted no less firmly that Cornwallis' army must pay the price for the lawless savagery of the Loyalists. The case aroused great interest in France and England as well as in America. The young man's mother wrote to Vergennes begging him to intercede on her son's behalf, and at the same time Rochambeau appealed to Washington. The combination of Vergennes, Rochambeau, and La Luzerne, who had a great influence on Congress and to whom Rochambeau had also written, secured Asgill's release. Washington was not a vindictive man and, though he was always prepared to think the worst of the Loyalists, he did not want to have an innocent man's blood on his hands. In any event he owed so much to his French friends he was glad to satisfy them in any way that he could.

On the first anniversary of their joint victory at Yorktown, Washington gave a farewell dinner for Rochambeau and his staff at his camp on the Hudson. Fortunately Closen was present on this occasion, and the entry in his diary shows that he was deeply affected: "There are few courtesies or kindnesses that General Washington has not shown us, and the idea that he must part, probably forever, from the French army seemed to cause him genuine pain, the more so because he had received the most convincing evidence of the respect, veneration and esteem, and even affection, that everyone in our army felt for him."[11]

The French troops were now under sailing orders and they marched north to Boston, stopping at familiar campgrounds and renewing old friendships on the way. Rochambeau gave another ball in Providence, at which for the first time he spoke publicly about the army's embarkation. The bulk of the army, under the command of the Baron de Vioménil, sailed out of Boston harbor on November twenty-fourth. Vaudreuil could not transport the whole French force on his crowded ships, which meant that a few units of siege artillery had to be left behind under the command of the Duc de Lauzun. The French admiral was to sail to Santo Domingo, join a Spanish fleet which would be waiting for him there, and renew the attack on Jamaica, which had been foiled by Rodney's victory earlier in the year. This ambitious project, which was to have included an attack on New York after the island of Jamaica had been captured, came to nothing. Peace preliminaries were signed before the various squadrons converging from Brest, Cádiz, and Boston had reached the rendezvous.

By this time even Washington agreed that the war was petering out. Wrangling at the peace table would continue for some time, but there would be no more fighting. The independence of the United States had already been conceded, but Spanish and French claims in Gibraltar and the West Indies still remained to be ad-

justed. Such things did not concern Rochambeau. He had carried
out the King's orders, and he was ready to go home. After a final
farewell visit to Washington at Newburgh, where they took leave
of each other "in the tenderest fashion," he made his way south-
ward hoping to find a ship for him either at Philadelphia or on the
Chesapeake. Within a few days of his starting down the Hudson
the British fleet sailed out of New York. Rochambeau had timed
his departure very exactly.

He sailed from the little town of Anne Arundel (Annapolis),
January 8, on the small frigate *L'Emeraude*. With him he took two
small field pieces, captured at Yorktown and presented to him by
Congress. Washington took immense pains over the inscription.

In less than an hour of his sailing the *Emeraude* was sighted by
a British frigate, evidently a more powerful vessel and a fast sailer.
It was only by throwing overboard her spare masts and part of her
artillery that the little *Emeraude* was able to escape. Evidently the
British had full warning that Rochambeau was on the eve of departure, since he and his staff were greeted on their arrival in
Annapolis with fireworks and artillery salvos. In his memoirs Rochambeau tells us how, after being pursued by the British frigate,
they were followed all the way across the ocean, and right up to
the mouth of the Nantes River, by gales and bad weather. All
hands were delighted when the frigate anchored off St. Nazaire on
the morning of February 10.

It was nearly three years since Rochambeau had sailed from
Brest. If he had been ready for retirement then, he was even more
ready for it now. Always a countryman at heart, he looked forward to spending the rest of his life in his beloved Vendôme. He
would have been aghast had he known what the next decade was
to hold in store for him and for his country. The King's decision to
go to the aid of the American colonists and to appoint him commander-in-chief of the expeditionary corps had presented him with
a challenge, but it was a challenge he had known how to meet. In
the American Revolution he had felt himself on firm ground, fight-

ing side by side with a man who kept his eyes fixed on the goal of independence, a man to whom the issues of the war were crystal-clear. Like everybody who has been away for a long time on active service overseas, Rochambeau was glad to be home, glad to be able to attend to his own affairs, glad above all to be with his wife after so many months of separation. But he was ill at ease too. Back in France he felt he was floundering in quicksands.

Rochambeau was not a philosopher, but he was a shrewd observer, and he was not pleased with what he observed in Versailles, in Paris, or even in Vendôme. Ruefully he notes that England was rising phoenixlike from her defeat while France, once more the arbiter of Europe, was plunging deeper and deeper into debt. The financial problems were not of themselves insoluble, but they were complicated by a moral and intellectual crisis that had stirred the nation to its depths. War he could understand. A victorious peace posed strange new difficulties that were beyond his ken.

Notes

1. Washington, *Writings*, XXIII, 241.

2. Rupert Hughes, *George Washington, the Savior of the States, 1777–1781* (New York, 1930), p. 680.

3. Elias Boudinot, *Journal of Historical Recollections of American Events during the Revolutionary War* (Philadelphia, 1894), p. 38.

4. Doniol, V, 583.

5. Closen, p. 166.

6. *Calendar of Virginia State Papers*, II, 601.

7. Wallace Brown, "Negroes and the American Revolution," *History Today* (August 1964).

8. H. W. Preston, *Rhode Island Historical Background* (Providence, 1930).

9. Doniol, IV, 686.

10. Rochambeau, *Mémoires*, I, 312.

11. Closen, p. 257.

Fifteen

ROCHAMBEAU'S RETURN TO FRANCE was almost an anticlimax. When he passed through Philadelphia on his way to Annapolis, he had received the thanks of Congress, and he had been even more gratified by the flattering words of a deputation of Quakers who had congratulated him not on his military achievements, in which they set little store, but on the good conduct of the troops under his command, which proved him to be a genuine friend of man. At Annapolis, where he went on board his frigate, he was given a magnificent send-off with an impressive display of fireworks. So well was this entertainment advertised that the British ships lying in wait for him off the Capes heard about it and very nearly succeeded in waylaying him. As noted, the *Emeraude* escaped only by throwing overboard the guns it mounted and the spare masts and sails.

By the time they dropped anchor at Nantes, on February 20, 1783, the peace preliminaries had been signed. It was a year and a half now since the victory *Te Deums* had been chanted, and Yorktown was an old story. There was no ripple of excitement over his return home. La Fayette had gathered all the laurels, and Rochambeau was not the man to claim anything for himself. He knew that he had the good opinion of the men he most respected—La Luzerne, with whom he had worked so closely in America; Ségur, the Minister of War in Paris, who had denied him the reinforcements he had been promised but whom he never criticized; and Vergennes. Ségur, who evidently felt that the services of Rochambeau and La Luzerne had not been fully appreciated, told his son

[253]

years later that "a juster posterity would honor as it should two men so useful to their country and would make up for the wrongs of their contemporaries."[1]

Though the general public may have ignored him, Rochambeau tells us that the King received him at Versailles "with great distinction." It was to him and to his victory over Cornwallis, said the King, that France owed the peace. Instead of bowing respectfully as was expected of him, Rochambeau replied that the King was no less indebted for the peace to Admiral De Grasse, without whose cooperation there would have been no victory at Yorktown. The King rather brushed aside these remarks about De Grasse, whose successful engagement off the Chesapeake had been overshadowed by his crushing defeat in the Battle of the Saints Passage. It was characteristic of Rochambeau to plead the case of a gallant officer who was under a cloud at the moment, but his loyalty to his old comrade was of no avail. De Grasse had made things more difficult for himself by trying to shift the blame for his defeat to the ship captains, some of whom, he maintained, had not obeyed his orders. Under these circumstances he would have to wait until the naval board of inquiry had ruled on his case before he could hope for any expression of royal favor. The King was well aware of the Admiral's services in the past, but on this particular occasion he wished to do honor to Rochambeau and to nobody else. Accordingly he graciously conferred upon his faithful servant the right of "entry to his chambers," a privilege highly prized by courtiers though it can have meant little to a man who disliked Court life as much as Rochambeau. A far greater distinction in his eyes was the *cordon bleu* of the Order of the Saint Esprit, the highest honor a King of France could bestow. Rochambeau had had to wait longer than he thought was just for it, but it was none the less welcome when it came.

The investiture, as described by John Adams, who was a fascinated observer at one of these ceremonies, must have been something of an ordeal. For one thing, the participants had to kneel bolt upright on the bare marble floor of the Sainte Chapelle for not less than two hours. To endure such torment four times a year seemed to Mr. Adams a high price to pay for a piece of blue ribbon, however honorable. Apparently he was not alone in this opinion, for Vergennes admitted to him that the pain was almost more than he could bear.[2]

As a more tangible recognition of his services, though the *cordon bleu* of the Order of the Saint Esprit was what he valued the most, the King assigned him to the command of the northern district, including Flanders, Picardy, and Artois, always the cockpit of Europe and destined to be fought over even more heavily in the First World War. It was, as he said, "one of the finest military commands in France" with the added advantage of a headquarters in Calais, through which all the ambassadors passed on their way to and from England. There was no better listening post in Europe than Rochambeau's headquarters.

The King also gratified him by awarding three months' extra pay to the regiments who had served with him in America and by promoting the Duc de Lauzun and a few other officers who up till then had been overlooked. Rochambeau was not required to assume his new duties until the following year. In the meantime there was much to occupy him in Vendôme and at his house in Paris in the rue du Cherche-Midi, which he had bought just before setting off for America. At last, for a few months, he was able to enjoy the life of a country gentleman. Like Washington, who wrote him that, thanks largely to the French, he could now sit down under his own vine and his own fig tree, and "enjoy those pleasures which are rarely to be found in the more active pursuits of life,"[3] Rochambeau expected to be left alone to cultivate his garden. Like Washington too he soon found that the peaceful old age he saw stretching out ahead of him was only a mirage. There was still work to be done in the world from which he could not escape.

The new threat he was called upon to face came from an unexpected quarter. As always at the end of a war, the peacemakers assembled in Paris really believed they had profited from the mistakes of the past. This time it was to be a peace of reconciliation. Since no nation was to be humiliated, no nation would again have recourse to war. Aside from the one great blow, the loss of the thirteen colonies, which satisfied the principal war aim of France and of the United States, Great Britain did not suffer heavily in the general peace. There were a few minor adjustments in the West Indies, and she relinquished the restrictions imposed on the French naval port of Dunkirk in 1763, but she retained Gibraltar, and her position in India was unchallenged. France emerged from the war victorious, but the tremendous effort she had put forth to secure American independence had left her financially crippled. The national deficit did not escape the attention of her ever-watchful neighbors. In the autumn of 1784 Austria, who had been playing the role of a neutral peacemaker, now threatened her with a serious conflict. The Emperor, master of Belgium, claimed to impose on the Dutch the free navigation of the Escaut in order to favor the development of Antwerp. Holland called on France for support, which put the French government in a difficult position. If things turned out badly, France ran the risk of another war she was in no position to face.

Vergennes submitted to the King a recommendation that France support Holland at any cost, and Rochambeau had no sooner arrived at Calais than he was ordered to be ready at short notice to march to the support of the Dutch Army. The French government was about to commit itself when Vergennes died. His policy of maintaining French preponderance in Europe died with him. France was appealing to an Assembly of Notables to find a remedy for her financial troubles, and was hardly in a position to add to those troubles by embarking on another war. Whether the decision to stand aloof decided the fate of Holland, as Rochambeau believed, it was from the point of view of Calonne, the new Minister of Finance, inevitable.

For the next few years, while the storm of the Revolution was

brewing, Rochambeau busied himself at Calais with the usual routine of Army life. Much of his time was taken up organizing reviews and parades in honor of the distinguished visitors who were
always passing through on their way to Paris or to London.
Among them was the Archduke Ferdinand, brother of Marie
Antoinette, for whom Rochambeau arranged a special review,
which to his great disappointment the Archduke failed to attend
because of bad weather. In addition to these ceremonial occasions
he directed maneuvers at the nearby camp of St. Omer under the
paternal eye of the Prince de Condé, who was soon to be heading
the army of émigrés on the Rhine. Wherever Rochambeau was in
command, the army always managed to put on a good show. The
Archduke Ferdinand in Calais was treated with no more and no
less distinction than the delegation of Indian warriors who had
visited his headquarters at Newport. They both offered him an
opportunity of showing off the excellent equipment of the French
Army and the flawless discipline of the crack troops under his
command.

Rochambeau thoroughly enjoyed the four years he spent in
Calais. He did not treat the post as a sinecure, but he felt free to
come and go as he pleased. Above all he was not bothered, as he
had been so often in America, by lack of funds. In the summer of
1787 he spent twelve days in England, visiting London and Portsmouth, where Admiral Hood greeted him as an old friend, accorded him full military honors, and allowed him to see as much of
the fortifications as he wished. This inspection was of great interest
to Rochambeau as it enabled him to verify the reconnaissance
made by Admiral d'Orvilliers at the time of his projected raid on
the south coast. He came to the conclusion that if the Admiral had
only shown a more aggressive spirit he could have captured the
roadstead at Spithead, landed his troops, and burned the ship-
yards. Such an opportunity, he added, was not likely to occur
again, as the defenses had been considerably strengthened. Rochambeau was delighted with his visit. The English would always

be enemies, but in the intervals of peace they could be friends too. In any case, the great game of war in all its ramifications was endlessly fascinating.

Rochambeau's duties at Calais were only as arduous as he chose to make them, but he seems to have had some difficulties with the city officials. They did not fail to compliment him on his victories, but they regretted that they were not in a position to furnish the house which had been assigned to him. One of the items he found himself arguing about was the supply of linen. After a year of discussion the mayor wrote him: "Forgive us, Monsieur le comte, if we argue with you at greater length over our sheets than our enemies have argued with you over their flags, but this new expense is very embarrassing to us."[4] It was unfortunate for Rochambeau that his predecessor, the Duc de Croy, was a rich man who entertained the city fathers lavishly at his own expense. The city fathers had rather hoped that the Duc de Croy's son would take his place, and the appointment of Rochambeau, in spite of his victories in America, was something of a disappointment. Rather than bicker with the mayor over his household expenses the old general went to stay with his daughter-in-law and his son, now a colonel of the Auvergne Regiment, which formed part of the Calais garrison.

As soon as the war scare over Holland had died down, Rochambeau spent almost as much of his time in Paris and at Vendôme as he did in Calais. One of the great events in the history of Calais, which he appears to have missed, was what the local newspapers referred to as "the conquest of the air." On the seventh of June 1785, John Jeffries, an American Loyalist resident in England, and a Frenchman, Jean Pierre Blanchard, crossed the Channel in a balloon from Dover to Calais. The arrival of the two aeronauts caused a sensation. It was the first time anyone had flown the Channel. Men spoke of it as an unparalleled triumph over space, a feat which would be remembered long after every other event in the age of Louis XVI had been forgotten.

One of the more agreeable duties that took Rochambeau to Paris was the organization of the French members of the Society of the Cincinnati. On January 7, 1784, just a year before Jeffries and Blanchard had flown across the Channel, two meetings of the newly admitted members of the Society of the Cincinnati were held simultaneously in Paris. Many of the senior officers who had served under Rochambeau, including the Vioménil brothers, Chastellux, and the Duc de Lauzun, met at his house in the rue du Cherche-Midi. Officers who had served under the commissions from the Continental Congress met at La Fayette's house in the rue de Bourbon, and after considering the claims of the various applicants proceeded in a body to unite with the other French Cincinnati under Rochambeau's roof. Some difficulties had to be ironed out, since no foreign order was then allowed in France, but the King was so much interested in the whole proceeding that he waived all objections. On certain occasions Louis XVI could act quickly and decisively, and this was one of them. "His most Christian Majesty," wrote Ségur to Rochambeau, "directs me to inform you that he consents to your acceptance of this honorable invitation. He wishes you also, on his behalf, to assure His Excellency General Washington that he will always regard with extreme satisfaction everything which may tend to maintain and strengthen the ties formed between France and the United States. The successes which have resulted from this union and the glory which has been the fruit of it has shown its advantages. You may therefore inform the general officers and colonels who served in the Army which you commanded, that the King permits them to join the Association of the Cincinnati."[5]

In the presence of Major L'Enfant, who would soon be drawing up plans for the new Federal City, but who had been chosen on this occasion to represent the American Cincinnati and to help organize the French chapter, Rochambeau distributed the golden eagles and the festival regalia to the officers who had qualified for membership. It was the kind of ceremony he liked, commemorating as it did the links of friendship forged on the battlefield. Rochambeau took great pride in the Cincinnati, but not everybody in France or in America agreed with him about its importance. Benjamin Franklin indulged in some ridicule of the institution and condemned the members as "forming an order of Hereditary Knights," but he thought better of it later and finally accepted honorary membership. In America, both Jefferson and John Adams were loud in their criticism. Jefferson felt that the Society was incompatible with the natural equality of man, and advised the members to "distribute their funds, renounce their existence, and melt up their eagles." To John Adams' suspicious mind the founding of the Society was "the first step taken to deface the beauty of our Temple of Liberty."[6]

In France too *"l'Ordre de Cincinnatus,"* which was at first hailed as a symbol of liberty, soon came under a cloud. By the time Robespierre came into power, when every sign of personal and hereditary distinction was being wiped out, any man known to be in possession of the eagle of the Cincinnati was in grave danger. A Society with so many aristocrats on its rolls was obviously a threat to the Republic. With the overthrow of the French monarchy on August 10, 1792, *l'Ordre de Cincinnatus* dropped out of sight, not to be heard of again until it was officially reconstituted in 1923. Many of the original members, including the President, Admiral d'Estaing, perished on the scaffold. What little survives of the original records is to be found in the Rochambeau papers now in the Library of Congress.

Rochambeau's letters to Washington after his return to France, written in his own very individual English, have never been published, and many of them are of great interest. Apart from the references to the Cincinnati, which show how seriously he took the affairs of the Society, he has a good deal to say about contemporary abuses in France. Like so many of the officers who had served in America, his eyes were opened to the necessity for radical changes in almost every department of the government. In a letter written from Paris on May 12, 1787, he reveals to Washington his anxiety over the ever-increasing deficit: "We are here in a terrible crisis of finances which has occasioned an assembly of chief men that last yet. You heard speak of the ministry of M. Necker and of the flourishing state where he had left our finances. A devil of a fool named Calonne, Minister of finances since four years, has believed to be bound to take contrary sense to his predecessor, and has made succeed to an economical administration, a prodigality and a devastation which has no example."[7]

If Rochambeau had been better informed he would not have said that Necker had left the finances in a flourishing state. All Necker had done was to postpone the day of reckoning. He was an honest man and, as both he and his friends knew how to make the most of his real virtues, he had the confidence of the public. He carried out some reforms, and he even published accounts, but instead of raising money by imposing taxes he raised it by a series of loans. That in itself might not have been disastrous if he had not always counted on the last loan to pay the interest on the one preceding. Necker's successors could only follow his example and present the mirage of wealth in the future, or reverse his policy and undertake to raise revenue the orthodox way, from taxes. Calonne, who became Minister of Finance in 1783, followed the first method up until the meeting of the Assembly of Notables, or "chief men" as Rochambeau called them, in 1787. He then adopted, or tried to adopt, a thoroughgoing reform of the taxes, but he was not a big enough man to impose his will on the Notables. The laws and customs in every province were different. Local privileges and exemptions had to be swept away, and Calonne did not have enough iron in him to carry out the housecleaning involved.

He was a plausible man with twenty years of administrative experience, and France expected great things of him. The *Almanach Royal* thought that the day he took office, November 3, 1783, would forever be remembered as a memorable date—5783 years, it pointed out, after the creation of the world, 4124 years since the flood, and 1363 years since the foundation of the French monarchy. Rochambeau, as we have seen, thought nothing of him and was delighted when the Notables demanded and obtained his resignation. The Assembly of Notables consisted of princes, bishops, great landowners, presidents of the provincial parliaments and other dignitaries, and a few mayors of the more important towns. The King nominated the Notables and the meeting therefore could hardly be called a great step forward. Yet it was a step, even if it was a small one, and at the news of it France began to rouse herself as from a long sleep.

The Notables had done nothing, but their assembly had momentous results. Calonne laid his new taxes before them, with other measures of much-needed reform, one of the most important being the establishment of provincial assemblies. At the same time he was obliged to reveal the deficit in the finances, a deficit which had increased tremendously since he assumed office. The Notables accepted a few of the reforms, but they resisted the moderate taxation of the privileged orders which Calonne had proposed. They called for further information, raised objections to Calonne's proposals, and ended by suggesting that only the nation had the right to tax. By their unwillingness to give up their special privileges the Notables sealed their own downfall. France could not grapple with her financial problems without a new constitution, and a new constitution could only be drafted by the States-General. Calonne's successor, Loménie de Brienne, Archbishop of Toulouse, tried to make out that the country had done very well without the States-General for a century and a half, and that the provincial assemblies would be far more useful than any States-General could be. Nevertheless, in answer to the popular demand, the King would be pleased to summon the States-General in five years. This gracious concession was received in silence. It was clearly the wish of the whole nation not only that the States-General should be summoned, but that it should be summoned at once.

Rochambeau watched all these proceedings with the deepest misgivings. Loménie de Brienne, knowing that the name of Rochambeau would be an asset to his government, invited him to become chairman of the new war council he was forming, but Rochambeau wisely declined. Dabbling in politics was not his affair, and he sensed that Loménie de Brienne, whom he distrusted as much as he did Calonne, wanted to use him for political purposes. It was a great relief to Rochambeau when, at the end of May 1789, Brienne was dismissed and, to the joy of all France, the popular Necker became Minister once more. The fact that Necker was Swiss and that he was a banker may explain the confidence he inspired in Rochambeau and in many others, but he was essentially a timid man. Confronted with a nation humming with discussion about the States-General and the Constitution it might, could, and should give the country, Necker could think of nothing better than to reassemble the Notables and consult them. Rochambeau was a member of this second Assembly and he recounts in his memoirs how he argued with one of the bishops on the impossibility of keeping the government permanently in the hands of the privileged class. On the basis of his experience in America, he warned the bishop against making the same mistake the English had made with their American colonists. The right of the people to decide how they should be taxed must be recognized. Maybe the parallel was not as exact as Rochambeau claimed, but on the main issue— that there should be as many deputies for the Third Estate as for the two other Orders and that they should all meet together—he took the position of common sense.

In one of the most famous pamphlets of the day the Abbé Sieyès had written: "What is the Third Estate?—Everything—What has it been in the political order up to the present?—Nothing—What does it ask?—To become something." Rochambeau was a soldier, not a clever phrasemaker like the Abbé Sieyès, but he was definitely on his side. Most of the officers who had served in America agreed with him, including La Fayette, but as he wrote Washington in January 1789, just before the meeting of the States General, "we have a great number of aristocratical men that are very interested to perpetuate the abuses."[8]

As the time for the meeting of the States-General drew near, fears of what was about to happen grew more definite. Rochambeau, who still believed that Necker might lead the way into the promised land of constitutional government, foresaw troubles. He regretted that the nation did not accept with thanks what the government offered so generously. While the provincial assembly of Orléans, to which he had been elected, had shown the right spirit, there were other provinces in France, Brittany among them, where the troops had to be called out to maintain order. It was in Brittany, and then again at St. Omer only a few miles from his own headquarters, that Rochambeau heard for the first time in his life of French troops arguing with their officers and refusing to obey orders. In America he had heard about troops mutinying, but such things could not happen in France. Though the disturbances at St. Omer did not turn out to be serious, he had the uneasy feeling that the celebrated *esprit de corps* of the French Army, which meant everything to him, was undergoing a change. The soldier's conception of duty was becoming more complicated. Officers could no longer expect absolute, unquestioning obedience. It was all very well to talk of restoring order, but if "restoring order" involved firing on civilians who had legitimate grievances or whom the troops thought had legitimate grievances, they might very well refuse to obey.

In the spring of 1789, during a brief lull before the storm, Rochambeau made another visit to England. The French ambassador in London at that moment was his old friend La Luzerne, who—in spite of his having played an important part in the victory of the American colonies over the mother country—seems nonetheless to have been *persona grata* to the British government. La Luzerne had invited him to London for the festivities that were to take place in connection with the King's recovery from a bout of insanity. In all the corporations of the city, in the clubs, and in the

foreign embassies, the convalescence of "Farmer George" was celebrated in the greatest style. Rochambeau was warmly greeted
by his old enemies, particularly by those officers of Cornwallis'
army who happened to be in London. Cornwallis himself was in
India at the time, but his officers, says Rochambeau, went out of
their way to express their gratitude for the many kindnesses they
had received from the French Army at the time of their surrender.

The visit to England, though it lasted only two weeks, gave
Rochambeau much to think about. During the King's illness Pitt
had governed in his name, and the Ministers had all remained at
their posts. Rochambeau was impressed by this evidence of loyalty
and stability. He was also impressed by the way Pitt had gone to
work to set the British finances in order. The war had cost England
more than it had France. How was it that England had recovered
more quickly? France was a rich country, richer in resources than
England. With a reasonable system of taxation the monarchy
might well have weathered the storm, but the taxes were badly
administered and unfairly assessed. The burden fell almost entirely
on the Third Estate, the great bulk of the nation—peasants,
workmen, soldiers, lawyers, doctors, everyone engaged in any
trade or industry. The Clergy and the Nobles were excused pay-
ment of certain taxes and paid others at a much lighter rate.

These evils, which Rochambeau noted in his memoirs and in his
letters to Washington, were brought home to him even more forci-
bly when he was relieved of his command in the north of France,
where popular discontent was felt in only a few localities, and
appointed to Alsace, which by 1789 had already become a hotbed of
revolution. When he arrived at Versailles on July 12, two days
before the fall of the Bastille, to report to the Duc de Broglie, the
new Minister of War, for last instructions, the Minister could tell
him nothing. "Get to your post as quickly as possible," said the
Duke, "and use your own judgment." Rochambeau returned to
Paris, where he learned that Necker, still a popular figure with the

crowd, had just been dismissed. "Having reached my house," he writes, "I heard shots from the direction of the Tuileries while I was packing."[9] In the streets he could see patrols from the Regiment of the Guards fraternizing with the crowds. Ringleaders were carrying on their shoulders busts of two men who were supposed to be champions of the people—Necker, an honest man but a temporizer, and the Duc d'Orléans, one of the most contemptible characters of the Revolution, who was thought to have paid the mob in the hope that the King would be deposed and he himself made regent. By parading these busts, snatched from the waxwork show of John Curtius, an uncle of Madame Tussaud, the ringleaders whipped up the crowds into a frenzy of destruction.

For a man like Rochambeau, to whom law and order were synonymous with decency, it was a disgusting spectacle. Since it was out of the question for a private carriage to cross Paris, and equally out of the question to find a stagecoach, he left the rue du Cherche-Midi on horseback. Traveling by a roundabout way via Fontainebleau and Sens, where the crowds were robbing the grain boats, Troyes and Langres, he finally reached Strasbourg on July 18. News of the capture of the Bastille and the dismissal of Necker, combined with exasperation over the high cost of bread, had already aroused what Rochambeau called a "general effervescence." On the next day when the mail brought the news of the recall of Necker the crowds bullied the mayor into ordering a public illumination. Rochambeau took the precaution of doubling the patrols, but the situation was already out of hand. The effervescence had grown into a riot. A mob armed with axes forced their way into the city hall, smashed the furniture, tore up all the documents they could lay their hands on, and burst open the wine casks in the cellars. Only after several rioters had been drowned in the wine did Rochambeau, at the head of the Alsace Regiment, succeed in clearing the city hall. While he was not an orator, he knew how to talk to troops, and his adroit appeal to their self-interest finally took effect. *"Mes enfants,"* he told them, "these are

your papers that they are throwing out of the windows, your con-
tracts that are being tossed on to the fire. Don't stand for it. Go in
there and drive them out with the butts of your rifles."[10]

For a few minutes it was touch and go. While he was harangu-
ing troops, the rioters threw out of the window a cast-iron stove
which barely missed him. Rochambeau thought himself lucky to
have escaped with a torn uniform. The significance of these riots
did not escape him. It was not the monarchy the mob was protesting against. As yet there was no quarrel with the King, whom the
people still looked upon as their friend. Nor was their anger directed primarily at the aristocracy, but rather at the middle men,
the contractors and the rich merchants, everyone indeed who was
exploiting the common man and living off his earnings. The peasants in Alsace were just as prone to attack Jewish merchants as
aristocrats or monasteries and convents. Unfortunately the troops
shared this feeling, and though they cleared the city hall even
Rochambeau could not get them to make any arrests.

The main source of the trouble was hunger. For several years
the harvests had been disappointing, and a fierce July hailstorm
had completed the damage. There is no question that the suffering
among the poor was severe, and rightly or wrongly the peasants
and the workmen believed that the rich contractors, backed by the
magistrates and all others in authority, had been hoarding food-
stuffs for their own use, allowing everyone else to starve. In Strasbourg itself Rochambeau placed guards on the houses of all the
magistrates, and these were protected, but the troops could not be
everywhere at once, and in the surrounding country many houses
of Jews were burned, chateaux were sacked, and abbeys robbed.

Soldiers do not necessarily make the best policemen, and it is
much to Rochambeau's credit that at the age of sixty-five he managed to cope successfully with problems that were entirely new to
him. If Alsace suffered less than other parts of the country, it was
because he taught the constabulary (*maréchaussées*) and the Regular Army to work together. The city magistrates did not always

make things easy for him. On one occasion when the quick action of the troops prevented the fires started by rioters from spreading, the magistrates wished to reward them with an extra twenty sous per man. Rochambeau warned them that with an extra twenty sous per head the whole garrison would be drunk by nightfall. In spite of his warnings the magistrates insisted on giving out the money; as he had predicted, the results were disastrous. By the end of the day troops were reeling about the streets shouting "Long live the Third Estate! It is our turn to command now."

No one could have felt the breakdown of discipline more keenly than Rochambeau. In America the good conduct of the French troops had been a source of pride to him and to every one of his officers. Now many of those same men were making spectacles of themselves. Wearily he waited until the twenty sous' worth of misguided generosity had spent itself. Then he and his staff, with the help of the more reliable noncommissioned officers, toured the city, collected the wayward brethren, marched them back to barracks, and restored order. No punishments were meted out, since Rochambeau considered the magistrates more to blame than the troops, but he moved the Hesse-Darmstadt Regiment, to which most of the offenders belonged, to a camp outside the city, where they were subjected to a two weeks' course of the most relentless training he could devise.

During his whole six months in Alsace Rochambeau received no orders from Paris. The King had no Ministers, and the government was at a standstill. "Used to a life of action," he was to write later, "I passed my time at my desk, dictating to four aides de camp and two secretaries the stream of orders that had to be sent out to every corner of the province." Barely did he find time to make his rounds and hold the necessary inspections. Under these conditions his health broke down again, and he asked to be relieved.

Rochambeau was never afraid of hard work and he might have overcome the ills of the flesh, the rheumatism and the painful swelling in the legs, and stayed on at his post, if he had felt that the government was supporting him. He had succeeded in re-establishing order throughout Alsace, but the trend of events in Paris proved to him that at any moment fresh disturbances might break out which he would be powerless to control. Nor could he well adapt himself to carrying out the orders of a government which did not know its own mind and had allowed its authority to be defied by the mob. Would he not be better advised to spend his few remaining years by his own hearthside, or at least to stay there until the gathering storm had blown itself out? There was no question about his loyalty, or about his readiness to serve the King again as soon as he had recovered his health, but he must know what was expected of him, and his authority over the troops assigned to him must be clearly defined.

Notes

1. Weelen, p. 123.

2. Page Smith, *John Adams* (New York, 1962), I, 405.

3. Washington, *Diaries,* XXVIII (Sept. 7, 1785).

4. Nelly Mulard, *Calais au Temps des Lys* (4 vols.; Calais, 1961), IV, 208.

5. Asa Bird Gardiner, *Order of the Cincinnati in France* (Providence, 1905), p. 10.

6. Edgar E. Hume, *La Fayette and the Society of the Cincinnati* (Johns Hopkins Press, 1934), p. 20.

7. Rochambeau Letters (unpublished), Library of Congress.

8. *Ibid.*

9. Rochambeau, *Mémoires,* I, 351.

10. *Ibid., Mémoires,* I, 353.

Sixteen

BY THE TIME Rochambeau got back to Paris after his six months in Alsace the first stage of the Revolution was over. The royal family had left Versailles forever and had settled down to an uneasy life in the Tuileries, a cold, bleak, half-furnished palace that had not been occupied for fifty years. Technically they were not prisoners, but they were kept under the eye of La Fayette and the National Guard. For the moment the mob was in a good humor. Having marched out from Paris to Versailles, burst into the palace and brought "the baker, the baker's wife, and the baker's boy" home with them, together with wagon-loads of bread, they were now confident, quite rightly, that they had gained the upper hand. The King put as good a face on it as possible. When Bailly, the mayor of Paris, offered him the keys of the city and told him that they were the same keys that had been presented to Henri IV when he came to conquer the people, but that today it was the people who were reconquering their King, he smiled as graciously as possible and replied that he too was glad to be back with the good people of Paris. Louis XVI was a kindly man, and genuinely anxious to relieve suffering, but it is one thing to grant such reforms as you think necessary and another to have the power of granting reforms taken away from you, especially if you and your whole family have always believed that this was a sacred power entrusted to you by the Almighty. All he could do was to summon the Assembly to follow him to Paris and to live in hope that the nation, led astray for a while by evil men, would sooner or later return to their old allegiance.

In Paris the Assembly sat in the Manège, the riding school originally built for Louis XV, a long narrow building on the north side of the Tuileries Gardens. The building was torn down by Napoleon in 1802 to make room for the rue de Rivoli. No body of men ever took their duties more conscientiously than the members of the National Assembly. The King's Ministers, whose business it was to carry on the government, took their cue from the King and did nothing. Consequently the Assembly, which had been called together to draft a constitution, soon found that every question to do with government was being referred to them. Meeting as they did seven days a week with never a Sunday off, there was no time for reflection. Edmund Burke thought they worked too hard, but since every matter great or small was discussed on its own merits and with reference to first principles, this was perhaps inevitable.

As the first winter of the Revolution set in, it looked as if the coming year would mark the consolidation of reform and the beginning of peaceful constitutional government. Provided that bread did not again become scarce, La Fayette was confident that there would be no further outbreaks in Paris. The Revolution had run its course. Writing to Washington, January 12, 1790, he assures his old friend that "a new political edifice is in process of construction. Without being perfect it suffices to guarantee liberty."[1]

Rochambeau was not so optimistic. After seeing his doctor in Paris he had gone back to his château near Vendôme to rest and convalesce. Like Antaeus he always gained strength from touching his native soil. Hard on his heels came a King's messenger with letters appointing him to oversee the elections in his department. It was not a difficult task. The Vendômois was one of the districts of France that had not yet been seriously affected by the Revolution, and the name Rochambeau commanded such respect that the elections passed off uneventfully. Unfortunately, the Vendômois was no criterion for the rest of France. If Rochambeau was less confident about the future than La Fayette it was because, being a professional soldier of long experience, he was far more aware than La Fayette of what was happening in the Army.

The new spirit of fraternity represented by the so-called federations, in which the National Guard of the various districts met to swear mutual friendship, was harmless enough, but the federations had gone on to undermine the discipline of the regular forces by bringing them under the direct influence of the revolutionary clubs. Everywhere soldiers were choosing regimental committees to manage their affairs, and sending deputations to their commanders to ask for redress of their grievances. Garrisons sent deputations to each other or to the National Assembly. Sometimes the men went further, put their officers under restraint and helped themselves from the regimental chest. The new fraternal spirit in the Army produced what one observer calls "a delicious intoxication," and the immediate result of that intoxication was the disappearance of the old patriarchal relationship between officers and men.

As Rochambeau points out, the officers in many cases had brought the trouble on themselves. They had begun by applauding the National Assembly as long as they thought its decrees were directed only at the Court set, the drones who buzzed about Versailles, but they became bitter enemies of the Revolution as soon as they saw their own privileges and their own titles being swept away. Rochambeau may have exaggerated the role of the Army, but he was certainly on the right track in insisting that the current frenzy over liberty was likely to prove a serious handicap, not only to the Army but also to the monarchy and to the nation. The disorders he had seen at Strasbourg were now being repeated on a larger scale at Metz and at Nancy. In those two towns the breakdown of discipline had gone further than anywhere else. Three regiments together with the National Guard of the district had revolted against their officers, and the situation was so serious that the National Assembly had to take note of it. The Marquis de Bouillé, who commanded in this area, was ordered to collect such troops as he could rely on and suppress the insurrection at any cost. Being a man of energy he succeeded, but only at a cost of forty officers and four hundred men. The mutiny of Nancy caused such alarm that both the King and the National Assembly published their thanks to Bouillé and the troops which had served under him. Three months later the Assembly withdrew its compliments, and the ringleaders of the mutiny who had been sent to prison were set free. By that time the Revolution was gathering momentum, and the Jacobins, following their new theory that there were no enemies on the left, announced that the revolting troops had been justified. From now on it was always the officers who were guilty. *"Pas d'ennemis à gauche."*

It was this refusal of the government to back up the man in the field that eventually drove Rochambeau to resign from the Army. After six months at home he was only just recovering from the dropsy which was to afflict him off and on for the rest of his life when he was ordered to Paris to take command of the Army of the North. Never had it been more difficult for him to tear himself away from his wife and family. How far would the Assembly support him in re-establishing order throughout the Army? The experience he had had in his own province, where the King had named him one of his representatives but had then refused to back him up when he had tried to bring to justice men who had been cheating the government, was not promising. If it had not been for the insistence of his old friends, he might well have refused the appointment. As it was, he set out for his new post with a heavy heart.

From the very beginning nothing went right. The position of La Tour du Pin, the new Minister of War who had suggested his name to the King, was very shaky. Within a few months La Tour du Pin gave way to General Duportail, at one time Washington's chief of engineers, an exceptionally able man whom Rochambeau knew and liked, but he too soon gave way to someone who would prove more accommodating. The King greeted Rochambeau so coldly that the old general begged to know whether the King really wanted him to take the post he was being offered. Unless he were the King's own choice, as he had been when he was picked for the command in America, he would prefer to go back to private life. It would be uphill work under any conditions to rebuild the French Army, and the task would be impossible unless he could count on the King's entire confidence.

Rochambeau's interview with the King at St. Cloud must have taken place at about the same time Marie Antoinette was conspiring with Mirabeau for the escape of the royal family from France. No doubt Rochambeau felt, as did Mirabeau, that the Queen was the only man the King had about him, yet when the King promised him his full support, Rochambeau could not refuse to serve him. The new command, stretching from Brest to Lille, was a tremendous challenge. Under ordinary conditions he would have welcomed it, but everything was changed now. Soldiers listened to politicians now as much as to their own officers. As an old soldier himself, rough and brusque in manner, Rochambeau was too independent to submit to the interference of politicians.

In spite of his misgivings Rochambeau was glad to be back in the Army. By the end of 1790 he had rebuilt the defenses of Dunkirk and laid out the fortifications along the Sambre and the Oise, the route so often taken by the German invader. But it was not enough to put the forts in repair. He must also bolster the morale of the armies which would defend them. One evening in January, just after returning from a tour of inspection to his headquarters in Valenciennes, Rochambeau was startled by a decree put out by the Assembly permitting, even encouraging, soldiers to join political clubs. He had protested against this particular decree and he had used all his powers of persuasion on the King to prevent him from signing it, but with no success. To offset the effect of this decree he now issued a proclamation of his own, which shows far more vividly than the terse statement in his memoirs how seriously he viewed the consequences of the Assembly's "liberalism":

Mes enfants, we are all equal in the eyes of God and of the law; but take the word of an old general who has passed fifty years in the service, a soldier like yourselves, who has seen the old world and the new.

There can be no society, there can be above all, no military life without discipline and subordination. Officers should conduct themselves among their troops as fathers in the midst of their families; it is their duty to punish all those who break military regulations; and in keeping of orders approved by the King they should respect all good soldiers who serve the King loyally. The same rules apply to noncommissioned officers. If they are to win the respect of the men in the ranks they must give an example of obedience to their officers. If I have achieved some success in my profession it is due to the discipline and to the courage of the men I have commanded. If, as I hope, we are destined to win still more victories in the future, it can only be by observing the same discipline that has stood us in such good stead in the past.[2]

As for himself, faithful to his own code of ethics which forbade him from meddling in politics, he confined himself more and more to his duties in the field. He was offered, early in 1791, the office of Minister of War, but he refused it without hesitation, knowing that he had neither the strength nor the talent to struggle against the warring factions in the Assembly. At the same time he realized that the new order of things demanded wide-reaching changes in military regulations. His experience in America convinced him, as it did many others, that promotion must be open to everybody, as it had never been under the *ancien régime*. Every soldier must be encouraged to feel he had a marshal's *bâton* in his knapsack. It was while Rochambeau was in Paris, drafting these changes with the Committee on Military Affairs, that he heard the news of the King's flight to Varennes. From his point of view nothing could have been more shattering. His whole conception of duty was founded on loyalty to the King. Since the outbreak of the Revolution Louis XVI, even if he had not always been as cordial as in the past, had appeared to treat him with confidence. Now, suddenly, without a word of explanation, he had run away.

The flight of the King at midnight on June 20, 1791, was intended to place him under the protection of the Army on the frontier commanded by Bouillé. Posts of loyal cavalry should have guarded the highway from Pont-de-Somme-Vesle to Montmédy, but someone had miscalculated. It was midnight when the coach lumbered into the deserted little town of Varennes, in the Argonne. Here the relay of horses had been stupidly removed from the place the couriers had been told they would find them. There was much hunting around in the dark, and the postilions refused to go further. By the time a detachment of Bouillé's soldiers appeared on the scene, the King had been recognized, and the National Guard was beginning to assemble. It was obvious that the King could not get away without bloodshed, and Louis hated bloodshed. Wearily he gave himself up, and his wife and his children and his sister, as prisoners of the people.

The ignominy of the "capture" of the royal family was as distressing to Rochambeau as the news of their flight. Was the King's position really so desperate that his only remedy was to break every promise he had made to the people? Whatever the rights and wrongs of the situation, Rochambeau could not help reflecting on how the natural honesty of the King's character had been vitiated by those around him. While he was still wondering how to adjust himself to a monarchy without a monarch, the Assembly passed a decree requiring a new oath of allegiance. To the President's question whether or not the course of events had changed his "patriotic intentions" only one reply was possible. Of course it had not. He would return at once to his post in the North to withstand the expected attack of the Austrian army. Inspired by his example most of the Deputies, including all those who had fought under his command in America, grouped themselves around him and took the oath to defend the country and to maintain the Constitution against enemies from without and from within.

The Assembly, by this time suspicious of everybody, delegated two commissioners to accompany Rochambeau and to administer the oath to all troops in the field. Most of these commissioners were highly critical of the generals to whom they were attached, but it is significant that the two men with Rochambeau paid a remarkable tribute to the energy he had infused into his command

and to the respect and affection in which he was held by all ranks. In spite of their commendation Rochambeau found the presence of these delegates irksome and the ceremonies attending the oath slightly ridiculous. The *Moniteur Universel* carried an account of one of these reviews which happened to take place in Lille in the pouring rain. The Assembly's commissioners, their chests crossed with tricolored scarfs, climbed out of their carriages; their plumed hats looking very bedraggled, and proceeded to explain to the volunteers the sacredness of their oath to uphold the Constitution. Then followed "a charming concert" made up of the shouts of the volunteers and the clinking of bayonets. The ceremonies wound up with the distribution of new flags bearing the device *Liberty or Death.*

The exaltation of the volunteers, founded more on good intentions than on any awareness of what they were fighting for, was tempered by Rochambeau's uncompromising insistence on Army regulations. Whatever was set down he would enforce—that and nothing more. One of the battalions of the Beauce Regiment, having added a tricolored ribbon to its uniform, was confined to its quarters in Arras in spite of the protests of Robespierre, the deputy of that city. In reply to the rumble of discontent Rochambeau announced that the cockade alone was specified in the Assembly's decree, and that as long as the tricolor was not specified he would not permit it. The matter of the tricolor was only one of the many difficulties that now bedeviled him and every other general in the French Army. Rochambeau had strongly disapproved of the soldiers' clubs. The next blow was the series of laws, known as the Civil Constitution of the Clergy, which transformed the religious organization of the country by making the priests elective officials paid by the state. Those who refused to take the oath to the Constitution would be dismissed from office. Down to this time a large proportion of the *curés,* resenting as they did the wealth and the idleness of many of the bishops, had been friendly to the Revolution. Most of them were now alienated, and Rochambeau complained that the civil population, as well as many of the soldiers, were becoming more and more discontented.

The Civil Constitution of the Clergy, followed by the growing influence of the Jacobins in the Assembly, marked the beginning of what Rochambeau called "the disease of emigration." In his army it began with the resignation of a number of Irish officers, who announced that the new laws offended their conscience and that they wished to return to Ireland. The disease spread rapidly. In the last three months of 1791 more than two thousand officers, disgusted with the general state of anarchy in the Army and the breakdown of responsible government, crossed the frontier to form a new army of their own at Coblenz, with which to return to Paris, restore the monarchy, and re-establish an orderly government. Altogether the Regular Army lost about one third of its officers through emigration.

Rochambeau was not one of them. Accustomed to complete obedience imposed by social hierarchy rather than military law, he now found himself in command of an army whose discipline had been weakened by two years of licensed insubordination, an army whose officers were viewed with suspicion by their own men. Yet emigration did not seem to him the answer. So long as he was physically able he would stay at his post trying, as best he could, to postpone an offensive for which his army was totally unprepared.

The new Minister of War, the Comte de Narbonne, had devised a scheme for bringing the Revolution to an end, which seemed to Rochambeau impracticable. An attractive, liberal-minded aristocrat, loyal to the King and at the same time sympathetic to the Revolution, the Comte de Narbonne brought to his job intelligence, honesty (a quality rare among his colleagues), and a capacity for hard work. He was handicapped by being too elegant, too much a man of the *salons,* to dominate the Assembly. Nor did his friends—Talleyrand, supposedly bishop of Autun, and the Duc de Lauzun, both men of notorious morals—inspire the King and Queen with any confidence in the new Minister. This was unfortunate; Narbonne was genuinely devoted to their cause.

In the autumn of 1791, at the time he was appointed, Narbonne felt that the monarchy was doomed unless something were done to retrieve the effect of the abortive flight to Varennes. The King and even more the Queen were suspected of still being in sympathy with the émigrés, and in spite of what they said, of not being converted to the Revolution. The only way to correct that impression was to declare war. Narbonne wanted to declare a "brushfire war" which could promptly be extinguished as soon as he had gained his objectives. The gathering of émigrés on the frontier furnished a pretext for an attack on the Elector of Trier. From this expedition across the frontier the Army would return victorious and regenerated. Having acquired confidence in its officers, it would be in a position to impose its will upon the Assembly, consolidate the gains achieved by the Revolution and restore the King to power. Even if the little war he had in mind should develop into something bigger, in which France found herself at war with Austria and Prussia, the very fact that the nation was at war would make it possible to reintroduce the idea of a congress of crowned heads, which Louis XVI had always wanted, and at which he would have a chance of recovering his authority. Such was Narbonne's ingenious scheme for saving the monarchy. How much of it he divulged to Rochambeau we do not know, but apparently enough to turn him against it. Under existing circumstances the Army was not capable of carrying out any such delicate operation.

Narbonne was not to be discouraged. He began by making an extended tour of the frontier. Even Rochambeau was impressed by the thoroughness of his inspection. Following this tour he created three armies, the Army of the North under command of Rochambeau, the Army of the Center under La Fayette, and the Army of Alsace which, in a moment of aberration, he entrusted to a certain Count Luckner, a bull-headed German Hussar who had fought against France in the Seven Years' War and then, like many other soldiers of fortune, as soon as the war was over had passed into the Army of his former enemies. Luckner was a born fighter, a *condottiere* who would have been at home in the Italian wars of the fourteenth century. He might well have been picked to lead a cavalry raid, but the idea of his commanding an army was preposterous. At a staff meeting his incompetence showed up immediately. After the plan of a campaign was explained to him, he would say: *"Oui, oui, moi tourne par la droite, tourne par la gauche, et marcher vite."*[3] On one occasion, when he tried to read a speech to the Assembly, the members began laughing and Narbonne had to save the situation by taking the manuscript himself and explaining that the Marshal, as he was then, had a heart more French than his tongue. By a curious chance it was to this German swashbuckler that the "Marseillaise" was dedicated. Eventually, muddled to the last, he was sent to the guillotine.

Why Narbonne should have chosen such a man to command one of the new armies is difficult to understand, except that he was popular with the troops and he had a great reputation for patriotism. It was also a great point in his favor that he chimed in with Narbonne's idea of an immediate offensive. Not only did Narbonne pick him for an important command, he also persuaded the Assembly to promote him, along with Rochambeau, to the rank of marshal. Narbonne made a great point of the occasion and traveled to Metz to deliver the *bâtons* himself. Rochambeau's satisfaction in the promotion, which he had coveted for years, was not enhanced by the fact of Luckner's receiving it at the same time. Apart from any personal feelings, he was appalled by Luckner's readiness to commit a French army to the attack without proper preparation. When asked how he planned to make his attack, and with what troops, Luckner would not reply. He merely remarked, like all charlatans, that that was his secret.[4]

Though Rochambeau had grave doubts about Luckner's qualifications, the three commanders were on good terms with one another and with Narbonne. Rochambeau, as the most experienced and most cautious of the three, recommended taking up a defensive position. Since the enemy showed no signs of attacking, surely the winter months (1791–92) should be devoted to training. He even went so far as to suggest to Prince Albert de Taxe-Teschen, commanding the troops opposite him, that since they were both commanding untrained volunteers, it would be just as well not to start shooting among the outposts. The death of these brave young men could have no effect on the outcome of the war. The proposal was gladly accepted.[5] In the days when war was conducted according to certain fixed rules, Rochambeau's proposal not to embark on hostilities until everybody was ready was not so fantastic as it sounds. Even in our own time, in the First World War during the long period of trench warfare, there were always recognized quiet sectors in which by tacit consent each army could rest and recuperate.

Rochambeau's position was perfectly clear. He did not believe the enemy would attack, since the Prussian and Austrian armies were as unprepared as the French were themselves. In a long memorandum to the King Rochambeau urged him to avoid a foreign war which would inevitably end in civil disturbances at home. Louis XVI may well have agreed with him, since there was nothing to be gained by antagonizing nations that were friendly to him and to his house. But the King was no longer his own master, and in any event he had drifted into the habit of agreeing with the last person who spoke to him. Luckner proposed war on all sides and demanded that he be given a free hand. La Fayette refused to commit himself, but Rochambeau suspected him of supporting Luckner. So difficult was it for Narbonne to get his three generals to agree that he was on the point of resigning. It speaks well for him that Rochambeau, who did not agree with his military plans, should have begged him to stay on at his post. Without his enthusiasm and his driving energy, thought Rochambeau, the whole military machine would collapse. It was mainly because of him that France still had any Regular Army left. Even so, Rochambeau compared his task to that of Penelope. Every day the emigration of officers tended to undo the work of the day before. While the artillery and engineer officers were not so much affected, the young bloods in the infantry and the cavalry and the greater part of the old staff of the Army had either retired or emigrated. In spite of his frantic efforts to plug the gaps as they occurred, Narbonne still insisted that the Army could and would find itself as soon as it crossed the frontier and made contact with the enemy.

At the beginning of 1792 France was about to enter on a war with an army composed partly of regular soldiers of the old ré-gime, partly of volunteers who had as yet little organization and less discipline, and with a general staff whose personnel was chang-ing at each fresh outburst of suspicion. Meanwhile the poor bewil-dered Louis XVI, who could never recognize a loyal supporter when he saw one, had dismissed Narbonne from office. Though Rochambeau and Luckner both supported him and had each ad-dressed a letter to the King requesting that he be retained, the King had somehow got it into his head that Narbonne was intriguing against him. His dismissal caused a great upheaval in the Assem-bly. In the course of the next six months five Ministers of War were appointed and dismissed. The plans, good or bad, of these ephemeral Ministers were constantly overridden by an Assembly which insisted on immediate results. If they did not produce vic-tories they had to go.

The most capable of the five was General Dumouriez, a brilliant adventurer who might have been a great man if he had had any convictions beyond the importance of using the Revolution to ad-vance his own interests. Like Rochambeau, Dumouriez had served in the Seven Years' War and been wounded in the battle of Clos-tercamp. In every other respect the two men could not have been more different. While Rochambeau stuck to soldiering, Dumouriez left the Army and came back to it whenever it suited him. At one moment he entered the service of the Duc de Choiseul, who employed him on various secret missions. Apparently Choiseul lost interest in him, for after his return from a mission in Poland he was clapped into the Bastille. On his release from this not-too-uncomfortable prison he got himself appointed commandant of

Cherbourg, where he laid out the fortifications. According to Rochambeau, who was admittedly hard to please in these matters, the results were not satisfactory. Clever, restless, and enterprising, Dumouriez was certain to rise in the Revolution. After a cool survey of the political scene he joined the Girondins, the party which stood between the Royalists and the Jacobins, and when a Ministry of that party was formed it was not surprising to those who knew him to see that Dumouriez occupied the key position of Minister of Foreign Affairs. At the same time he was never thoroughly at home with the Girondins. They were idealists, they made eloquent speeches about Liberty, but they were incapable of acting swiftly and decisively. Dumouriez quickly reached the same conclusion as Narbonne—that France must declare war, or embark on a crusade if the Girondins preferred it that way, in order to achieve a sense of unity at home.

By the middle of April 1792 he had got what he wanted. As Minister of Foreign Affairs he persuaded the Assembly, and compelled the King, to declare war against Austria. The old Emperor, Leopold II, brother of Marie Antoinette, had just died. He had been too cautious to go to war to help his brother-in-law, but his son, the twenty-four-year-old Francis II, was thought to be altogether too sympathetic with his aunt in the Tuileries. Austrian and Prussian troops were concentrating on the frontier, and General Dumouriez decided the time had come to accept the challenge.

Apparently he did not consult Rochambeau, who was in Paris at the time recovering from one of his periodic bouts of dropsy. When Rochambeau finally heard of what was going on behind his back he was aghast. Such plans, he told Dumouriez, could only have been drawn up in the Petites Maisons (the well-known Paris lunatic asylum). Rochambeau could never understand that not everybody was as honest and straightforward as he. The fact that Dumouriez might be in secret correspondence with one of his generals never occurred to him.

The general in question was none other than the Duc de Lauzun

—he now called himself General Biron—a man as fond of intrigue as was Dumouriez. For some reason which he never divulged to Rochambeau, Biron had convinced himself that the Austrian Netherlands, or Belgium, was ready for a general insurrection against the Austrians, and that a general desertion could be provoked among the Austrian troops. Biron sent one of his staff to Paris, an Adjutant General Beauharnais whose wife Josephine was soon to become more famous, to treat secretly with Dumouriez. Counting on Rochambeau's being too much of an invalid to rejoin his army, he confessed that he could see no one but himself to replace the Marshal. Suddenly, to the discomfiture of the plotters, Rochambeau instead of fading out of the picture announced that he was well enough to go back to his headquarters and take up his duties. That meant that he had to be informed of the plan of campaign, which involved his army and about which he had been purposely left in the dark.

Rochambeau had been ordered to appear at the Assembly just before the declaration of war to reaffirm his loyalty to the King and to the nation, and he had availed himself of that opportunity to report on the needs of his army. Mathieu Dumas, his aide de camp in America and now a general himself, tells us that his report was received with unanimous applause. Rochambeau returned to his headquarters in Valenciennes thinking that he had made his point about the necessity of further tactical training. Except for a brief campaign in Corsica and what he called "partial" war in America, meaning that only a few thousand men had been engaged and that the casualties had been negligible, French troops had had no experience of war for thirty years. Hardly had he reached Valenciennes when a messenger, who had been traveling close behind him, delivered a new bundle of dispatches changing everything he believed to have been decided.

At the last moment Rochambeau had been overruled. Further delay was out of the question. All that was necessary for the success of the invasion was, as Dumouriez put it, "to employ celerity rather than method."[6] Rochambeau could only shake his head in despair. He would do his best to supply the "method" that Dumouriez scorned. According to the plan of campaign there were to be two real and two false attacks. La Fayette, with an army of ten thousand men which had been assembled at Givet, was to take possession of Namur, where there was only a single battalion of Walloons, which was said to be ready to desert on the appearance of the French. From then on he was to use his own judgment whether to march on Brussels or Liège. General Biron was to set out simultaneously from Valenciennes to occupy Mons. Those were to be the two main prongs of the invasion. At the same time there was to be a tentative advance from Lille in the direction of Tournai, with orders to halt if the Belgians did not seem friendly, and an advance from Dunkirk toward Furnes, "to feel the pulse of the Flemings."

The success of this sketchily planned campaign depended entirely on the effectiveness of the Dumouriez propaganda machine. The proclamations he issued are still worth reading as representing the first attempt by a French army to do something that has since become standard procedure in every revolutionary movement. Dumouriez hoped to win his objective by sapping the morale of his enemies rather than killing them. To the people of Belgium Dumouriez said: "Our armies are on your frontiers; they bring war to tyrants, and liberty to peoples. Let the Belgian lion rouse himself. People of Belgium, we swear to make you free." The appeal to the soldiers was more specific: "The French people are free. Do you want to be free too? Come over to us. How are you fed? Worse than our dogs in France. Your officers look upon you as wild beasts to be made to fight whenever it pleases them. Come, brave soldiers, come and see for yourselves the mildness of our laws. Divide up the lands and properties of the Comte d'Artois and the Prince de Condé and the other *'coquins'* [*émigrés*]. But first, stamp them out. Clean the world of these creatures, and then come to live and die with your French brothers."[7]

Dumouriez' propaganda did not work. To be successful, propaganda must have some hint of truth about it, and in this case there was none. The enemy did not throw down their arms, and the Belgian civilians did not mingle happily with the French troops, as Dumouriez had expected. On the contrary, at the first sign of resistance the hastily recruited French volunteers, believing they had been betrayed by their officers, turned tail and fled. On the evening of April twenty-eighth General Théobald Dillon, a member of the famous Irish family who had been in the service of France for a hundred years, was advancing from Lille toward Tournai when he met a small force of the enemy. Following Dumouriez' orders, since this was not intended as a genuine attack, he gave the order to withdraw. The enemy fired a few shots, whereupon his troops, suddenly panic-stricken, broke and fled back to Lille, shouting that their officers were aristocrats and that they had been betrayed. Dillon, who only the day before seemed to enjoy the respect and confidence of his men, was set upon and massacred. General Biron's experience was only slightly less disastrous. He was not murdered, but his troops were seized by the same unaccountable panic as those of Dillon. At the first sign of the enemy they broke and ran. Fortunately they headed back to Valenciennes where Rochambeau, suspecting that something of the kind might happen, finally succeeded in checking the panic and restoring order. Fortunately for France the Austrian Army was completely bewildered by its unearned success and was unable to take advantage of it.

La Fayette suffered from the same demoralization. Dumouriez complained that he could well have taken Namur, but that as soon as he heard of the disasters of the northern army he gave up and marched his troops back to Givet and did nothing. Patience in adversity was not one of his virtues. In the long stalemate that followed, his heated imagination conjured up a picture of himself, the hero of two worlds, appearing in the Assembly and by the sheer force of his personality stemming the tide of the Revolution. The National Guard hailed him enthusiastically, but the effect of his entry into the Assembly was spoiled by one of the Girondin deputies remarking that when he saw La Fayette in Paris he supposed the Austrians must have been beaten. There was nothing more to be said, and the hero of two worlds returned to his army the next day. Rochambeau could have told him to decide once and for all whether to be a soldier or a politician, but that was a decision La Fayette could never quite bring himself to make.

As for Rochambeau, the satisfaction of having been proved right in his controversy with Dumouriez was no compensation for the reverses his army had suffered. He had argued that since no one was threatening France, except for the émigré officers who had no army at their disposal, the Assembly would have been better advised to spend at least a month training the new recruits in the entrenched camps behind the frontier. Unable to answer Rochambeau's arguments, but determined on war, Dumouriez had induced the Assembly to approve what he called the plan of his campaign for the invasion of Belgium. When Rochambeau's predictions were proved true, Dumouriez blamed the failure of his plans on everybody except himself. "Rochambeau's age had blunted his faculties, and an habitual state of ill health had deprived him of all his activity." Biron was "a very brave man . . . but he did not possess great military talents." La Fayette had not carried out orders. "His ill-humour began to display itself in complaints against the ministry, and more especially the author of the plan of the campaign, which he had not executed."[8] The complaints of Dumouriez about the lack of support he received might almost have been written by Sir Henry Clinton.

Some of his criticisms of Rochambeau have been repeated by modern historians. Albert Mathiez, among others, thinks that Rochambeau was too old and that he showed a lack of energy in this campaign.[9] That was not the opinion of the men who served under him. Biron, for instance, who had never liked Rochambeau, pays tribute nevertheless to his amazing activity and to the confidence the soldiers had in him. Baron Closen, who was still his aide; Berthier, now a colonel; and Dumas, a general and a member of the Assembly had no doubts about his ability to command an army. Dumas in particular speaks of Rochambeau with the highest admiration and deplores the fact that "the ambitious Dumouriez, eager to justify by prompt and brilliant success the rashness of his political measures, disdained the prudent advice of the Nestor of our armies."[10] Certainly it is true that his health was breaking and that he was a sick man during most of the campaign, but except for Dumouriez there was no one who did not think that Rochambeau was still the ablest general in the French army. Berthier, indeed, very nearly got into trouble when he arrived at the Assembly to report that Rochambeau had requested to resign. Théodore Lameth, one of three brothers who had served under Rochambeau in America and was now a Deputy, leaped to his feet to demand that the request be refused: "The retirement of M. de Rochambeau would be a public calamity, the greatest misfortune that could befall the army."[11]

Rochambeau, however, was not to be dissuaded. The loyalty of the old soldiers who had served under him and knew him best must have given him great satisfaction, but his relationship with Dumouriez had become impossible. In his letter to the King requesting that his resignation be accepted as soon as possible, he went straight to the point. He could not remain in command of the Army as long as all the decisions were being made in General Dumouriez' office in Paris without any regard to his advice or to his recommendations. The most convincing proof of Rochambeau's qualifications in spite of his illness was that no one wanted to step into his shoes. Dumouriez offered the command to Biron, but though at one moment Biron had been intriguing against Rochambeau and hoping to take his place, he now decided that the position was too much for him. He would rather be killed as a soldier than hung as a general.

Luckner, whom Dumouriez approached next, was equally reluctant. He would have preferred to serve as second in command under Rochambeau, but Rochambeau declined this arrangement. It is amazing how many of those who had criticized him in the past hated to see him go. Even the temperamental La Fayette decided that he too would rather serve under the old general than command an army on his own. Dumouriez, aware by now that he had made a mistake in ignoring a man everybody trusted, a man who had been only too anxious to help him, tried to repair the damage by offering him the command of all troops within the kingdom, in which case he would have acted as a military elder statesman, but it was too late. Rochambeau was sick at heart as well as sick in body. The recurrent fevers and the swelling in his legs would perhaps respond to treatment, but there was no cure for the ache in his heart. His world had crumbled. He was disillusioned with the monarchy, impatient of the Girondins, and disgusted by the Jacobins. The qualities he had to offer—his competence, his indifference to public opinion, and his absolute integrity—were no longer in demand.

Notes

1. Marquis de La Fayette, *Memoirs, correspondence and manuscripts of General Lafayette* . . . (3 vols.; London, 1837), II, 422.

2. Archives de la Guerre, Dossier of the Comte de Rochambeau.

3. Captain Ramsay Weston Phipps, *The Armies of the First French Republic* (London, 1926), p. 69.

4. Rochambeau, *Mémoires*, I, 395.

5. "La Dernière Campagne du Mar. de Rochambeau," *Revue des Questions Historiques*, XXVI N.S. (July 1901).

6. General C.-F. Dumouriez, *The Life of General Dumouriez* (3 vols.; London, 1796), II, 287.

7. Albert Sorel, *L'Europe et la Révolution Française: Deuxième Partie: La Chute de la Royauté* (Paris, 1889), p. 481.

8. Dumouriez, II, 289, 299, 301.

9. Annales Révolutionnaires: Organe de la Société des Études Robespierristes. Vol. 13: Albert Mathiez, *L'Intrigue de La Fayette et des Généraux au Début de la Guerre de 1792* (1921).

10. Dumas, I, 191.

11. *Ibid.*, I, 194.

Seventeen

———◦◦∞◦◦———

ROCHAMBEAU SPENT the month of May 1792 at his house in Paris recovering from a severe attack of erysipelas and a "hydropsy of the chest."[1] Dumouriez had counted on his resigning his command, but he had not expected him to act so quickly. Nor had he anticipated the demonstrative welcome which greeted him in the Assembly. The collapse of the touted invasion and the tragic death of General Dillon proved that Dumouriez's cheery optimism was no substitute for Rochambeau's insistence on the training of recruits, and on establishing confidence between them and their officers, before demanding that they face the seasoned troops of Prussia and Austria. To offset this popularity, which threatened to undermine his own position, Dumouriez gave it out that Rochambeau had wanted the attacks to fail and that he was a member of a mysterious group of people known as "the Austrian Committee" who met in the Tuileries and directed the conduct of affairs in the interests of Austria. Actually there was no such committeee, though no doubt the Queen, if not the King, sympathized with the Austrians and may even have let the Austrian ambassador, now in Brussels, know where Dumouriez meant to attack. Rochambeau challenged the Ministry to produce any proof of Dumouriez's innuendo. He had no intention of boring the public with such rubbish, but he warned the Ministry that if they were foolish enough to bring up the case in court he would defend himself like a lion, and that he had material in his files, or as he expressed it, "artillery in his portfolio,"[2] which they might not care to face.

By the middle of June he was sufficiently recovered to travel the hundred-odd miles from Paris to his beloved château at Thoré, near Vendôme. He had never had any liking for politics or any understanding of politicians, and as he watched the steady whittling away of the King's authority he was more than ever determined to bury himself in the country and never again to become involved in public affairs. Though he was anything but an anglophile, a constitutional monarchy on the English pattern would probably have suited him better than any other form of government, but the King could never bring himself to accept that conception of his role. It was not that he was autocratic by nature. If Louis XVI had had anything of the dictator in him, he could have saved the monarchy with a "whiff of grapeshot" on more than one occasion, but that was not his way. He could be obstinate and he could be unselfish, but he could not conceive or carry out a consistent policy. Rochambeau found him impossible to serve. He invariably yielded when he should have taken a firm stand, and he dug his toes in and refused to budge when it was to his own interest to be conciliatory.

During the month Rochambeau spent in Paris, unable to leave his room, it must have wrung his heart to read in Marat's *L'Ami du Peuple* or in any of the other inflammatory journals of the day of the way the King was being provoked into vetoes which could only lead to his downfall. At the end of May, the Assembly passed a law authorizing the deportation from France of any priest who had not sworn to obey the Civil Constitution of the Clergy, if twenty voters of the canton where he lived petitioned for it. Being a deeply religious man, Louis refused to sanction this law. It went against his conscience. His Ministers begged him not to use the veto, but this was a question of principle and their arguments fell on deaf ears.

Two days later the Assembly passed another law abolishing the royal bodyguard, into which several well-known enemies of the Revolution had imprudently been admitted. The King and his friends regarded the disbanding of his household troops as a dangerous attack upon himself, but he approved this decree nonetheless, and it was carried out. Having got rid of the bodyguard, the Assembly went on to propose the formation of a camp, beneath the walls of Paris, of twenty thousand of the National Guard from all parts of France. The National Guard of Paris was offended by the implied criticism of their powers of keeping order in the capital. They got up a petition against the camp, called "the petition of the eight thousand" from the supposed number of signatures. A camp so near the city was obviously a political rather than a military move, specially designed to overawe the Court.

Once again Paris was in a ferment. The King had consented to the dissolution of his bodyguard, which from the point of view of his own safety was a great mistake, whereas he refused to sanction the decree establishing the new National Guard camp. Apparently he was influenced by the protest of the eight thousand, but whether he was morally justified in exercising the veto or not, the effect on his own fortunes was disastrous. Perhaps he realized that by now it was impossible for him to make any decision, or take any course of action, that was not disastrous. If he had not vetoed the decree about the priests, he would have condemned seventy thousand of them to deportation, and if he had authorized the camp the Assembly had in mind he would have been putting the throne, himself, and his family, at the mercy of men determined to destroy him. On the other hand, the people of the two faubourgs Saint-Antoine and Saint-Marceau, who were always impatient of the veto, were infuriated by the King's actions and spoiling for blood.

The Assembly and the King being at loggerheads, the people determined to see what they could do to end matters. On this occasion the demonstration took a peaceful form. Early in the morning of June 20 a mob headed by the formidable Santerre, a popular brewer of the faubourg Saint-Antoine, paraded through the Manège, overflowed into the garden of the Tuileries, and forced an entrance into the palace itself. The King, surrounded by a few faithful friends and accompanied by his sister Madame Elisabeth, met them with calm, stolid courage. He consented to place a red cap on his head and to drink the health of the nation, but he betrayed no weakness in the matter of vetos and made no promises to the crowd. After the baiting of the King had been going on for some hours, it began to occur to the authorities that the insurrection was hanging fire, and that if it were not to end in failure they had better pose as champions of order. Finally at six o'clock in the evening, Pétion, the mayor of Paris, who had been waiting to see what would happen, persuaded the mob to withdraw. At eight o'clock the King was able to leave the hall and rejoin the Queen, who had been undergoing similar treatment in another room of the palace.

So ended the insurrection of June 20. At first the King seemed to have profited from his ordeal, for his courage was much admired, and addresses of sympathy poured in from the provinces. At the same time the agitators and the rioters had profited too. They had learned that they could force an entrance into the Assembly and into the Tuileries without much difficulty. Given time and further organization they knew they could depose the King, overawe the Deputies, and dictate their will to the nation.

These events all took place while Rochambeau, delighted to leave Paris behind him, was rumbling across the Beauce plains in his post-chaise. He may have thought, or at least have hoped, that his own lovely countryside had not been affected by the mad bitterness of the Revolution. If so, he was very quickly disillusioned. By now the poison of class hatred was seeping into every village in France. He arrived home to find that his wife had been shrewd enough to offer to the town of Vendôme the two cannon presented to him by Congress in honor of his victory at Yorktown. Under other conditions Rochambeau would have hated to part with them, but at this moment when the foundations of his world were crumbling, the loss of these treasured souvenirs of his greatest victory was of small importance. If the Comtesse de Rochambeau thought that the authorities would be more kindly disposed to the family on account of this gift, she too was mistaken. Like so many other towns in that part of France, Vendôme was the victim of Republican fury and Royalist counterfury, which meant that there was no peace or security for honest people, whatever their political opinions might be. Any letters that reached the family were opened before being delivered, horses were stolen out of the stable, the fields were ravaged, and one of Rochambeau's personal friends, a solicitor named Chéroute, who had tried to protect his estates in his absence, was assassinated.

In spite of their hatred of him as an aristocrat the town council of Vendôme did not hesitate to call on *"citoyen Vimeur, dit Rochambeau"* when it came to defending the town against a troop of Royalists. The old marshal did what he could, but the walls of the city, extending from the château, were in ruins and it would have taken more time than he was given to construct any adequate system of defense. Such services as he was able to give did not protect Rochambeau from slanderous denunciations. In December 1792 he was obliged to go to Blois to clear himself. By that time the monarchy had been abolished. "Kings," said Grégoire, the Bishop of Blois, "are in the moral order what monsters are in the physical world." Grégoire, an ardent republican but also a zealous churchman, had just been elected president of the Convention. Rochambeau did not share the views of the Abbé Grégoire, but he respected him as a brave man who refused to abjure his religion or vote for the death of the King.

As we follow the course of the Revolution in the pages of Rochambeau's memoirs we can see that he was torn between his disgust over what was happening in Paris, the attack on the Tuileries in which the gallant General Vioménil, his second in command in America, had been mortally wounded, and his admiration for the spirit of the Revolutionary armies. Never, even in America, had he seen troops imbued with such passionate enthusiasm for the justice of their cause. What other country, asks Rochambeau, could have kept twelve armies in the field and repulsed every attempt at invasion in spite of civil war at home and treason among so many of its generals. If ever a man's patriotism was indestructible, it was Rochambeau's. His faith in the ultimate wisdom of the French people is all the more remarkable when we remember the treatment of his son in the West Indies, not to mention the tyranny to which he himself was subjected, culminating in the ordeal of the Conciergerie.

The injustice to his son afflicted him even more than his own hardships. The Vicomte de Rochambeau was just the kind of son he should have had, a *beau sabreur* utterly devoted to his profession. After serving under his father in America as lieutenant-colonel of the Bourbonnais, he had gone up the ladder until, in 1792, he was promoted lieutenant-general and appointed to the command of the Windward Islands. For the next two years he fought against the British in the West Indies with varying success, until early in 1794 he was besieged in Martinique by an overwhelmingly superior army and navy and forced to surrender. Though technically a prisoner he was accorded full honors of war and allowed to reside in America until he could be exchanged. By one of those odd coincidences which occurred more than once in the Napoleonic wars, he was exchanged with his old acquaintance General O'Hara who, after being captured at Yorktown and set free by the peace had again been captured, this time by the French, at the siege of Toulon.

On his return to France in 1796 General Rochambeau was immediately ordered back to the West Indies, to occupy that part of Santo Domingo ceded to France by the Spanish. By this time Frenchmen in the colonies were quarreling among themselves. General Rochambeau had embraced the Republican cause, and possibly for that reason he was not acceptable to the Governor. With no troops at his disposal he was not in a position to combat the civil authorities by whom he was arrested and sent back to

France. To his amazement as well as his disgust the Directory confirmed the sentence. For four years this brilliant officer who asked nothing more than to serve his country remained under a cloud, until finally Bonaparte brushed aside the charges that had been made against him, reinstated him with the rank of general of division, and used him to good effect in the Army of Italy.

Rochambeau's own treatment was even more inexcusable. The Committee of Surveillance at Blois sent him away with a certificate of good citizenship, but the village of Thoré, of which the Rochambeau château was almost a part, had its own committee of ruffians who took a savage pleasure in insulting him. They claimed the right to examine his collection of maps and deeds, and in the name of the Republic they confiscated his silver plate. The old marshal bore these indignities as stoically as he could, but he was living from day to day, and his very name and the names of the men he had been associating with counted heavily against him. By the beginning of 1793 every aristocrat was suspect. La Fayette, soon to be followed by Dumouriez, saved his own life by skipping across the frontier. Biron and Luckner were not so fortunate. Having been defeated by one of the Royalist armies, they were consigned to the guillotine. Robespierre had no use for unsuccessful generals.

The King himself was executed on January 21. If it had not been for the *émigrés* and for the "help" of the Austrian and Prussian armies he might well have survived the Revolution. There had been a reaction in his favor, but the extraordinarily inept manifesto of the Duke of Brunswick, threatening the citizens of Paris with an "exemplary and never-to-be forgotten vengeance" in the event of a further violation of the Tuileries, alienated the sympathy of the moderates and sealed the King's fate.

Rochambeau watched all these events with mingled feelings. He was proud of the French Army and generous enough to admire Dumouriez who, profiting by experience, had finally succeeded, as Rochambeau himself would have succeeded if he had been given

the chance, in forging an army worthy of France. Verdun had
fallen in September, but Dumouriez had prevented the Prussians
from marching on Paris by holding the passes of the Argonne,
through which lay their route to the capital. At the battle of Valmy
he taught the world that whatever crimes Frenchmen might commit in the name of liberty, France was still a nation to be proud of.
The Allies had expected an easy victory. The march on Paris was
to have been more of a parade than a military campaign. No one
in Vienna, Potsdam, or London dreamed that it would take them
twenty-two years to reach their destination.

Along with the *levée en masse* that provided the recruits for the
Revolutionary armies, and which Rochambeau could only compare with the crusades of St. Bernard, a life-and-death struggle was
going on in Paris between the Girondins and their ruthless opponents on "the Mountain," so called because they sat in the
highest seats of the amphitheater. The Gironde and the Mountain
were agreed upon foreign policy. Both were anxious to doom the
enemies of the Republic to death, but the massacres in Paris,
inspired by the fear of invasion and by the Duke of Brunswick's
manifesto, had raised a hopeless barrier between them. The
Girondins had not put a stop to the massacres, but they tried to
convince themselves they were blameless by protesting their
abhorrence of bloodshed. In the end they voted for the death of
the King, and again tried to hedge by recommending that the
execution be delayed. Their downfall was inevitable. Though they
were men of ability individually, and though they had a majority in
the Convention, they had shown themselves incapable of govern-
ing.

In his dry report of what was happening in Paris, Rochambeau
casually lets drop that he occupied a front-row seat at all these
tragedies. While he was not an old man by modern standards—he
was sixty-seven when the King was executed—he had acquired
something of the serene detachment we associate with old age. He
did not expect to be overlooked by Robespierre's minions, and he

was not overlooked, but it never occurred to him to emigrate or to go into hiding. On the morning of April 4, 1794, the day Danton went to the guillotine, four commissioners of the Committee on Public Safety presented themselves at the château and showed a warrant for his arrest. Rochambeau examined it carefully. Yes, he was the former marshal, a colleague of Luckner and La Fayette. Satisfied that they had the right man, the commissioners proceeded to ransack the house and to go through all his papers, in which even they could find nothing incriminating. Since they had other culprits to round up they confined the Marshal upon his own estate under the surveillance of the town council of Thoré, until their return.

Rochambeau took advantage of this delay to draw up documents in his own defense. He had been arrested in accordance with one of the most terrifying laws the Convention ever voted, the law defining suspects. All who had shown themselves partisans of tyranny and federalism (a blow at the Girondins), all former nobles, together with relatives and agents of émigrés, who had not shown constant attachment to the Revolution, were suspect. Also suspect were those who talked about the misfortunes of the Republic as well as those who, having done nothing specific against liberty, had yet done nothing for it. This extraordinary law, known as the "procuress of the guillotine," did little more than sanction what the Revolutionary Tribunal was already practicing, for any evidence was being admitted, and with the shortness of the trials the defense had become a mere farce. The only punishment the Tribunal could award was death.

By the terms of this law Rochambeau must have realized that he would almost inevitably be convicted, but he set to work methodically to build up the best defense he could. Ten days after his arrest he obtained the following certificate from the health officer of his canton: "I, citizen Ourry of Villiers canton, certify that citizen Rochambeau bears the marks of several serious wounds which he received in the various engagements in which he has

taken part; one on the left temple, one in the right thigh made by a
bullet which passed through the leg, and another in the left arm
which the said citizen Rochambeau is obliged to keep open to
protect himself from the fits of blood vomiting to which he is
subject, and which do not fail to recur when the aforementioned
wound is allowed to close—the said infirmities, together with a
swelling of the legs to which he is also subject, necessitate a very
strict diet, and do not permit him to travel."[3]

In spite of this certificate and in spite of his petition to the
Committee on Public Safety stating that his only son was at that
moment in command of Republican troops and fighting the battles
of the Republic in the West Indies, the representatives of the
Committee, on their return to Vendôme, added Rochambeau—
with his servant and his secretary, who refused to leave him—to
the haul of suspects they had already made and drove them all to
the jail in Chartres. There they deposited the less important members of the batch, and drove on to Paris with the prize victims. On
the twenty-first of April the dreary procession wound its way along
the banks of the Seine to the Palais de Justice. As a dangerous
enemy of the Republic Citizen Vimeur Rochambeau, the last man
to be appointed a Marshal of France by Louis Capet, was to be
housed in the Conciergerie.

The great pile of buildings on the Quai de l'Horloge known as
the Palais de Justice may well claim to include the most beautiful
chapel, as well as the most infamous prison, in France. The Kings
of France, who built the palace and occupied it up to the end of
the fourteenth century, were determined that the Sainte Chapelle
and the Conciergerie were to be models of their kind. It was a wise
decision, since the chapel and the prison, representing security in
this world and the next, were the most essential elements in a
feudal castle. Today the very word *Conciergerie* conjures up visions of human degradation, but it was not always so. John
Howard, the English philanthropist who visited the Conciergerie in
1783, found it a very up-to-date institution, far better than most of

the prisons in his own country. He gives the credit (there is an unconscious irony in his tribute) to the King. Shortly after he came to the throne, Louis XVI had made a tour of the prisons of Paris and had come to the conclusion that they were unworthy of the most civilized nation of Europe. Howard declares that the King's declaration on the subject, dated the thirtieth of August 1780, "contains some of the most humane and enlightened sentiments respecting the conduct of prisons."[4] Howard was particularly impressed by the airy paved courtyard "with a fine piazza" where the prisoners were allowed to exercise and by the fact that a benevolent society issued clean linen to the prisoners once a week.

If he had visited the Conciergerie eleven years later, at the time Rochambeau was admitted, he would have had a very different story to tell. By that time there were seven thousand prisoners herded together in the ten prisons of Paris (in Howard's day there were fewer than a thousand), and the Conciergerie, through which all suspects passed on their way to the Revolutionary Tribunal, had become known as the "vestibule of the guillotine." Howard describes the jailers he talked with as being men of a good class, generally honest and humane, but the jailers who received Rochambeau looked and acted like executioners. They treated him as a common criminal who had already been condemned to death, and they were going to leave him in the prison courtyard until the tumbrils called for him when a few old soldiers insisted that he be given a corner in their room.

There were two categories of prisoners in the Conciergerie, the *pistoliers,* who paid for their room and board, and the *pailleux,* who slept on straw in the courtyard, which was changed once a month, and who, not being able to pay for their food, were fed on bread and soup.

In these horrible surroundings Rochambeau was delighted to hear a friendly voice: "Good heavens, Monsieur le Maréchal, what are you doing here?" It was Malesherbes, a former minister and one of the outstanding liberals of the day. Although the King had never followed his advice when he was minister, Malesherbes had offered to defend him before the Convention, and it was because of his eloquent speech on that occasion that he now found himself in the Conciergerie. The principal charges against him were, first, that he had defended the King, in itself a treasonable act, and second, that the defense had been subsidized by Pitt's Cabinet. When he was confronted with these charges, Malesherbes remarked to a friend who stood near him: "Surely they could have put a little more semblance of truth into them."[5]

Only a day or two after Rochambeau's arrival at the Conciergerie the tumbrils called for Malesherbes, his daughter, his son-in-law, and their children—as many of the family as Robespierre had been able to lay his hands on. Along with them went three of the famous orators of the Revolution: Thouret, at one time president of the Assembly; Chapellier, a prominent member of the Jacobin Club; and d'Esprémesnil, a dark, fiery man with a silvery voice who had been an important figure at the meeting of the States-General and had afterward developed a hatred of all reform. Rochambeau knew them all, though perhaps not so intimately as their warm welcome seemed to indicate. In the Conciergerie all acquaintances became old friends. Two duchesses, the Duchesse de Grammont and the Duchesse de Châtelet, went up before the Revolutionary Tribunal at the same time as the Malesherbes family and the three deputies. It was a good batch. They were all convicted and sentenced to death within half an hour. In the old days Fouquier-Tinville, the public prosecutor, had liked to conduct matters formally, but the guillotine had warmed to its work by now, and there was no time for legal niceties. Suspects were tried and convicted *en bloc*.

Like many others, Rochambeau was struck by the extraordinary gaiety of the prisoners. Only a minority of those condemned could be called aristocrats, and many of the victims were men and women of humble origin who had somehow fallen foul of the all-powerful Committee of Public Safety. Not all of those arrested were innocent—some of them were really guilty of high treason. Nor did they all act like heroes. Madame du Barry was one of those who shrieked and begged for one more minute as she was being dragged to the tumbrils, but generally speaking the guillotine brought out the best in its victims. It was as if, while the Revolution was trying to make a clean sweep of the past, even changing the calendar to help the nation get rid of "superstition" by effacing Sundays and saints' days, the prisoners, knowing they were marked for death, were determined to maintain not only their own time-honored code of behavior but also the tradition of graceful gaiety that had always made French society the envy of Europe. So it was that even after they had been condemned, they talked and flirted, played cards and dominoes, supped and drank, recited poetry, sang, listened to music, and in other ways behaved as civilized people in every walk of life have always behaved in their hours of relaxation.

Rochambeau quotes the story of Malesherbes stumbling over a step as he went up before the Revolutionary Tribunal. "This is what they call an evil omen," he remarked. "A Roman, if he were in my place, would go no farther." On the way to the guillotine he offered his arm to his daughter, who was then murdered before his eyes. The Duc de Lauzun, now known as General Biron, was another of those who remained in character to the end. Though in a moment of weakness he had thrown in his lot with the Revolution, as a former *grand seigneur* he was suspected of still being in sympathy with his old associates. He had already passed through the "vestibule of the guillotine" before Rochambeau had arrived, but the story of his death must have gone the rounds of the Conciergerie. It seems that the executioner had interrupted him while he was enjoying a particularly good dinner. "You don't mind if I finish my oysters?" said Lauzun, at the same time offering him a glass of wine. "Your business must make you thirsty."[6] The executioner was only too ready to oblige, and the two men spent a pleasant half-hour together before getting on with the day's work.

After the first few days in the Conciergerie, when it was obvious that he was a very ill man, Rochambeau managed to have a surgeon look at his wounds. The surgeon insisted that his patient be transferred to the Archbishop's hospital. The old wounds, which had been bothering him for so long, may well have saved his life. The physical care he received in the hospital was at least adequate, and the fresh air and the clean rooms a welcome relief after the stench of the Conciergerie. With him in the prison van from the Conciergerie came Loménie de Brienne, the ex-Minister whom Rochambeau had not thought much of when he was in power but whom adversity had transformed into a friend, and a number of members of the Montmorin family whom Rochambeau had also known, and whose daughter had married a son of La Luzerne. The Montmorins had been accused of sheltering in their cellar Rochambeau's former second in command, the Baron de Vioménil, who after being wounded in the Tuileries had dragged himself to their house to die.

The party, including a few convalescents already in the hospital, amounted to thirteen in all. Rochambeau was delighted when he found they were to have two rooms allotted to them, and for two weeks they forgot they were prisoners as well as patients and enjoyed the comparative privacy of their two rooms. Then the blow fell. "Fifteen days after our arrival," Rochambeau writes, the court bailiffs brought us twelve writs of accusation, which really amounted to twelve burial certificates. Those twelve were to accompany Madame Elisabeth, sister of Louis XVI, to the Tribunal the next morning. I was leaning on my stick, waiting for my name to be called, when the head bailiff, accompanied by the hospital surgeon, called out to me: 'You did not hear what I said when I came in, Marshal? There's nothing for you.' 'I'm deaf,' I replied, 'but it won't hurt you to say it again.'"[7]

For some reason Rochambeau's name had been omitted. No
doubt he would be included in the next batch. He spent the night
going over the prisoners' writs of accusation with them, and the
next morning they embraced and said their last good-bys with a
courage that stayed with them and helped disguise the horrors of
the guillotine. Two days after the execution of these twelve friends
Rochambeau was brought back to the Palais de Justice to be questioned, in the presence of the public prosecutor, by Gabriel de Liége,
a trail judge. The books of the Conciergerie recorded that he had
been jailed under the title of "the last Marshal of France by the appointment of the last tyrant."[8] At this period, in the spring of 1794,
when the Revolutionary Tribunal was dispatching nearly a thousand victims a month, that entry against his name might well have
condemned him, but De Liége seems to have been one of the
unusual judges of this court in that he demanded evidence of
guilt.

A prolonged examination by the registrar of the court elicited
facts about Rochambeau's career, and more especially his recent
activities, that convinced De Liége, as it must have convinced even
Fouquier-Tinville, that they had no case against the old marshal at
all. It appeared that since resigning from the Army he had been
living quietly at home. He had not corresponded with La Fayette
since La Fayette had fled the country, nor did he have any children
who were émigrés. On the contrary his only son, now a general in
the Army, was at this moment serving the Republic in the Windward Islands.

De Liége concluded the questioning by reminding Rochambeau
of the letter of resignation which he had sent to the National
Assembly, saying "that he recalled it very well as having been
widely applauded at the time." Rochambeau's spirits began to rise.
Since the judge admitted that he had nothing against him and that
he could not understand why he had been arrested, Rochambeau
began to hope that he might be set free, but that was asking too
much of the court. The Revolutionary Tribunal was jealous of its

authority. In the interests of liberty it might hurry prisoners to the guillotine, but it must not itself be hurried. Those who pressed for their release too urgently were suspected of trying to interrupt the course of justice and were very likely to be judged guilty of starting a prison conspiracy.

For the next three months, while Rochambeau was wondering whether his release would ever come through, the Revolutionary Tribunal was more active than ever. Robespierre seems to have had no difficulty in persuading the great mass of Frenchmen, himself among them, that he was leading the nation to victory and safety and that the only alternative to the guillotine was the sword of foreign despots. His policy was to keep order by regulated terror. Probably he would have liked to restrain the bloodshed, but new enemies of the Republic were always cropping up, and he discovered, like all dictators, that having started along a certain track he had to go on to the end.

In April, May, and June 1794, Robespierre's power was absolute. He seemed to be more incorruptible, more invulnerable than ever. Women, money, pleasure, or relaxation of any kind played no part in his life. There was only one danger he could not guard against, and it proved fatal. The men who were supposed to be supporting him were terrified. Fouché, the butcher of Lyon; Barras and Fréron, the butchers of Marseilles and Toulon; and most of all Tallien, who had hounded the Girondins to their death, and whose mistress, the beautiful Terésa Cabarrus, was already on trial, knew that it was his life against theirs, and that they must act quickly. Robespierre knew he was in danger but he made the fatal mistake of threatening instead of striking. On the eighth Thermidor (July 26) he made a long, rambling speech in the Convention about immorality and public virtue, concluding with vague denunciations of all counterrevolutionaries.

The effect of this speech was electric. Every man in the Convention felt that he was standing on the edge of an abyss. Joseph Cambon, the watchdog of the Treasury and one of the most honest

men in the Convention, rose to reply: "What paralyzes the Republic is the man who has just spoken." His courage proved con-
tagious. The decision to print and distribute the speech, as Robespierre had demanded, was repealed, and he sank back on his seat
murmuring, "I am a lost man." From then on events moved
quickly. He made the same speech that evening before the Jacobin
Club, where it was received with some enthusiasm, but he was
never again able to get the ear of the Convention. On the following
day, whenever he tried to speak he was howled down. His voice
grew hoarse with the effort. "The blood of Danton is choking
him," shouted one of Danton's friends. An obscure member proposed his arrest, and it was voted unanimously. Though he was
rescued from prison and taken to the Hotel de Ville, the strong
men in the Convention were not to be thwarted. The National
Guard forced its way into the Hotel de Ville, seized Robespierre
(who had tried to commit suicide) and a few of his supporters,
and delivered them to the Revolutionary Tribunal. The fact that
Robespierre was an outlaw was quickly proved. There was no need
for a trial. He was executed with his brother, with Saint-Just, and
nineteen adherents on the evening of the tenth Thermidor (July
28). Only two days before he had been all-powerful. Men trembled when he looked at them. Now, within forty-eight hours, he
was a broken man going to his death.

These events took place so quickly that the prisoners in the
Conciergerie can hardly have known what was happening, but the
announcement of Robespierre's death must have caused an explosion of joy in all the prisons. Even more welcome was the arrest of
Fouquier-Tinville, the public prosecutor, who had sent more innocent victims to their death than any other man in Paris. Fouquier-
Tinville was impeached on August first, three days after the death
of Robespierre. Rochambeau hurried to the bedside of an old
friend and former president of the Assembly, Angran d'Alleray,
who had received his writ of accusation the day before, and told
him the good news. "Well, then," said the old man, smiling, "the

ticket I have in my pocket isn't good any longer." His brother, not so fortunate, had been sentenced to death, for sending money to émigrés, only a few months before.

The prisoners were right in thinking that the death of Robespierre signaled the end of the Reign of Terror, but the prison gates opened slowly, and it was months before Rochambeau got his release. The farmers and workmen, as obviously innocent, were sent back to their villages first. Rochambeau would have preferred their society to that of the cutthroats and criminals who took their places, but he was a patient man and he knew he must wait until the new president of the court and the new public prosecutor had had a chance to visit the prison. Finally they came, and he went over the old ground all over again. He had fought for liberty in two continents, he had never had any dealings with émigrés, and he had never conspired in any way against the Republic. Those facts had all been established. "I do not doubt," he wrote the president of the court after still another month had gone by, "that you are very busy, but I cannot believe that in this era of equality a former aristocrat has no rights except to march to the scaffold before anybody else, and to be the last man to be allowed to prove his innocence. Those are not the principles I learned from Washington, my colleague and my friend, when we were fighting side by side for American independence."[9]

This last appeal struck home. The president of the court knew that Rochambeau should never have been arrested, and there was no excuse for detaining him any longer. On the sixth Brumaire (October 27), after an ordeal that had dragged on for six months, the Revolutionary Court ordered that Jean-Baptiste-Donatien Vimeur Rochambeau be released at once. The doors of the Conciergerie swung open, and "the last Marshal of France by order of the last tyrant" walked out a free man.

Notes

1. Rochambeau, *Mémoires,* I, 419.
2. *Ibid.,* II, 420.
3. Archives Nationales. W 475, No. 317.
4. John Howard, *The State of the Prisons* (Everyman Edition, 1929), p. 126.
5. J. M. Allison, *Malesherbes* (New Haven, 1938), p. 165.
6. Lauzun, *Mémoires,* p. 36.
7. Rochambeau, *Mémoires,* II, 40.
8. *Ibid.,* II, 41.
9. *Ibid.,* II, 50.

Eighteen

———•◦◦∞◦◦•———

I N THAT STRANGE welter of idealism, stupidity, heroism, and
cruelty that goes to make up the French Revolution, nothing
is more striking than the way those who had been imprisoned
and who, like Rochambeau, had brushed the guillotine came
home and took up their lives again as if nothing had happened. It
is often said that the wounds of the Revolution have never healed
and that those who know France well can still see the scars, but it
would seem to be the grandchildren who looked back and nursed
their grievances rather than the sufferers themselves. When asked
what he had done during the Revolution the Abbé Sieyès is said to
have replied, "I lived through it." Rochambeau might have made
the same reply. He was glad to be alive, and though he would not
have denied the horrors of the Conciergerie, there was much that
he could look back on with pride.

It was characteristic of him to dwell on the heroism of Malesherbes and Madame Elisabeth and not to pass judgment on the
Deputies, many of them friends of his, who had acquiesced in the
travesty of justice that sent Malesherbes and Madame Elisabeth to
their death. An easy way for Frenchmen to free themselves of
any sense of guilt for the crimes of the Revolution was to find a
scapegoat. Fortunately the scapegoat was ready at hand. It was
Robespierre. To him and to his satellites every crime was at-
tributable. The French people were not guilty.

Patriotism may not be enough for some of us, but it was enough
for Rochambeau. France in her adversity was still a *nation unique*.
Never had his country seemed to him move lovable or more ad-

mirable. At home once more, in his own library overlooking the river Loir, surrounded by his books and maps, he became so absorbed in the wars of the Revolution and the Empire that when, at the request of his son, he sat down to tell the story of his life he ended by chronicling the exploits of the French Army. For the readers of his memoirs this is disappointing. When he is writing about his own campaigns in Germany, in America, and more recently in Flanders, we follow him eagerly step by step, but the secondhand accounts of Napoleonic victories that filtered down to Vendôme through the Paris newspapers and found their way into the memoirs are not what we want from him. No doubt Rochambeau would have argued, and he would have been quite wrong, that from the moment he left the Conciergerie he was a private citizen again and that his personal affairs could be of no interest to posterity.

We learn that he and his friend Foulon d'Écotais, a former Intendant of Martinique, were set free by the same writ. They had traveled together as suspected enemies of the Republic, shepherded by Robespierre's agents, from Chartres to Paris, and they drove home together as free men. What were their impressions, what did they talk about? All the trivial details about the homecoming that we long to hear Rochambeau keeps to himself. He would have said that he wrote his memoirs as a contribution to French history, not as a human-interest story.

Except for the references to his son in the West Indies, Rochambeau has nothing to say about his family, and tantalizingly little about himself. Nor does he give us any insight into such things as the life of a country gentleman at the end of the Revolution. How did he get on with the petty officials of Vendôme who had so recently ransacked his château? The Rochambeaus had always been one of the great families of the neighborhood. When he had resigned from the Army and come back to live among his own people, *Monsieur le maréchal* was the most respected man in the community. Then, gradually, the atmosphere had changed. As an aristocrat he came to be considered an enemy of the people, even before the Committee on Public Safety had trumped up their charges against him and condemned him to the Conciergerie. With Robespierre's death the wheel of fortune had come full circle again. The Vendômois greeted him as their most distinguished citizen, a man they were delighted to honor.

Even though the Paris prisons emptied very gradually, the reaction had set in long before he reached home, and so far as possible the wrongs were being set right. It is significant that Rochambeau had no difficulty in adding to his estates. He had been a great landowner before the Revolution, and on his return home he took advantage of the sale of national properties to acquire four more tenant farms.[1] Not only Rochambeau, but everybody else in his little world, the farmers and peasants as well as the landowners, was anxious to wipe out the memory of the class hatred engendered by the Reign of Terror and to get back to the orderly hierarchical life of the past. The pretext for the Terror had been the fear of invasion, and now as everyone knew, the victorious armies of the Republic were dreaded by all Europe.

In other parts of France, particularly in the South, a new White Terror, supposed to be connected with a revivalism of royalism, took the place of the Red Terror, but in the Vendômois passions seem to have cooled more quickly. The Republic was a going concern. It had come to stay. Its gains must be consolidated, but the structure of society was to remain the same.

Granted that Rochambeau is far too reticent for modern taste, when it came to drafting his will he could not help revealing himself. This document is dated July 1, 1805, the day on which he completed his eightieth year. Since no letters between Rochambeau and his wife have yet come to light, what he says about her in his will is worth repeating: "I give to my wife the use of all that I possess. After fifty-five years of the happiest marriage, and after having received from her a large dowry which has been spent upon my estate, this is the least expression of gratitude that I can show her. In addition I give and bequeath to her all that the law allows me and will allow me to give her. I desire my children and grand-children to show every confidence in her and to do away with any expense of inventory. She has proven herself worthy of this trust."[2]

From this charming tribute, along with the short passage in the Memoirs about their marriage, which is the only other occasion on which Rochambeau mentions his wife, we can assume that they were a most devoted couple. We would like to know more about the Comtesse, but evidently she did not care to be known outside the family. The only letter of hers which survives, and which is now in the Library of Congress, was written to President Washington, November 18, 1790, soliciting membership for Baron von Closen in the Society of the Cincinnati. Washington replied with his usual courtesy that he would like to grant her request, but that the Society had decided to refer such applications from "Gentle-men of the French Nation" to Counts Rochambeau and D'Estaing and to the Marquis de La Fayette, who were better acquainted with the merits of their countrymen.[3] It would be interesting to know why the Comtesse wrote to Washington about Closen when her own husband could have told her the answer, that membership in the French branch was restricted to officers of the rank of colonel or higher. Possibly she did not want to bother Rocham-beau, who had just taken command of the Army of the North and who, though he was devoted to Closen, presumably had other and more important things on his mind than Closen's membership in the Cincinnati. Eventually the matter must have come up to him, for it was finally agreed in February 1791 that all French lieu-tenant-colonels or majors of that date would be eligible for mem-bership. The appointments of Baron von Closen and thirty-six other officers were approved by the King early the next year. It was the last appointment to the Order that Louis XVI was des-tined to make.

That the Comtesse de Rochambeau had her admirers is indi-

cated by the dedication to her of a poem about Yorktown. *"La
Double Victoire,"* as this poem was called in honor of the "double
victory," on land and sea, of the French and American forces, is
the work of Caron du Chanset, an obscure Paris journalist of the
day. The poem has no great literary merit, but as the editor of the
recent reprint, Howard C. Rice, Jr., of the Princeton University
Library, points out, its very timeliness makes it interesting! "Caron
du Chanset was less concerned with what he said or how he said it
than he was with getting his story into print while it was still
'news'. . . . Cornwallis surrendered at Yorktown in Virginia on
October 19, 1781. The Royal Censor's permit to print Caron du
Chanset's poem is dated December 15, 1781. *'La Double Victoire'*
must therefore have been in the hands of some readers, at least, by
New Year's Day 1782. Perhaps, indeed, the author intended it as
an *étrenne* for the Comtesse de Rochambeau, to whom he dedicated it. It was quick work, in every sense of the word."[4]

Rochambeau's will also tells us something about his three
grandchildren. During his son's imprisonment in England, which
lasted for seven years, these grandchildren, Augustine, Thérèse-
Constance, and Philippe de Vimeur, had lived with their grand-
parents. The daughter-in-law had received Fouché's permission to
join her husband in England, and the arrangement that the grand-
parents should bring up their children must have suited everybody.
When they were old enough to marry, the Comtesse picked out
suitable husbands, and Rochambeau gave them each a good
dowry. To Philippe the grandson, who was studying at the artillery
school in Strasbourg, he bequeathed the château and most of the
property, "in view of how little my son cares for the property."
That one sentence in the will conjures up a familiar picture. We
can imagine the old man shaking his head as he reflects on the
changing times. To him the Rochambeau château and the surrounding countryside was home, the spot that beckoned to him in
all his dreams. Evidently his son had different tastes. Rochambeau
would not saddle him with a property he did not want.

General Rochambeau, to distinguish him from his father the Marshal, remains something of an enigmatic figure. His father was proud of him, and he was certainly a capable officer, but he was not popular in the Army, possibly because he was one of those who had changed his allegiance from the monarchy to the Republic too quickly. When the news of the King's execution reached Martinique, General Rochambeau had immediately posted addresses of congratulation to the Convention throughout the island. This anxiety to conform to whatever party was in power made no difference to Napoleon, but it was not forgotten by his brother officers.

After serving with distinction in the Army of Italy he was again sent to the West Indies for the third time, this time as second in command to General Leclerc, the husband of Napoleon's sister Pauline. When Leclerc died of yellow fever, General Rochambeau took his place as commander-in-chief of the Army of Santo Domingo, and in the following year he was promoted to captain-general of the colony. Again, there was no question about his ability, but he made an unenviable reputation for himself, not only with the black population but also with the French colonists, many of whom were still loyal to the old order. Though he succeeded in stamping out the struggle for freedom headed by the Negro patriot, Toussaint l'Ouverture, he was himself driven out of Santo Domingo by the British and compelled to surrender.

During the next seven years General Rochambeau was a prisoner in England, and his father never saw him again; that was the great sorrow of his old age. No doubt the grandchildren made the house gay, but they could not compensate for the absence of one who, even if he had drifted away from the family, was still very dear to him, and who was now wasting away the best years of his life in an English prison. In desperation Rochambeau wrote to Cornwallis in the hope that, remembering how well the French had treated him after his capitulation, he might use his influence to get the son of his old enemy exchanged. There was no answer to his

appeal. Cornwallis died in India in 1805, and the letter probably
never reached him.

The General was not exchanged until 1811, four years after
Marshal Rochambeau's death. Napoleon did not make use of him
at once, but after the Russian campaign, when he was short of
officers, he called him to the colors again and gave him command
of the 19th Infantry division of the 5th corps. It was at the head of
this division that he was mortally wounded in the battle of Leipsic.
During this last campaign of the year the Emperor made up for his
previous neglect of General Rochambeau by making him a Baron
of the Empire and awarding him the Officer's Cross of the Legion
of Honor. Nothing could have given his father greater pleasure.

Rochambeau was one of Napoleon's most uncritical admirers.
Others might admire the Emperor and yet admit his mistakes—his
treatment of the Pope, his cruelty to Toussaint l'Ouverture, or the
unforgivable execution of the Duc d'Enghien—but so far as Rochambeau was concerned there were no faults. This was partly due
to his ignorance of what was going on, either in France or abroad,
except what he read in the government-controlled press. But there
was another reason as well. On the rare occasions Rochambeau
went to Paris, Napoleon loaded him with honors. Nobody knew
better than the Emperor how to win men to his side. The old
marshal was presented to him first in 1801. Rochambeau had been
in correspondence with Fouché about his sister, who had gone to
Switzerland with her husband in the early days of the Revolution
and had been living there ever since on account of his health.
When she wanted to return to France after the death of her husband, Madame Dessales found herself classed as an émigré. Rochambeau had pleaded her case with Fouché, and after a great
many letters had passed to and fro the barriers were let down and
the sister was allowed to come back.

It was on this occasion that the well-known interview took
place. The First Consul, as he then was, received Rochambeau
with "the greatest distinction" in the presence of Berthier and a

number of other officers. "General," cried Napoleon, "here are your pupils!" Rochambeau rose to the occasion magnificently. "The pupils," he replied, "have far surpassed their master."[5]

Two years later, at the first meeting of the Council of the Legion of Honor, he was unanimously elected a member of the new Order. Gratified as he was by what he considered a tribute to his old age, he begged that the honor might go to his son rather than to himself, but this suggestion did not meet with approval. Napoleon was not to be argued with, even on matters of detail. Rochambeau had already been offered, and had refused on account of deafness, a flattering appointment to the Senate. Accordingly, when by a stroke of the pen Napoleon created a new peerage, complete with dukes, counts, barons, and chevaliers, and at the same time proclaimed Rochambeau *"ancien maréchal de France"* and grand officer of the Legion of Honor, there was nothing for it but for him to accept. The Emperor was determined to link the old aristocracy with the new, and if Rochambeau had refused to go along with him, it might very well have jeopardized the chances of his son ever being exchanged.

Nonetheless he did respectfully decline, on account of his infirmities, Napoleon's invitation to attend his coronation. He hoped that the Emperor would excuse him. He was in his eightieth year, crippled with gout and rheumatism, and in no condition to drag himself to Paris, even for this great occasion. He would of course be proud to take the oath of allegiance, and to accept the grand cross of the Legion of Honor. Napoleon sent him the insignia, which were delivered to him while he was in bed, suffering from one of his worst attacks of gout. The story is that Rochambeau himself pinned on his shirt the five-pointed star bearing the device *Honneur et Patrie.* As he lay back in bed he might well have reflected that his whole life had been built around those two words.

There were not many of his contemporaries of whom that could be said. Some had gone into exile because they associated the idea of *honneur* with a king rather than with the *patrie*. Some, who had crossed the ocean with him to fight for American independence and who had returned to France imbued with new ideals of freedom, had become disillusioned with freedom and had lost faith in their country. The guillotine had taken its toll of others. Like many of his friends, Rochambeau had sympathized with the Revolution in its early stages. Later he had been appalled by its excesses, but he had never, even when confined in the Conciergerie, wavered in his devotion to the *patrie* or in his faith in the ultimate sanity of the French people.

Just after his return from Alsace he had written a letter to Washington reminding him of their first dinner together. The French officers had burned their mouths on the soup, while the Americans waited until it cooled. "Our nation has not changed since then," says Rochambeau; "we go very fast—God will we come at our aims."[6] Washington's reply had been encouraging: "If there shall be no worse consequence resulting from too great eagerness in swallowing something so delightful as liberty, than that of suffering a momentary pain, or making a ridiculous figure with a scalled mouth, upon the whole it may be said you Frenchmen have come off well, considering how immoderately you have thirsted for the cup of liberty."[7] The consequences of swallowing liberty too quickly had unfortunately been more serious than Washington had foreseen, but he had said what Rochambeau wanted to hear.

Rochambeau's last letter to Washington, February 6, 1796,[8] was written in a different vein. As the Revolution pursued its course, American enthusiasm for France had cooled. The churches in America denounced French atheism and French savagery. British agents were making the best of the situation, and a treaty favorable to the British interpretation of the rights of neutrals was signed in 1794. By 1795, America and France were not far from a state of war. Rochambeau lamented the state of friction between the two countries. He complained that the government of the

United States was drawing near to England, "which has always been the enemy of France." There was something childlike, or at least very unworldly, in his approach to foreign affairs. Forgetting that allies drift apart, sometimes with regret and sometimes with a sigh of relief, as soon as the common danger is removed or the common objective won, he had assumed that the loyalty, affection, and respect he and Washington felt for each other would forever hold true for their two countries as well.

In his own profession Rochambeau was very much a realist, but when he ventured into politics the wish became father of the thought. It was natural enough that it should be so. France had passed through the furnace of the Revolution, and a new nation was rising phoenixlike from the old. He had good reason to be proud of his country. As an old soldier he took immense satisfaction in the succession of Napoleonic victories, but there was more to it than that. The Emperor had harnessed the traditions of the monarchy to the ideas of 1789. The new laws and the new institutions were obviously more equitable than the old. Surely everyone must feel, as he did, that France, after all she had been through, was once more marching in the van of civilization.

Rochambeau was fortunate, more fortunate than most of those who were dazzled by Napoleon, in that death came to him at the right time, before the cracks in the façade of the empire had begun to show. The spring of 1807 was late in coming. It was a wet spring, and Rochambeau, sitting in the window of his library, watching for the first signs of good weather, caught a bad chill. Sieur Fournier, the doctor from Vendôme, prescribed the usual remedies, but this time the usual remedies failed to work. The cough persisted and the heart began to falter. The eighty-three-year-old marshal had come to the end of the road. He died on the twelfth of May at two o'clock in the afternoon. It was an easy death. At one moment he was comfortably ensconced in his armchair, reading the newspaper and exchanging a word now and then with the Comtesse. Then, suddenly, he slipped away.

It could hardly be called a tragic death. Not many men of his age were able to contemplate the past and peer forward into the future with such equanimity. His son was still a prisoner. That was a sorrow, but eventually he would be exchanged and in the meantime he had just heard that his grandson, twenty-year-old Philippe, had distinguished himself on the field of battle. Marshal Davoust had written him about the young man, how he had had his horse killed under him in a cavalry charge and how he had then endeared himself to a company of grenadiers by plunging into their midst and leading them in an attack on an enemy battery.

How familiar it all was and how true to the family tradition! The old man could close his eyes and think back to that day, more than sixty years ago, when he had first ridden across the Rhine to fight the battles of France. Perhaps, as he sat there in his pleasant room turning over the pages of his mind, he thought too of the American adventure, of his aide, that clever fellow Berthier who was now the great man's chief of staff, of the headstrong young La Fayette, back in France again, they told him, but he should never have emigrated; of his good friend De Grasse, who had met with such misfortunes; of the utterly reliable General Washington and of the long road to Yorktown. Yes, it had been a good life. He could say, like Ulysses, that he had been a part of all that he had known, even of the terrible convulsion which had swept away the old monarchy. Friends sometimes asked him about his six months in the Conciergerie, but he did not remember them very clearly. Recent events were blurred in his mind. Anyway he was at home now, looking out through the windows at the winding Loir. What glorious news that was about Philippe! He would be home soon now, and by that time summer would be here again and the sun would be shining.

Notes

1. Weelen, p. 176.
2. Weelen, p. 185.
3. Closen, p. xxx.
4. Caron du Chanset, *La Double Victoire* (intro. Howard C. Rice, Jr., Washington, 1954).
5. J. F. Michaud, *Biographie Universelle* (Paris, 1843–1865).
6. Rochambeau Papers, Library of Congress (April 11, 1790).
7. Washington, *Writings*, XXXI (August 10, 1790).
8. Rochambeau Papers, Library of Congress (February 6, 1796).

Bibliographical Note

Rochambeau's life can be conveniently divided into three periods —before, during, and after the Revolution. For the first and third periods the main sources of information are Rochambeau's memoirs, and the life by Jean-Edmond Weelen, translated by Lawrence Lee (New York, 1936). Mr. Weelen includes in his biography an unpublished journal by Rochambeau's son dealing with the war in America. The Archives de la Guerre at Vincennes, and the Archives Nationales in the Hotel de Soubise, Paris, contain important information about Rochambeau's military career. Rochambeau's memoirs are disappointing. Except for the passage in Volume 2 in which he describes his six months in the Conciergerie, he confines himself largely to a chronicle of historical events. The two volumes run to 794 pages, of which only 80 deal with his experiences in America.

For the two and half years he spent in this country, from July 1780 to January 1783, Doniol's *Histoire de la Participation de la France à l'Établissement des États-Unis d'Amérique* is more valuable than the memoirs. Most of Rochambeau's correspondence, from the time of his appointment to command the expeditionary force to the end of the siege of Yorktown, will be found in Volume 5 of this monumental history. Many of Rochambeau's officers kept journals, or wrote *Souvenirs,* and these are more interesting and more revealing than anything Rochambeau wrote himself. They are listed in the bibliography below.

Washington's *Diaries,* edited by John C. Fitzpatrick, are useful for records of conferences with the French. *The Writings of Wash-*

ington, 39 volumes, also edited by John C. Fitzpatrick, contain all the letters Washington wrote to Rochambeau. The replies to these letters are printed in Doniol.

The Rochambeau Collection in the Manuscripts Division of the Library of Congress consists of six volumes of miscellaneous documents, including statements about the pay and quarters of troops, orders for marches, a "Journal of the operations of the French corps since August 15," a "Journal of the Siege of York in Virginia," etc. These six volumes, together with the splendid collection of Rochambeau papers recently acquired by Mr. Paul Mellon, enable the reader to follow the course of the Yorktown campaign in great detail. Many of the items in this collection are in the handwriting of Washington and Rochambeau. The final letter from Washington, dated February 1, 1784, telling Rochambeau of the evacuation of New York by the British, differs in many respects from the letterbook copy in the Fitzgerald edition of the writings (XXVII, 316-17). This letter contains Washington's memorable tribute:

I shall recollect with pleasure that we have been contemporaries and fellow labourers in the cause of liberty, and that we have lived together as brothers should do—in harmony and friendship.

The part Rochambeau played in the French Revolution, and more particularly in the 1792 campaign, is discussed by two of his contemporaries, Generals Dumouriez and Mathieu Dumas. Dumouriez is critical of Rochambeau for remaining on the defensive. Dumas disagreed with Dumouriez and believed that subsequent events justified Rochambeau's tactics.

Rochambeau's memoirs contain no information on the last years of his life. For this period Weelen's biography remains the principal source. Most of the Rochambeau source material is now in America, either in the Library of Congress or in the Paul Mellon collection.

Selected Bibliography

PRIMARY SOURCES

Annual Register, a Review of Public Events at Home and Abroad . . . , The. London, 1781.

BERTHIER, ALEXANDRE, *Journal de la Campagne d'Amérique. 10 Mai, 1780–26 Août, 1781.* Edited by Gilbert Chinard. Washington, D.C.: Institut Français de Washington, 1951.

Berthier, who was later to become Napoleon's chief of staff, served in America as adjutant quartermaster and cartographer. He supplied Rochambeau with beautifully executed maps and plans of the camp sites occupied by the French army. One set of these maps is in the Library of Congress, another in the Princeton University Library, and a third has recently been acquired by the Paul Mellon Library at Upperville, Va.

His journal gives an excellent picture of the life of a young officer at Rochambeau's headquarters.

BIRON, ARMAND LOUIS DE GONTAUT, DUC DE LAUZUN, *Mémoires du Duc de Lauzun, Général Biron.* Edited by Edmond Pilon. Paris, 1928.

Gay memoirs of the leader of the Lauzun Legion. His account of his own exploits is not always trustworthy, but Washington seems to have had confidence in him. He complains that Rochambeau treated him badly.

BLANCHARD, CLAUDE, *Guerre d'Amérique, 1780–1783; Journal de Campagne.* Paris, 1881.

One of the most interesting of the journals kept by French officers. As commissary quartermaster Blanchard found Rochambeau a difficult man to please, but he admits he knew his business: ". . . s'il n'est pas un administrateur habile, c'est un général très actif, ayant un excellent coup d'œil . . . et entendant parfaitement la guerre."

BOURG, BARON CROMOT DU, "Diary of a French Officer," *Magazine of American History,* IV, Nos. 3–6 (March–June, 1880), VII No. 4 (October 1881).

Du Bourg served as an aide-de-camp to Rochambeau. His journal ends shortly after the siege of Yorktown.

BROGLIE, PRINCE VICTOR CLAUDE, "Narrative of the Prince de Broglie," *Magazine of American History*, I (1877).

One of the young French liberals marked for the guillotine. What he saw in America made a great impression on him. His dying admonition to his son was to remain faithful to the principles of the French Revolution, however unjust and ungrateful.

CHASTELLUX, FRANÇOIS JEAN, MARQUIS DE, *Voyages . . . dans l'Amérique Septentrionale dans les Années 1780, 1781, et 1782*. Paris, 1786.

A first edition of 24 copies was printed in Newport, 1781, at the Imprimerie Royale de l'Escadre.

A revised translation with introduction and notes by Howard C. Rice, Jr. was published by the University of North Carolina Press in 1963.

The references in the text are to the French edition of 1786.

CLINTON, SIR HENRY, *The American Rebellion. Sir Henry Clinton's Narrative of his Campaigns, 1775–1782, with an Appendix of Original Documents*. Edited by William B. Willcox. New Haven, 1954.

The British general's apologia.

CLOSEN, BARON LUDWIG VON, *The Revolutionary Journal of Baron Ludwig von Closen, 1780–1783*. Translated and edited with an introduction by Evelyn M. Acomb. Chapel Hill: University of North Carolina Press, 1958.

The fullest and most interesting of the French journals of the period.

DEUX-PONTS, COMTE GUILLAUME DES, *My Campaigns in America: a Journal . . . 1780–81*. Translated and edited by Samuel A. Green. Boston, 1868.

The best account of the Yorktown campaign by a French officer. Deux-Ponts led the attack on Redoubt No. 9.

DUMAS, LT. GEN. COMTE MATHIEU, *Memoirs of His Own Time*. Philadelphia and London, 1839. 2 vols.

An aide-de-camp to Rochambeau and one of his greatest admirers. In the French Revolution he acted with La Fayette and the constitutional liberal party.

DUMOURIEZ, GENERAL C.-F., *The Life of General Dumouriez*. London, 1796. 3 vols.

English Historical Documents. General editor, David C. Douglas. Oxford University Press, 1957. 12 vols.

Vol. X deals with the period of the American Revolution.

FAY, BERNARD (ed.), *"L'Armée de Rochambeau Jugée par un Français"* *Franco-American Review*, II (1937).

An anonymous article found in the municipal library of Troyes written by an *Officier du Génie*. Critical of Chastellux and Vioménil.

FERSEN, HANS AXEL VON, COMTE DE, "Letters of Fersen, Written to His Father in Sweden, 1781–1782," *Magazine of American History,* III (May–July 1879).

A vivid and sometimes querulous account of his life as one of Rochambeau's aides.

GRASSE, FRANÇOIS JOSEPH PAUL, COMTE DE, "Account of the Campaign of the Naval Armament under the Comte de Grasse," *Magazine of American History,* VII (1881).

This account was first printed on board De Grasse's flagship, the *Ville de Paris.*

HEATH, GENERAL WILLIAM, *The Heath Papers,* Massachusetts Historical Society Collections, 7th series, V (1905).

Letters dealing with the arrival of the French in Newport.

LA FAYETTE, MARIE JOSEPH PAUL YVES GILBERT DU MOTIER, MARQUIS DE, "Letters from La Fayette to La Luzerne, 1780–82," edited by Waldo G. Leland and Edmund C. Burnett, *American Historical Review,* XX (1914–1915).

LEE, HENRY, *Memoirs of the War in the Southern Department of the United States.* New York, 1870.

The author, more familiarly known as "Light-Horse Harry" Lee, was the father of Robert E. Lee.

MONTBAREY, PRINCE DE, *Mémoires Autographes.* Paris, 1826. 3 vols.

MONTESQUIEU, CHARLES DE SECONDAT, BARON DE, *"Quelques Lettres du Baron de Montesquieu sur la Guerre d'Indépendance Américaine,"* edited by E. de Levis Mirepoix, *Franco-American Review,* II (1938).

A grandson of the famous philosopher, Montesquieu served as an aide to Chastellux.

PERRON, JOACHIM DU, COMTE DE REVEL, *A Map of Yorktown.* Edited by Gilbert Chinard, R. G. Albion, and L. A. Brown. Princeton, 1942.

Three surveys of the Yorktown campaign by an officer on the *Languedoc.*

PONTGIBAUD, CHEVALIER MORÉ DE, *Mémoires.* Paris, 1898.

Pontgibaud was not in Rochambeau's army. He was a volunteer who came over shortly after La Fayette. Apparently he regretted the results of their American experience on some of his brother officers: "When we think of the false ideas of government and philanthropy which these youths acquired in America, and propagated with so much enthusiasm, and such deplorable success, . . . we are bound to confess it would have been better for themselves and for us if these young philosophers in red-heeled shoes had stayed at home in attendance on the Court."

ROBERNIER, LOUIS JEAN BAPTISTE SILVESTRE DE, *Journal of the War in America, 1780–83*. Translated by Edouard R. Massey. Rhode Island Historical Society Collections. Vol. XVI (July 1923).

Robernier was a lieutenant in the Soissonnais. The manuscript of his journal is in the Rhode Island Historical Society Library, Providence.

ROBIN, ABBÉ, *Nouveau Voyage dans l'Amérique Septentrionale en l'Année 1781; et Campagne de l'Armée de M. le Comte de Rochambeau.* Paris, 1782.

The Abbé was Rochambeau's chaplain. His journal includes a list of the marches and camp sites of Rochambeau's army from Providence to Yorktown.

ROCHAMBEAU, JEAN-BAPTISTE-DONATIEN DE VIMEUR, COMTE DE, *Mémoires Militaires, Historiques et Politiques.* Paris, 1809. 2 vols.

The manuscript of the *Mémoires* is now in the possession of Mr. Paul Mellon.

SÉGUR, LOUIS PHILIPPE, COMTE DE, *Mémoires, Souvenirs et Anecdotes.* Paris, 1824–1826.

STILES, EZRA, *Literary Diary.* New York, 1901. 3 vols.

THACHER, JAMES, *Military Journal, during the American Revolutionary War from 1775 to 1783.* Hartford, 1854.

Interesting for its account of contacts between the Americans and the French. Thacher was a doctor attached to Scammell's Light Infantry Regiment.

VOLTAIRE, *Précis du Siècle de Louis XV.* Kehl edition, 1785–89. 70 vols.

WASHINGTON, GEORGE, *The Diaries of George Washington, 1748–1799.* Edited by John C. Fitzpatrick. New York, 1925. 4 vols.

WASHINGTON, GEORGE, *The Writings of George Washington.* Edited by John C. Fitzpatrick. Washington, 1931–1944. 39 vols.

WASHINGTON, GEORGE, *Correspondence of General Washington and Comte de Grasse.* Edited by the Institut Français de Washington. Washington: U.S. Government Printing Office, 1931.

SECONDARY SOURCES

ADAMS, RANDOLPH G., "The Burned Letter of Chastellux," Franco-American Pamphlet Series No. 7. New York, 1935.

BALCH, THOMAS, *The French in America during the War of Independence of the United States, 1777–1783*. Philadelphia, 1891–1895.

BALZAC, HONORÉ DE, *Louis Lambert*. Paris, 1832.

BONSAL, STEPHEN, *When the French Were Here*. Garden City, N. Y., 1945.

CARLYLE, THOMAS, *Frederick the Great*. London, 1858.

CASTRIES, DUC DE, *Le Testament de la Monarchie: L'Indépendance Américaine*. Paris, 1958.

CHEVALIER, LOUIS EDWARD, *Histoire de la Marine Francaise pendant la Guerre de l' Indépendence Américaine*. Paris, 1877.

FLEMING, THOMAS J., *Beat the Last Drum*. New York, 1963.
A vivid account of the Siege of Yorktown based on contemporary sources.

FORBES, ALLAN and PAUL F. CADMAN, *France and New England*. Boston, 1925. 3 vols.
Contains interesting article on the marches and campsites of the French army in New England.

FORBES, ALLAN, "Marches and Camp Sites of the French Army beyond New England during the Revolutionary War," *Proceedings of the Massachusetts Historical Society*, LXVII (1945)

FREEMAN, DOUGLAS SOUTHALL, *George Washington: a Biography*. Volume Five: *Victory with the Help of France*. New York, 1952.

GABRIEL, CHARLES N., ABBÉ, *Le Maréchal de Camp Desandrouins, 1729–92*. Verdun, 1887.
Biography of the man who commanded the engineer corps under Rochambeau. Most of the book is taken up with Desandrouins' service in Canada under Montcalm, but Chapter 17 deals particularly with the

Yorktown campaign. Desandrouins makes it very clear that Yorktown was Rochambeau's project. The book consists in large part of extracts from his diary.

GACHOT, E., "Rochambeau," *Nouvelle Revue,* new series, 16 (June 1902).
Deals with Rochambeau's career in the War of the Austrian Succession and in the Seven Years' War.
Rochambeau speaks of some of the officers inflicted on his regiment by Madame de Pompadour as "petits maîtres incapables dans le métier des armes et irrespectieux envers leur colonel."

GALLATIN, BARON GASPARD DE, "With Rochambeau at Newport," *Franco-American Review,* I (1937).

GANNIERS, ARTHUR DE, "La Dernière Campagne du Mar. de Rochambeau," *Revue des Questions Historiques,* new series, 26 (July 1901).

GARDINER, ASA BIRD, *The Order of the Cincinnati in France.* Providence, 1905.

GAXOTTE, PIERRE, *La Révolution Française.* Paris, 1962.

———, *Le Siècle de Louis XV.* Paris, 1933.

GOTTSCHALK, LOUIS R., *Lafayette and the Close of the American Revolution.* Chicago, 1942.

GUTHRIE, WILLIAM D., "General Count de Rochambeau, Commander of the French Army in America during the American Revolution, 1780–1782," *Franco-American Review,* II (1938).

HUGHES, RUPERT, *George Washington, The Savior of the States, 1777–1781.* New York, 1930.

JAMES, CAPTAIN WILLIAM M., *The British Navy in Adversity.* London, 1933.

JOHNSTON, HENRY P., *The Yorktown Campaign and the Surrender of Cornwallis.* New York, 1881.

JUSSERAND, J. J., *With Americans of Past and Present Days.* New York, 1917.
Contains an article on Rochambeau, making use for the first time of the Rochambeau Papers in the Library of Congress.

LA BEDOYERE, MICHAEL DE, *Lafayette, a Revolutionary Gentleman.* New York, 1934.

LACOUR-GAYET, GEORGES, *La Marine Militaire de la France sous le Règne de Louis XVI.* Paris, 1905.

LA FAYETTE, MARQUIS DE, *Memoirs, correspondence and manuscripts of General Lafayette, edited by his son George Washington Lafayette.* London, 1837. 3 vols.

LEWIS, CHARLES LEE, *Admiral de Grasse and American Independence*. Annapolis: United States Naval Institute, 1945.

MAHAN, ALFRED THAYER, *The Influence of Sea Power upon History, 1660–1783*. Boston, 1890.

MATHIEZ, ALBERT, *La Révolution Française*. Paris, 1924.

MERLANT, CAPTAIN JOACHIM, *La France et la Guerre de l'Indépendance Americaine*. Paris, 1918.

MONTMORT, ROGER, COMTE DE, *Antoine Charles du Houx, Baron de Vioménil*. Baltimore, 1935.

NOAILLES, AMBLARD MARIE R. A., VICOMTE DE, *Marins et Soldats en Amérique pendant la Guerre de l'Indépendance des États-Unis*. Paris, 1903.

O'DONNELL, WILLIAM E., *Chevalier de la Luzerne*. Louvain, 1938.

PADOVER, SAUL K., *The Life and Death of Louis XVI*. New York, 1939.

PALVEY, FRANK D., "The Battle of Chesapeake Bay," *Franco-American Review*, II (1938).

PATTERSON, A. TEMPLE, *The Other Armada*. Manchester: Manchester University Press, 1960.

An account of the Franco-Spanish attempt to invade Britain in 1779.

PELL, CLAIBORNE DE B., *Rochambeau and Rhode Island*. Providence, 1954.

PERKINS, JAMES B., *France in the American Revolution*. New York, 1911.

PHIPPS, CAPTAIN RAMSAY WESTON, *The Armies of the First French Republic*. London, 1926.

POTTET, EUGÈNE, *Histoire de la Conciergerie de Paris*. Paris, n.d.

PRESTON, HAROLD W., *Rhode Island and the French Troops in Providence*, Rhode Island Historical Collections, Vol. 17.

RENARD, MAURICE CHARLES, *Rochambeau, Libérateur de l'Amérique*. Paris, 1951.

SÉRIGNAN, LE COMTE DE LORTE DE, *Un Duc et Pair au service de la Révolution, le Duc de Lauzun (Général Biron)*. Paris, 1906.

———, *Les Préliminaires de Valmy, la Première Invasion de la Belgique*. Paris, 1903.

SMITH, PAGE, *John Adams*. New York, 1962. 2 vols.

STEVENS, JOHN A., "The French in Rhode Island," *Magazine of American History*, III (1879).

———, "The Operations of the Allied Armies before New York, 1781," *Magazine of American History*, IV (1880).

———, "The Route of the Allies from King's Ferry to the Head of Elk," *Magazine of American History*, V (1880).

———, "The Return of the French, 1782–1783," *Magazine of American History*, VII (1881).

STONE, EDWIN M., *Our French Allies . . . from 1778 to 1782*. Providence, 1884.

SUSANE, CAPTAIN LOUIS, *Histoire de l'Ancienne Infanterie Française*. Paris, 1848–53.

TREVELYAN, SIR GEORGE OTTO, *George the Third and Charles James Fox. The Concluding Part of the American Revolution*. London, 1914. 2 vols.

WEELEN, JEAN-EDMOND, *Rochambeau, Father and Son . . . with the Journal of the Vicomte de Rochambeau (hitherto unpublished)*. Translated by Lawrence Lee. New York, 1936.

WILLCOX, WILLIAM B., "The British Road to Yorktown—A Study in Divided Command," *The American Historical Review*, LII (October 1946).

———, "Rhode Island in British Strategy," *Journal of Modern History*, XVII (1945).

———, *Portrait of a General: Sir Henry Clinton in the War of Independence*. New York, 1964. An absorbing study of the personalities of Cornwallis and of Clinton, to which all students of the Revolution are indebted.

Index